The Hidden War

The Hidden War

Crime and the Tragedy of Public Housing in Chicago

SUSAN J. POPKIN
VICTORIA E. GWIASDA
LYNN M. OLSON
DENNIS P. ROSENBAUM
LARRY BURON

RUTGERS UNIVERSITY PRESS
New Brunswick, New Jersey, and London

Library of Congress Cataloging-in-Publication Data

The hidden war : crime and the tragedy of public housing in Chicago / Susan J. Popkin . . . [et al.].
        p. cm.
    Includes bibliographical references and index.
    ISBN 0–8135–2832–1 (cloth : alk. paper) — ISBN 0–8135–2833–X (pbk. : alk. paper)
    1. Chicago Housing Authority.   2. Housing authorities—Illinois—Chicago.   3. Public housing—Illinois—Chicago.   I. Popkin, Susan J.
HD7288.78.U52 C44 2000
363.5'85'0977311—dc21

                                                                    99–056789

British Cataloging-in-Publication data for this book is available from the British Library

Manufactured in the United States of America

Contents

List of Photos, Figures, and Tables

Photos

Figures

Tables

Foreword

Although the title of this book indicates that it's about fighting crime, in reality the book is about much more. This book represents the culmination of a remarkable project, in which the authors talked with and surveyed residents and observed life in three Chicago housing projects over a period of four years. The results provide a portrait of life in some of the worst neighborhoods in the United States; they give a feel for what life is like when lived amid bullets, graffiti, and broken plumbing. The stories are outrageous; they evoke deep anger that such conditions exist and even deeper despair as repeated efforts to improve these projects prove inadequate. The stories depict an environment in which no one should live, but where some of America's poorest citizens have become mired and from which there is no easy escape.

The book sends a humbling message to policymakers and prognosticators who claim to know the right way to "solve poverty." Here is the story of how policies undertaken with largely good intentions—urban renewal of slum housing and the provision of modern high-rises for poor families—can end up failing miserably. The public housing projects described here have become synonyms for lost lives. They display the result of a series of disastrous policy decisions, from high-rise construction, to the racial politics that determined their siting, to the decades of poor management and underfunding that led to today's crumbling and crime-ridden projects. The efforts to improve the maintenance and the safety of these buildings fail again and again, as the stories here indicate. But these efforts are typically short-term, poorly funded, and often ill-suited to the nature of the problem they are facing. No one believes that there are easy ways to "fix" America's high-rise public housing projects. But this book is a testimony to how ill-designed efforts can often make things worse.

This is also a book about the complexity of the lives that women live in these projects. The book does not flinch from recognizing that at least some of the blame for this environment must fall to its residents. The women and their children are victims of the violence around them, but they are also closely connected to its perpetrators. The racial segregation and social isolation of these projects' residents creates a bind from which too few can escape: Suspicious of the outside world of seemingly inaccessible (if not actively hostile) authority, people cling to the community they know, however inadequate and dangerous it may be.

Finally, as the title promises, this is also a book about crime and crime fighting. More specifically, this book chronicles a series of efforts to control crime in these public housing projects and describes why these efforts ultimately failed.

The welfare reform discussion of the past decade has focused heavily on the need to help single mothers move into employment and toward greater economic self-sufficiency. We should rightfully celebrate the progress we have made toward that goal for many public assistance recipients. But this book indicates the complexity that such programs face among at least that portion of the population living in these areas of intense poverty and crime. Finding and holding a stable job for these women requires much more than job training. It requires organizing a stable work life in the midst of a chaotic and dangerous environment, a challenge that would tax persons with far greater skills and support. This book underscores the necessity to think in much more complex terms about how welfare-to-work programs should operate in highly disadvantaged communities.

As the story this book records ends in the late 1990s, a number of these high-rise projects are undergoing demolition and renovation. Low-rise and scattered-site housing units are replacing the crumbling towers. Whether this policy change alleviates any of the multiple problems faced by these neighborhoods and their inhabitants remains to be seen. Unfortunately, the evidence in this book leaves one skeptical.

Rebecca M. Blank
Dean of the School of Public Policy, University of Michigan
and former member of the President's Council of Economic Advisors
September 1999

Acknowledgments

When Victoria Gwiasda, Lynn Olson, and I first conceived of this project in 1992, we never imagined it would grow from a small evaluation of the Chicago Housing Authority's (CHA) Drug Elimination program into a multiyear study that would eventually result in us writing this book. Audrey Chambers of Northwestern University's Institute for Policy Research had passed us the RFP and thought it would fit our interests in crime in public housing. As the project grew, Dennis and Larry joined the team, and many others made important contributions to our work; without their help, this project could not have been completed.

The National Institute of Justice (NIJ), the U.S. Department of Housing and Urban Development (HUD), and the John D. and Catherine T. MacArthur Foundation provided financial support for this research. The first phase of the project was funded under NIJ grants number 93–IJ-CX-0037 and 95–IJ-CX-0011. In 1995, HUD provided funding to add two additional waves of surveys under contract number DU100C000018374, Task Order 6. Finally, support for the follow-up assessment of the Henry Horner Homes was funded under HUD contract number DU100C000018374, Task Order 8, and by a grant from the John D. and Catherine T. MacArthur Foundation. We wish to thank our Project Officers, Rosemary Murphy of NIJ, Robert Dalzell and Harold Holzman of HUD, and Susan Lloyd of the MacArthur Foundation for their enthusiastic support. Of course, the conclusions reported here are those of the authors and may not necessarily reflect the opinions of these agencies.

We wish to extend a special thanks to the many current and former

CHA staff who provided information and assistance over the years, particularly Theresa Lipo, DePriest McCary, and Sharon Elliot. The especially helpful staffs of the CADRE centers in Rockwell Gardens, Henry Horner Homes, and Harold Ickes Homes graciously offered their space to us so we could conduct interviews.

Many colleagues made important contributions to this project. Wendell Johnson served as the project's ethnographer, providing us with keen insights into life in CHA housing. Judie Feins, Jean Amendolia, Cristopher Price, and Satyendra Patrabansh of Abt Associates all made substantive contributions to the data collection and analysis; Jean took most of the photographs that illustrate this volume and created an enormous database of *Chicago Tribune* coverage of the CHA that greatly enhanced this research. Gloria Chapa-Resendez, Dena Al-Khatib, Elise Martel, and Nina Taluc of the Survey Research Laboratory of the University of Illinois at Chicago did an outstanding job of overseeing the data collection; we are indebted to them for the high quality of the survey data and the impressive response rates we achieved. Carol Dellios and Valerie Lorimer, by transcribing hundreds of hours of tapes for this project, enabled us to tell our story through the words of the residents. Finally, we wish to extend a very special thanks to the Survey Research Laboratory field staff and interviewers (mostly CHA residents) who administered the surveys for this project. The excellent quality of the data speaks to their impressive level of dedication in working in extremely stressful and unpleasant conditions.

Many other colleagues provided assistance along the way. Gordon Hanson, Patricia Meaden, Susan Bennett, Donald Hedeker, Arthur Lurigio, Andrea Anderson, and Ruth Carter all participated in data collection and analysis at various points during the project. Wesley Skogan and Susan Hartnett of the CAPS Project at Northwestern University generously shared their data and their insights.

We wish to thank the Urban Institute for the time and support it took to finish writing this book. We particularly want to thank Marge Turner for her enthusiasm and generous support, Diane Levy for her insights into mixed-income housing, Aaron Graham and Shawnise Thompson for helping with all the little tasks involved in the final stages, and Diane Hendricks for formatting the final document.

We are grateful to our agent (my mother), Julie Popkin, who encouraged us to turn our research report into this book and helped us to negotiate our way through the arcane world of publishing. Phyllis Edelman did a fantastic job of editing the final manuscript and helped us to overcome the challenges of making an incredibly complex story comprehensible. Marlie Wasserman and Martha Heller and the staff of Rutgers University Press helped make this a much stronger book.

My coauthors and I wish to extend a special thanks to the many family members, friends, and colleagues who have patiently listened to our horror stories and provided us with much-needed support as we attempted to make sense of the huge piles of data we had collected. In particular, I wish to thank Norman Hall for his patience, his unwavering faith in my abilities, and for taking on many household responsibilities so I could finish this project. I also want to thank my children, Zachary and Rachel Popkin-Hall for putting up with their mother spending so much time in Chicago—and in front of the computer. Victoria Gwiasda would also like to thank Martin Berger for his encouragement and support.

Finally, we wish to thank the many CHA residents who participated in the surveys and in-depth interviews for this project. We have benefited greatly from their generosity in sharing their stories and experiences with us and hope that this book will help to give them a voice in the debate over how to replace CHA's developments. We especially want to acknowledge the contributions of Mr. Wardell Yotaghan of Rockwell Gardens and resident leaders in Horner and Ickes (who remain anonymous) who inspired us with their dedication to their communities. It is our profound hope that their efforts will finally help to bring about a brighter future for CHA residents.

Susan J. Popkin

The Hidden War

1 | Introduction

It seems like I've kind of given up hope.... It's like there's no hope, like I'm fighting for myself a lot of times.... When you call [the police] and make them [the drug dealers in her hallway] leave, and then it's like they come right back. So what can you really do? What else can you do?... They [the gangs] watch you.... That's why I was—kind of giving up— just working on getting out, moving.

LaKeisha, Henry Horner Homes

I really don't want them [my kids] to grow up in here.... Children like to play on the ground. It's okay to be on the ramp porch sometime, but you wanna be downstairs, you know, where they can rip and run and play in the dirt and in the grass and stuff like that. And right now it's really not safe for them to be there. They have to play on the porch, and a lot of time, when the shooting start, the big boys run upstairs, and so you just snatching your kids in the house and closing the door. 'Cause you don't know which way the bullets gonna go.

Regina, Henry Horner Homes

LaKeisha and Regina are residents of the Chicago Housing Authority's (CHA) Henry Horner Homes. Chicago's public housing is among the worst in the nation—poorly constructed, poorly maintained, and extremely dangerous. A complex layering of problems has left the people who live in these developments mired in the most destructive kind of poverty. These problems include extreme racial and economic segregation and inadequate public services, particularly police, schools, and sanitation. The national economic boom has left these residents behind. The neighborhoods that surround CHA's developments have few services or stores and even fewer jobs. Most residents are unemployed; they depend on public assistance or the underground economy. Only a few older, stable individuals are capable of enforcing standards of acceptable behavior. Without this underlying social structure, there is little mutual trust and cohesion that can encourage or even allow residents to unite to fight their common problems.

Starting in the late 1970s, Chicago's notorious street gangs—among the most lethal in the United States—have filled this social void by gradually coming to dominate the CHA's eleven enormous high-rise developments. The gangs have created a social order and economy in which most of the residents—voluntarily or involuntarily—have become enmeshed. CHA's developments have proven to be ideal drug markets. The residents provide a base of customers and a vulnerable pool of young recruits for the drug business. The location of the developments near major expressways and the open and unsecured buildings and grounds provide easy access for customers and ready hiding places from police. The gangs, having fought many battles to control this lucrative turf, have turned these developments into urban war zones.

Hidden inside these forbidding developments lies a humanitarian disaster. Thousands of vulnerable families live in these troubled communities, many because they have no other alternatives. These families include tens of thousands of children: the CHA has long been one of the only places to find affordable housing for large families, and the majority of the residents of its high-rise developments are eighteen or younger. Many young residents have been permanently damaged as a result of the poorly maintained housing: poisoned by lead paint that was never removed, killed falling out of windows of high-rise buildings that had no screens or window guards, plagued with asthma after living in cockroach-infested buildings, burned by unprotected radiators or injured on broken elevators or darkened stairwells. Still more are victims of the overwhelming social disorganization, abused or neglected by drug-addicted parents, killed or injured in the gang wars, arrested or incarcerated for their involvement in the drug trade, or permanently traumatized by the stress of coping with the constant violence and disorder.

By now, the problems in the CHA's developments are so layered and deep, and the residents so troubled, that no obvious answers and no simple solutions exist. Many other well-designed, well-intended efforts to revive communities in less distressed inner-city neighborhoods have failed. The only types of programs that seem to have even a modest impact on the lives of poor families who live in these types of ghetto neighborhoods require costly long-term supportive services (Blank 1997; Halpern 1995).

This book tells the story of the CHA's efforts to contend with the overwhelming problems in its developments over the past decade. By the late 1980s, the disaster in CHA housing had reached tragic proportions. Years of managerial incompetence and neglect had left the buildings in an advanced state of decay. Most working families had abandoned CHA housing years before, and had been replaced with younger, more dysfunctional households. The crime and violence were overwhelming, and the gang dominance nearly absolute.

Faced with such circumstances, the CHA administrators who inherited these problems believed the only way to reclaim the developments was to declare war on the gangs and drug dealers. Without reducing the danger, they reasoned, they could not expect residents to help maintain order or janitorial crews to perform adequate work. Thus, in 1988, the CHA began its first all-out battle against the gangs, pouring millions of dollars into police, security guards, and metal detectors. By the early 1990s, this effort had become a state-of-the-art community crime-prevention program called the Anti-Drug Initiative. However, as the stories in this book show, by the mid-1990s, it was evident that the problems in CHA's developments were so severe that even this very expensive effort had little impact. At the same time, the U.S. Department of Housing and Urban Development (HUD), attempting to deal with troubled public housing on a national level, began providing funding to the CHA to demolish and "revitalize" its worst developments. Even as this redevelopment initiative got underway, the level of crime remained extreme. Thus, whether this dramatic policy change will benefit the people whose stories we tell in this book—especially the thousands of children who still live in CHA housing—remains unclear.

We tell the story of the CHA's struggle against crime in its developments presented through the eyes of the residents who suffered through life in these communities. The stories in this book poignantly document the tremendous toll that violence has taken on these individuals and the ways in which the gang-dominated social order has undermined any efforts to improve conditions.

This project began in 1992 as a small evaluation of the CHA's anti-crime programs. Other research had convinced us of the key role that crime played in preventing CHA residents from being able to take basic steps to improve their lives. A survey of CHA residents who had moved to the suburbs through a housing desegregation program found that participants consistently mentioned safety as the major benefit of their move; feeling safer helped them feel less depressed and more secure about leaving their children to go to school or work (Popkin, Rosenbaum, and Meaden 1993). Likewise, research on Project Match—a nationally recognized welfare-to-work demonstration program that worked with CHA residents—documented the many ways that crime and fear hampered participants' efforts to become self-sufficient (e.g., Olson and Herr 1989). Because of these findings, we became increasingly interested in the problem of how to control crime in public housing.

We quickly discovered that evaluating the CHA's programs was considerably more complicated than originally anticipated. The agency was in a nearly continuous state of management turmoil during the 1990s and its anticrime programs were constantly changing. We intended to compare the effects of the CHA's anticrime programs across three different developments hoping to identify the factors that led specific elements of the program to succeed or fail. However, the more time we spent in these developments, the more we came to appreciate the complexity of life in CHA housing and the subtle nuances that made the circumstances of each development unique.

Furthermore, we came to understand why traditional assumptions about community crime prevention did not hold in these settings. Community crime-prevention initiatives like the ones that the CHA tried to implement start with the idea that the goal is to get residents to work together to confront a common, outside enemy, for example, drug dealers who have chosen to open up shop in a house on a block. These models also assume that residents have sufficient resources and confidence to successfully cooperate in an organized crime-prevention effort. Finally, these models assume that residents will be able to work together to enforce an agreed-upon set of social norms.

But these assumptions do not apply in the dire circumstances of CHA housing. Here, as in other extremely troubled neighborhoods, an entirely different set of social rules apply (Bourgois 1995). Most of these criminals are not outsiders; instead, they are residents—or their friends and relatives. Drug dealers and gang members are nearly the only people in the community with power and resources; therefore, even law-abiding residents tolerate their presence (Patillo 1998). Because the criminals are such a powerful part of the community, confronting them brings great dangers, and, without adequate protection from the police, most residents are unlikely to willingly take such risks. As the stories in this book show, rather than working together to confront their common problems, the realities of their social world force CHA residents to focus primarily on survival, "minding their own business," and protecting themselves and their children from the war around them.

Because each CHA development is really its own closed social world—each with its own set of resident leaders and dominant gangs and each affected by different types of CHA interventions—we have chosen to tell this story as a series of three comprehensive case studies. Using the voices of the residents, this book paints a picture of daily life in three of the CHA's high-rise developments and describes the extent to which the pervasive drug trafficking and gang violence control the social world. Looking in-depth at three different developments allows us to explore the range of CHA's attempts to grapple with these challenges, from traditional law enforcement actions to drive out crime to community crime-prevention efforts intended to "empower" residents to extensive community revitalization initiatives. We use the case studies to highlight the factors that kept even some of the agency's most comprehensive and best-intended efforts from having much significant long-term impact on the lives of individual residents. Finally, we explore how variations in the level of social organization—some developments or individual buildings are less violent and more organized than others—affected the impact of the CHA's efforts.

The first case study presents the story of Rockwell Gardens, the development where the CHA first tested its aggressive law enforcement strategies against the gangs. Rockwell Gardens was extremely violent, dominated by three different gangs. At the same time, Rockwell had a core of older, activist residents who struggled to maintain order and managed to turn one building into an oasis from the violence. The second case study tells the story of the Henry Horner Homes, a development literally split by the gang war and so devoid of resources that residents were forced to rely on the gangs to provide protection for their buildings. Horner eventually became the site of the CHA's first effort to revitalize one of its high-rise developments. Finally, the third case study tells the story of the Harold Ickes Homes, a development where a combination of a core of older, stable tenants willing to participate in crime-prevention activities and effective CHA security services maintained a relative peace for several years. However, when budget cuts and changes in HUD policy forced the CHA to cut back its security services, Ickes residents were left vulnerable, and tenant activists could no longer hold back the gangs and violence.

To tell these stories, we draw on a variety of different sources. These include:

Six waves of surveys of Rockwell, Horner, and Ickes residents conducted in May 1994, January 1995, May 1995, December 1995, December 1996, and December 1997;

Six rounds of in-depth, qualitative interviews conducted at three-to-six month intervals with "key informants" from each development—residents who were community leaders and/or viewed as being well informed about conditions in their developments.[1] We conducted life history interviews with seven of these residents in May 1996. In addition, we conducted interviews with small numbers of these residents from the three sites in 1998 as part of follow-up research.

Interviews with CHA site management staff and senior CHA

administrative staff involved in anticrime and redevelopment efforts in 1994 and 1996; we interviewed a smaller
group in 1998 as part of follow-up research.

Observations from a professional ethnographer who observed
daily life in Rockwell, Ickes, and Horner over a period from
May 1995 to August 1996.

A review of CHA-related newspaper articles in the *Chicago Tribune* and *Sun-Times* from 1988 through mid-1999.

The Hidden War in CHA Housing

To make sense of the case studies, it is important to
understand the larger context, both the incredible level of problems that
occur in CHA's developments and the policy changes that are currently
reshaping the public housing environment. The kind of violence that
occurs in CHA's high-rise developments is incomprehensible to most
Americans. Most horrors are hidden from outsiders, but some of the worst
make the newspapers or television news. These were a few of the stories that made the news during an especially violent four-month period
between January 1 and April 30 of 1997:

A nine-year-old girl (labeled "Girl X" by the media), was kid-
naped, sexually assaulted, poisoned, and left for dead in
Cabrini-Green (*Chicago Tribune*, January 10, 1997);

CHA police and drug dealers in Cabrini-Green engaged in a
shoot-out, ending with the police firing into an occupied
building (*Chicago Tribune*, March 5, 1997);

The head of the Chicago public schools announced a plan to
transport children from an elementary school in Cabrini-
Green to another location to escape constant gunfire (*Chicago Tribune*, April 12, 1997);

A thirty-one-year old man was killed in the Henry Horner Homes
in a gang-related shooting (*Chicago Tribune*, April 14, 1997);
and

A five-year-old boy was sexually assaulted by six ten-year-olds
in a community center in the Robert Taylor Homes (*Chicago
Tribune*, April 21, and April 23, 1997).

These were only the crimes that made major headlines. Many other serious crimes never make the newspapers, and even more are never reported to the police. Ironically, in April 1997, the Bureau of Justice
Statistics announced a dramatic decrease in violent crime in Chicago
(*Chicago Tribune*, April 14, 1997).

But incomplete as it likely is, this list demonstrates that in CHA developments extraordinary violence is routine. Gang conflicts and peace treaties have more impact on residents' quality of life than anything the police or the CHA tries to do to improve conditions. Residents are often caught in the gang crossfire, with bullets even shot into their apartments.

Children are frequent victims, sometimes hit by a wayward bullet, but even children who are not themselves direct victims witness countless beatings, fights, and shootings. They are continually exposed to the rampant drug dealing and substance abuse. It is not surprising that children growing up in CHA housing may become victimizers as well; some are involved in gang shootings and assaults, and a few in even more horrifying incidents of preying on other children, such as the two young boys who murdered five-year-old Eric Morse in the Ida B. Wells Homes in 1994 or the six ten-year-olds who sexually assaulted another child in the Robert Taylor Homes in 1997. Unlike the mostly white, middle-class victims of mass shootings in towns such as Littleton, Colorado, or Jonesboro, Arkansas, children who live in CHA housing, constantly exposed to violent crime, are not regarded as "brave survivors"; these urban children receive no trauma counseling or support to help them cope with their continual pain and fear.

In CHA housing, victims generally know the criminals, there is little privacy, and reporting crime to the police or even trying to keep the criminals away from your building brings great risks. One of the worst aspects of this situation is that, unlike urban guerrilla wars in other countries, the war in CHA's developments is not being fought *for* anything (Garbarino, Kostelny, and Dubrow, 1991). There is neither a greater cause that residents can use to justify their suffering nor any hope that the violence might lead to a greater good.

CHA residents have developed their own vocabulary to describe the war around them. A gang "truce" or "a peace" represents a period of relative calm. "Territory" refers to gang turf, as in "that building is in Disciples territory"; "challenges" are attempts to get new residents to show how well they fight. Residents describe their individual apartment units as their "refuge." Survival is foremost on residents' minds: the main survival strategy is to "mind your own business" and refuse to acknowledge or report the surrounding violence.

This war is largely hidden from the rest of the city. Most Chicago area residents never venture into—or even near—CHA developments; the closest most people come is driving by them on the expressway. Occasionally, a particularly shocking incident, especially one involving a small child, makes headlines. Two successful books were published during the 1990s focusing attention on the terrible plight of children growing up in CHA housing. In *Our America* (1997), LeAlan Jones and Lloyd Newman, both teenagers growing up in the Ida B. Wells Homes, created a poignant account of their attempt to come to terms with the killing of Eric Morse. Several years earlier, *There Are No Children Here*, Alex Kotlowitz's (1991) moving account of two boys growing up in the Henry Horner Homes, was a best-selling book and made into a television movie starring Oprah Winfrey. However, these brief flurries of media attention had little effect on day-to-day life for residents. Most days, the war continued, unnoticed by anyone but those most directly affected—the residents, the gangs, CHA staff, and the police.

The Transformation of CHA Housing

Even as the war continues, public housing in Chicago—as in many cities across the nation—is currently in the midst of an incredible transformation. Recent changes in federal policy have made it easier for housing authorities to demolish and redevelop their worst properties. Indeed, since 1997, federal law has required that housing authorities demolish all developments where the cost of replacement exceeds the cost of providing all current residents with Section 8 vouchers to use in the private rental market. The CHA, with its large numbers of developments in terrible condition, has been more affected by these changes in federal housing policy than any other housing authority in the nation. Nearly nineteen thousand of its units, including almost all of its high-rise developments, have failed the "viability assessment" and must be demolished during the next ten years. Some sites are being redeveloped, replaced with a combination of new townhomes and rehabilitated mid- and high-rise buildings that will become mixed-income housing for higher-income tenants and the working poor. Many current tenants will receive Section 8 vouchers and relocation assistance.

However, the problems in CHA housing are so profound and so damaging to the current tenants that it is likely that most people represented in this book will never benefit from these dramatic changes. The stories in this book show that traditional community revitalization initiatives and counseling programs are as unlikely to succeed for this population as were community crime prevention initiatives. Thus, the people who live in CHA housing face an uncertain future, one that may even increase the dimensions of the humanitarian disaster in CHA housing today.

———

This book tells the story of the CHA's struggles against the crime and disorder in its developments. Chapter 2, describing CHA housing and its history, explains how the situation grew so bad that the only alternative seemed to be demolition. Chapter 3 discusses the CHA's anticrime efforts in the context of what is known about effective crime-prevention strategies in poor communities. Chapters 4, 5, and 6 are the case studies of the Rockwell Gardens, Henry Horner, and Harold Ickes developments. In each, we describe conditions in the developments: the level of crime and community organization; the CHA's efforts to control crime; and residents' perceptions of how the situation changed over time. Finally, Chapter 7 draws lessons from the three case studies and suggests a framework for ways to think about helping these very vulnerable families.

2 | The Chicago Housing Authority

The Chicago Housing Authority (CHA) is the third largest public housing agency in the country with more than forty thousand housing units in seventeen family developments; only Puerto Rico and New York City have more public housing. Eleven of the CHA's developments consist of enormous, prisonlike highrises, with some buildings housing more than 150 families. Three developments—Robert Taylor, Cabrini-Green, and ABLA Homes—have more than three thousand units each, larger than some small towns. Other cities have had serious problems with what policymakers call "severely distressed" public housing, generally large, isolated developments located in inner-city neighborhoods (National Commission on Severely Distressed Public Housing 1992a), but few other developments approach the level of crime and social decay found in nearly all of CHA's family housing.

The resident population in CHA's family developments is virtually all African-American and consists almost entirely of single-parent, female-headed households, many with several small children or teenagers. In 1997, almost one-fifth of the households had five or more people living in the same apartment, more than half the residents were children, and only 6 percent of the households were headed by a married couple. Only 15 percent of the households had an employed member, and the average income in CHA's developments was $6,936 per year (CHA 1997); by comparison, the federal poverty line for a family of four was more than twice as high at $16,400.

Unmanageable Developments

A number of factors make the CHA's developments almost impossible to manage. The buildings in its enormous family developments are literally crumbling. They are relatively old; most construction occurred during the 1950s and early 1960s. The original materials were cheap and have not held up well over time. Further, buildings are poorly designed, with exterior hallways and elevators that have proven extremely difficult to maintain.

Because the exterior hallways of the high-rises are covered with metal grates, the buildings look like prisons. Many apartments (and some entire buildings) are boarded up because their major systems—plumbing, heating, electrical—have failed. The grounds and hallways are often filled with refuse and reek of human waste. The buildings are infested with vermin, including rats, mice, roaches, and even feral cats. Lights in interior hallways, elevators, and stairwells are vandalized regularly, leaving these areas dark twenty-four hours a day. The buildings' exteriors, halls, and stairwells are often covered with graffiti or, in the better-maintained developments, the evidence of the janitors' attempts to paint over the mess.

The apartments themselves are grim and institutional. They generally have cinderblock walls, bare light bulbs, and black linoleum floors. In most buildings, they lack basic amenities such as closet doors and showers. Without constant vigilance, it is nearly impossible to keep the units clean. In addition to the dirt that blows in from outdoors, it is not uncommon to see apartment walls literally crawling with roaches. Most apartments also have serious maintenance problems, owing to years of neglect and failed structural systems. For example, in some units, it is impossible to turn off the hot water in the bathrooms, so the walls now have severe moisture damage.

The fact that most CHA developments are concentrated in areas isolated from the more prosperous parts of the city compounds the agency's problems. On the South Side, a four-mile strip of public housing high-rises (the State Street corridor) runs along an expressway, interrupted only by the campus of the Illinois Institute of Technology. This strip begins with the Ickes Homes and includes the 4,400-unit Robert Taylor Homes, the largest public housing development in the world, and three other high-rise developments.

The History of Public Housing in Chicago

To understand how CHA housing ended up in such miserable condition, it is important to know something about the history of the agency. Chicago did not always have bad public housing;

indeed, during its first three decades—until the 1960s—the CHA was regarded as a model of efficiency and good management (Meyerson and Banfield 1955). The agency was founded in the 1930s to provide decent homes for the poor. Elizabeth Wood, the executive director of the CHA during the 1940s and early 1950s, and Robert Taylor, the first African-American chairman of the board who served with her, were both New Deal social reformers who saw it as their mission to replace slum housing, for both poor whites and poor blacks, with better apartments in good neighborhoods.

Wood and Taylor fought a losing battle to prevent Chicago's city council from locating public housing exclusively in poor, black communities (Hirsch 1998). Taylor particularly opposed building large, high-rise developments on "superblocks," that is, huge plots of land cut off from the regular street grid (Meyerson and Banfield 1955). But, like much of the country, Chicago was caught up in a "high-rise fad" (Bowly 1978). This emphasis on creating a "bold new environment" disregarded the fact that housing types appropriate for single people or childless couples might not be appropriate for families with children.

After a protracted struggle, the city council ultimately overruled the housing authority and voted to build the vast majority of new public housing in poor, black communities. This decision had far-reaching ramifications for both Chicago and the CHA. The new construction resulted in widespread slum clearance in some expanding black neighborhoods in Chicago. These changes effectively blocked the growth of working-class black communities. Families displaced by these urban renewal efforts were often relocated to the newly constructed public housing, thus reinforcing existing patterns of segregation and creating a "second ghetto" (Hirsch 1998). To save money and provide as much housing as possible for poor blacks, the local government chose to make these new developments extremely large. Most were eventually cut off from the neighborhoods around them by new expressways or expanding subway lines. In essence, these developments became "reservations for poor blacks" and created previously unimaginable geographic concentrations of poverty (Massey and Denton 1993).

Where CHA administrators had envisioned modern, attractive neighborhoods, the city constructed enormous blocks of grim concrete towers. Instead of providing pleasant places for children to play, the public areas were unattractive and alienating (Halpern 1995). Although they initially met city codes and were thus better than the housing they replaced, the CHA's developments were harder to maintain and deteriorated rapidly. Further, because these artificially constructed communities were isolated and lacked any formal social structure or leadership, they were extremely vulnerable to crime (Halpern 1995).

The CHAs eleven high-rise developments were constructed between 1950 and 1969. The cost was tremendous—about $20,000 per unit in 1960 dollars. The politically connected developers, who used cheap slab construction, shoddy materials, and poor workmanship, allegedly siphoned off huge sums of cash to line their own pockets (Baron 1969). Both Taylor and Wood, forced out by the city council by the mid-1950s, were replaced by leaders with strong connections to city hall and Chicago's notorious Democratic machine (Meyerson and Banfield 1955; Baron 1969; Hirsch 1998). Ironically, despite Chairman Robert Taylor's strong opposition to constructing large developments in poor black neighborhoods, the CHA named its biggest and most isolated high-rise development after him.

The Swibel Era

In the early 1960s, Charles Swibel, a crony of Mayor Richard J. Daley, became the chairman of the CHA board. Widely known as a slumlord and real estate promoter, he had connections to some of the most powerful politicians and union officials in the city. Despite ample evidence of malfeasance during his tenure, he retained his position for more than nineteen years, until HUD finally forced him out in 1982.[1] Under his stewardship, conditions in CHA housing rapidly deteriorated. By the 1970s, many observers regarded the high-rise developments as worse than the slum housing they had replaced (Metropolitan Planning Council 1990).

Crime in CHA housing began to increase catastrophically in the late 1970s and early 1980s. By 1981, the violence was so bad that Mayor Jane Byrne moved into the Cabrini-Green development for three weeks to show her determination to reduce gang crime. Well-received at the time, this dramatic gesture had no long-term effect, and crime continued to escalate.

CHA management had become abysmal; repairs went undone, and the agency's finances were in a shambles. By 1982, the CHA claimed a $33.5-million deficit even though $50 million intended for repairs sat untouched in low-interest bank accounts. HUD tried to salvage the situation by forcing the ouster of Swibel and the rest of the CHA board. After a lengthy struggle, Swibel finally resigned in 1982 (Gittelson 1982).

The Gautreaux Case

One legacy of the Chicago city council's control over public housing was the nearly complete segregation of CHA's developments.

Blacks lived in the huge high-rise developments concentrated on the south and west sides of the city, and the few whites lived in four small developments. The *Gautreaux* case,[2] a civil rights lawsuit filed against the CHA and HUD in 1966, had a profound impact on the history of the CHA. Dorothy Gautreaux, a CHA resident who was active in the civil rights movement, led a group of other residents in alleging discrimination in site selection and tenant assignment (Rubinowitz 1992; Rubinowitz et al. forthcoming). The case against the CHA was first settled in 1969, with the federal court ruling for the plaintiffs. The court ordered the CHA to provide a substantial amount of small-scale, scattered-site housing, primarily in white areas of the city. This ruling immediately stopped the construction of large-scale public housing in black neighborhoods. Further, because the CHA made little progress in building such scattered-site units, this ruling essentially stopped the construction of *any* new public housing in Chicago until the late 1980s, when the court finally appointed a receiver to oversee construction.[3]

The case against HUD eventually moved to the Supreme Court and was not settled until 1976. Instead of ordering the CHA to desegregate its housing, the court ordered relief in the form of 7,100 Section 8 certificates—subsidies that could be used to rent private-market housing.[4] These Section 8 certificates were to be used for current and former CHA residents to move to neighborhoods that were less than 30 percent black (Rubinowitz 1992). The Leadership Council for Metropolitan Communities, a fair housing organization, was awarded a contract to provide counseling to families who received the special Section 8 certificates. The *Gautreaux* program, as it came to be known, lasted for more than twenty years and became the model for other public housing desegregation cases.[5]

The Role of Federal Housing Policy

The situation in CHA housing was exacerbated by federal policies during the 1970s and 1980s, which helped to concentrate the neediest families in public housing. That is, legislation aimed at preventing homelessness required public housing authorities to adopt federal preferences in admission requirements to serve the poorest households. For example, the Brooke Amendments limited tenant payments for rents to 25 percent of income in order to make public housing affordable to very low-income families;[6] housing authorities were required to give priority to extremely needy households;[7] and ceiling rents were eliminated, which increased the rents that working families had to pay to live in public housing.[8] In Chicago, as in other cities, with no financial incentives to stay, working families quickly abandoned public housing. By 1991, nearly one-fifth of public housing tenants nationwide had incomes that were less than 10 percent of the local median (Fosburg, Popkin, and Locke 1996); in CHA housing, the median income was only about $6,000 (CHA 1991a).

Other federal policies inhibited the CHA from demolishing and replacing its developments. To maintain the supply of public housing units, the "one-for-one replacement rule" required housing authorities to build a new unit for every unit they demolished, regardless of occupancy. This policy made demolition prohibitively expensive. Without sufficient funding for demolishing and replacing units, the CHA either continued to place tenants in these deteriorating buildings or let them remain vacant. In Chicago, any decisions about demolition were further complicated by the *Gautreaux* decision because the CHA would have been able to construct replacement housing only in nonminority areas.

The Mid-1980s: The Downward Spiral Continues

The election of Harold Washington as Chicago's first African-American mayor in 1983 in a three-way race seemed to herald a new era of hope for the CHA.[9] But the white aldermen on the city council blocked him from appointing his allies to the CHA board. During this power struggle, the agency endured a series of short-term executive directors; meanwhile, conditions in CHA developments continued to worsen. Mayor Washington died suddenly in 1987, just months after having been reelected; he had had little impact on what was already recognized as a disastrous situation.

With the city government in flux as a result of the mayor's untimely death, and HUD threatening to take control of the CHA, the Metropolitan Planning Council, a civic group long concerned with public housing in Chicago, put forth a plan to rescue the troubled agency. Because demolishing the CHA's developments was both politically and financially unfeasible as a result of the *Gautreaux* case and the federal one-for-one replacement rule, the Council sought ways to bring about short-term improvements in management and security. As part of this plan, the group proposed that Vincent Lane, an African-American developer of low-income housing who chaired the group's CHA Management Committee, become both the executive director and chairman of the CHA board in 1988 (Metropolitan Planning Council 1990).[10] Although Lane resigned his position as executive director in 1991, he retained his position of chairman and dominated the agency until he was forced out by a HUD takeover in May 1995.

Vincent Lane's War on Crime

After his appointment in 1988, Lane and the new CHA board were given a mandate to address serious problems at the CHA and turn the agency around (National Commission on Severely Distressed Public Housing 1992b). Lane faced tremendous challenges; he had no public housing management experience, and, by the late 1980s, the CHA's problems were overwhelming.

Lane quickly made clear that improving security was his first priority; he declared war on the gangs within the first months of his administration. This effort, the first serious attempt by a CHA director to address the problems with crime and violence that plagued the CHA's developments, became the theme of Lane's administration. By the mid-1990s, Lane had diverted such a large proportion of CHA's management funds to his war on crime that the agency lacked sufficient funds for major repairs in its developments.

In 1988, Lane launched Operation Clean Sweep, his first major attack on the gangs, in Rockwell Gardens. All of the CHA's family high-rises—as well as some high-crime, low-rise developments—were "swept" for drugs, weapons, and illegal tenants at least once between 1988 and 1994. Lane described his rationale for "the sweeps" in 1994: "When they're [gangs] taking over apartments from legitimate leaseholders, it calls for drastic measures. Gangs are telling women. . . . 'We're going to use your apartment for drug dealing. Either you can take some money for it or you can just leave.'"[11] Lane's original strategy was to take control of the high-rise developments, one building at a time.[12] Operation Clean Sweep initially consisted of a joint inspection by police and CHA staff to search for illegal weapons and drugs, to determine that all residents were legal tenants, and to determine the maintenance needs of individual units. CHA resident programs staff participated in the sweeps, conducted needs assessments, and attempted to link residents with social services. The program also involved installing new building security systems and implementing a restrictive visitation policy.

Operation Clean Sweep was immediately controversial and brought Lane national attention. The CHA was widely accused of violating residents' civil rights in the name of better security. In 1988, the American Civil Liberties Union (ACLU) filed a class-action lawsuit against the housing authority on behalf of the tenants, seeking to stop the sweeps.[13] Despite the controversy, Lane viewed the early phases of the program as a success: "As a result of the curfew policy, a lot of guys who are living in apartments [illegally] had to leave. . . . Ninety-three percent of our households are female-headed. We're not naive; we know the men are there somewhere. So this whole group of guys who were living with their girlfriends had to leave when we had the sweeps. . . . I think that standards and controls will lead to changes in behavior. I believe we should maintain high standards, and people will live up to them—not all, but most."[14]

The Anti-Drug Initiative

In late 1989, the CHA began expanding Operation Clean Sweep into a state-of-the-art community crime-prevention program called "the Anti-Drug Initiative." Lane intended the Anti-Drug Initiative to serve as a national model for crime prevention in public housing. The program encompassed many elements researchers and practitioners believed were necessary for success. Buildings targeted under the CHA's Anti-Drug Initiative received a range of programs and services, including law-enforcement interventions (sweeps, in-house police and security forces, security guards), community crime-prevention interventions (tenant patrols), and drug prevention and treatment centers. In addition, the CHA installed metal detectors, secured doors, and guard booths in each building (CHA 1991b).

However, the expansion of Lane's war on crime placed increasing pressure on the agency's resources. Operation Clean Sweep alone was extremely expensive; the cost of a single sweep was estimated at $175,000 per high-rise building, excluding the costs of the Chicago police (National Commission on Severely Distressed Public Housing 1992b). In addition to the sweeps, the CHA created its own police and security forces in 1990 and hired private security guards for many high-rise developments. The agency's relatively small "drug elimination" grants from HUD (less than $10 million per year) covered only a fraction of these expenses; these funds were also being used to cover the entire cost of the drug treatment and prevention centers that the agency began opening in 1989.[15]

Costs for the Anti-Drug Initiative escalated as the CHA used sweeps to respond to many serious gang-related incidents. For example, in 1992, snipers in Cabrini-Green shot seven-year-old Dantrell Davis. He was the third student from his elementary school to be killed that year, and the crime received substantial media attention. The CHA responded by sweeping the entire development at once, one building at a time, violating its own policy of conducting random sweeps, and drastically increasing its security costs.[16]

By 1994, Lane's war on crime was costing the CHA more than $78 million each year. Because of these enormous costs, the CHA had no alternative but to divert a substantial portion of its HUD funds for operating costs and repairing and refurbishing buildings toward its security programs. This strategy meant the agency had little ability to address its other pressing problems, such as city code violations or failing heating and plumbing systems in its developments.

Sweeps Controversy

In addition to draining the agency's resources, Lane's war on crime became an increasing source of controversy by the mid-1990s. In the summer of 1993, several children fell to their deaths from unprotected windows in the Robert Taylor Homes. After a public outcry, the CHA launched an emergency program to install window guards in all of its high-rises.[17] In August, gang members fired on the crews installing the window guards in Taylor. In response, the CHA and Chicago police conducted what they called an "emergency sweep," which included searches of apartments for weapons. During this sweep, officers drilled open some doors and searched residents' personal belongings. Vincent Lane described the CHA's rationale for this extreme reaction:

> We reallocated some funds and carried out the emergency installation of child guards at Robert Taylor. Then I heard we had to pull the contractors out because the gangs had run them off. The reason the gangs ran them off is because the police often used TAC [tactical] teams dressed as workmen. So the gangs said, "To hell with the kids, you can't come in here." The staff was going to try again in a few weeks and see if they couldn't sneak the crews in. I said that was unacceptable. So, . . . I decided to look for weapons because there were a lot of guns in Taylor. It was a very hot summer, and they were shooting all the time. The police had to shut down State Street because of all the gunfire.[18]

Following the CHA's actions in Taylor, the ACLU once again filed a class-action suit against the agency,[19] and a federal judge issued an injunction preventing the CHA from conducting warrantless searches (*Chicago Sun-Times*, February 15, 1994). At the end of March, a major gang war erupted in Robert Taylor; more than three hundred shooting incidents were reported during a five-day period (*Chicago Sun-Times*, March 29, 1994). Faced with this situation, the CHA asked the judge to lift the restraining order, but the request was denied.

In April, President Clinton intervened, asking the judge to reconsider permitting the sweeps. Despite the high-profile support, the events in Taylor—coupled with concerns about costs—gradually stopped the CHA's sweeps. The CHA continued to sweep some buildings using a modified approach during 1994 and 1995, but these actions became much less frequent. Instead, the agency dramatically expanded its police patrols in the high-rises, with teams of CHA and Chicago police walking through the hallways and stairwells of specific buildings for weeks at a time.

Financial Scandals

During the following year, Lane gradually lost control over the agency. The CHA experienced a series of financial scandals during the summer of 1994, many involving the CHA's contract security guard program, one component of the Anti-Drug Initiative.[20] As the problems mounted, Mayor Richard M. Daley, the son of the first Mayor Daley, appointed one of his aides as executive director with a mandate to deal with the financial mess. Lane reportedly "ousted" him within six months, and concerns increased about the chairman's management ability (*Chicago Tribune*, April 29, 1995).

Worry about Lane's possibly inappropriate linkages to the Nation of Islam heightened his problems. In May 1994, the CHA announced that it had contracted with Moorehead and Associates, a property management company, and New Life Self-Development Company, a private firm affiliated with the Nation of Islam, to manage and provide security for two developments (Maplewood Courts and Rockwell Gardens).[21]

In May 1995, HUD announced an investigation of a possible conflict of interest involving Lane and New Life. The *Chicago Tribune* (May 17, 1995) alleged that Lane had struck a deal with the Nation of Islam to lease a store for one of its enterprises in a shopping mall Lane had developed, saving him from major financial problems. Lane reportedly offered to give New Life the security contracts for the Maplewood Courts and Rockwell Gardens developments as a quid pro quo for helping him out with his personal financial problems. Although Lane admitted discussing the two transactions at the same meeting, he denied that they were linked. Despite his denial, many observers believed that something unethical had occurred.

HUD Takeover

As a result of both these controversies and the evidence of on-going, serious management problems, HUD officially took control of the CHA at the end of May 1995. HUD officials demanded the immediate resignation of Lane and all other CHA board commissioners, and a management team comprised of senior HUD officials from Washington, D.C., assumed responsibility for the agency. With Mayor Daley's agreement, Joseph Shuldiner, the head of the interim management team and the former HUD assistant secretary for Public and Indian

Housing, was officially appointed executive director in September 1995. HUD's takeover ushered in a four-year period that brought the biggest change for the CHA since the construction of the high-rises in the 1950s.

The Shuldiner administration initially focused much of its efforts on cleaning up the CHA's management, particularly the agency's perpetually mismanaged finances. Because of the enormous costs, the new administration gradually dismantled Lane's Anti-Drug Initiative. Some major changes included implementing a community policing initiative in the high-rises, reducing reliance on security guards, and reorganizing the tenant patrols. Claiming it was increasing police patrols, the CHA nearly stopped using contract security guards and laid off much of its own inhouse security force (*Chicago Tribune*, May 20, 1998) as part of a drastic cost-cutting effort. In mid-1998, the agency began laying off some of its upper-level police officers as well, in an attempt to cut an additional $12 million from its security budget (*Chicago Tribune*, July 30, 1998).

The High-Rises Begin to Come Down

Instead of focusing on fighting crime directly, the Shuldiner administration sought to bring about much more fundamental change: it wanted to replace the CHA's unmanageable developments with a combination of new and revitalized public housing and Section 8 vouchers. In theory, these revitalized developments would be much safer than the housing they replaced. They would follow current thinking on the best ways to design public housing for families while minimizing crime, including designs intended to maximize "defensible space" that would be easier for tenants to control (Newman 1972, 1996) and constructing smaller developments of townhouses and mid-rise buildings. However, given the enormous expenditures—one proposed plan for a revitalized Cabrini-Green was estimated to cost over $1 billion—and the logistical difficulties of rehousing thousands of residents, the CHA had only made modest progress on its revitalization plans by the end of the decade.

The fact that Shuldiner was even able to attempt to reshape CHA housing was the result of a series of changes in federal housing policy during the mid-1990s, all intended to address the crisis situation in public housing (Popkin, Buron, and Levy 1999). Congress repealed the one-for-one replacement rule in 1995. This meant that the CHA was only required to replace any occupied units; further, the agency had the option of replacing them with either new housing or Section 8 vouchers that could be used in the private market. In 1993, the federal government created the HOPE VI program, providing an extraordinary infusion of resources to revitalize distressed public housing around the nation.[22]

The CHA, one of the biggest beneficiaries of the HOPE VI program, by 1998 had received nearly $160 million dollars in HOPE VI grants to initiate revitalization efforts in six developments: Cabrini-Green, Henry Horner Homes, Robert Taylor Homes, Ida B. Wells, Washington Park, and the ABLA Homes. However, the CHA's developments are so large that the HOPE VI funding will finance only a modest proportion of their revitalization.[23]

Shuldiner, pushing ahead with demolition almost immediately after taking control of the CHA, began with two buildings in Horner in August 1995. The Horner effort is one of the most ambitious public housing redevelopment initiatives in the country. Unlike CHA's other HOPE VI sites, Horner was the subject of a class-action lawsuit filed by a group of Henry Horner residents in 1991.[24] Shortly before the HUD takeover, the CHA signed a consent decree to resolve the lawsuit. The consent decree called for a comprehensive $200-million redevelopment of the Horner site, with new mixed-income town homes to be constructed on-site and in the surrounding community.[25]

By the end of 1998, the CHA had demolished small numbers of buildings in each of the first four HOPE VI sites, as well as buildings in several other developments. A number of high-rise buildings were closed, awaiting demolition. But a new federal law meant that the agency faced increasing pressures to close its worst properties. Starting in 1997, all housing authorities were required to conduct a "viability" assessment of any of their properties with more than three hundred units and a vacancy rate greater than 10 percent to determine whether the cost of rehabilitation exceeded the cost of demolition and replacement with Section 8 vouchers.[26] Under the law, developments that fail the viability assessment are supposed to be demolished and their occupied units "vouchered out" within a five-year period. The CHA, with its many large developments in terrible condition, was hit particularly hard by this new law. Nearly nineteen thousand of its units failed the viability assessment, and the agency scrambled to develop a plan to deal with replacing this housing in relatively short order.

By the end of the decade, it was unclear what the future would hold for the CHA. In particular, it was uncertain whether it would be feasible to house such large numbers of severely troubled low-income residents in private-market housing. Conditions in the high-rises remained terrible, worsening as they aged and as the CHA stopped investing in any major repairs. Finally, in mid-1999, the CHA faced yet another management takeover, as Mayor Richard M. Daley was poised to retake control of the still-troubled agency.

No Easy Answers

This review of the agency's history shows that there is no simple explanation for how CHA's public housing ended up in such disastrous condition. Certainly local politics have played an integral role in the CHA's demise, but local politicians can bear only partial blame for the disaster. A combination of federal policies and poor management drove out residents who had the means to live elsewhere; they left behind a younger, more dysfunctional population.

The failure of the Chicago police to provide sufficient service to residents compounded the problems. Some, including Lane, accused the police of not responding to calls for service from CHA developments because of the dangers from the gangs. Without adequate police protection, residents were forced to depend on local gang members for protection. Other city services failed CHA residents as well; fearful for their own safety, fire and ambulance crews sometimes refused to enter CHA developments. Many public schools in and around the developments were abysmal, and the public parks near the developments were usually crime-ridden as well. Even the U.S. Postal Service sometimes refused to deliver mail because of the dangers; more often, letter carriers, faced with rows of broken mailboxes, left the mail piled on the lobby floor. The indifference of government officials and other Chicago residents allowed the terrible problems to go unchecked.

Finally, CHA residents themselves were clearly responsible for many problems in their developments. As we show in the case studies of Rockwell Gardens, Henry Horner, and Ickes, the relationship between victims and perpetrators was complex; many criminals were the brothers, sons, or partners of other residents. Many of the worst criminals, who grew up in CHA housing, were well known to other residents. Some young gang members vandalized buildings, shattering light bulbs and defacing walls with graffiti. Residents who were not directly involved in the violence allowed gangs to use their developments as safe havens for their business, because of either their relationships with gang members or their fear of retaliation. A substantial number of CHA residents were addicts and depended on the gangs for their own supplies of illegal drugs. Because the drug dealers were among the only people in the developments with extra money, even those who were not addicts often depended on them for economic support.

Just as there is no simple answer to the question of how CHA housing ended up in such miserable condition by the 1990s, there are also no simple solutions. Lane, taking an aggressive stance against the gangs and crime, spent hundreds of millions of dollars on police and security. Shuldiner tried to revamp these programs to make them more efficient and at the same time began a massive reshaping of CHA develop-ments. The three case studies describe the limited effects of very costly efforts to control the crime in CHA's high-rise developments. These case studies show that in this environment, even the best designed commu-nity crime-prevention programs were doomed to failure, overwhelmed by the powerful gangs, the social disorganization, and the internal poli-tics that undermined virtually all of the agency's efforts.

3 | # Fighting Crime
in Public Housing

By the late 1980s, the CHA's high-rise developments had become national symbols of what many policy-makers were coming to view as a crisis situation: the concentration of extremely poor and troubled families in neglected, high-crime public housing developments in cities across the country. These troubled communities seemed to be particularly vulnerable to a range of social ills, including extremely high rates of unemployment and welfare dependence (National Commission on Severely Distressed Public Housing 1992a).[1] As in Chicago, many urban areas experienced severe problems with drug trafficking, violent crime, and gang activity, in part because of the large pool of vulnerable youths who were easy for the gangs to recruit (Bursik and Grasmick 1993). Exacerbating the situation, the crack epidemic and the increasingly violent drug market of the late 1980s and early 1990s overwhelmed public housing developments in many cities.

Despite the escalating crime, HUD and the Congress focused relatively little attention on the growing crisis in public housing. During the 1980s, HUD was an agency beset by problems, including the Reagan administration's lack of support for housing assistance, poor internal management, and corruption. Under these circumstances, it was difficult for HUD to take effective action.

Congress finally authorized a new program in 1988 called the Public Housing Drug Elimination Program, which was designed to provide grants to housing authorities to create crime- and drug-prevention programs.[2] Because of the extreme nature of its problems and because of CHA Chairman Vincent Lane's increasing prominence on the national scene—he was appointed cochair of the National Commission on Severely Distressed and Troubled Public Housing in 1989—the CHA's struggle to contain the crime in its developments received widespread attention.[3] At least on paper, the CHA's Anti-Drug Initiative programs reflected the latest thinking about crime prevention in public housing: creating a comprehensive range of programs, encouraging collaboration between residents, management, and police, and target hardening (that is, making the buildings less accessible to criminals). Using their Drug Elimination grants, many other housing authorities followed the CHA's lead by instituting sweeps, hiring security guards, organizing tenant patrols, and, in a handful of cases, creating their own police forces.

Several years later, in 1993, Congress increased funding for public housing modernization and, based on the recommendations of the National Commission, created the HOPE VI program to provide large grants (up to $50 million) for housing authorities to revitalize their severely distressed developments (Fosburg, Popkin, and Locke 1996). The CHA's battle against crime occurred in the context of these larger shifts in housing policy. The national war on drugs added urgency to the CHA's efforts, and the increase in funding allowed the agency to create what it hoped would be state-of-the-art anticrime programs. However, even the best-designed community crime-prevention efforts were unlikely to succeed in the violent, chaotic context of CHA's high-rise developments.

Crime and Disorder in Public Housing

Policymakers and researchers have offered various explanations for the prevalence of drug trafficking and violent crime in public housing. Yet, most agree that the physical and social isolation of many large developments contributed greatly to the problems. As in Chicago, during the high-rise craze of the 1950s and 1960s, housing authorities across the country constructed huge developments on superblocks, intentionally separated from the surrounding neighborhood. These developments were often physically barricaded by expressways or rail tracks (Fosburg, Popkin, and Locke 1996).

In addition to the physical isolation, in Chicago as elsewhere, housing authority policies often determined that these developments would be completely racially segregated (Massey and Denton 1993). By 1977, more than half of the family developments across the nation were predominantly African-American; in cities like Chicago, the segregation was even more extreme (Coulibaly, Green, and James 1998). Public housing was economically segregated as well, likely to be located disproportionately in poor neighborhoods where unemployment was high and income was low (Newman and Harkness 1999). Predominantly African-American developments, like those in Chicago, were particularly likely to be located in very low-income, minority neighborhoods (Goering, Kamely, and Richardson 1997).

Compounding the problems of isolation and racial segregation, these developments were artificially created communities; they lacked any existing social structure that might have reinforced social norms of acceptable behavior. As in CHA housing, gangs often filled the void, and the lack of other economic activity allowed the drug trade to flourish (Halpern 1995; Hagedorn 1998). The physical design and poor construction of many developments exacerbated the problems with crime and drugs.

Federal housing policies also contributed to the concentrated problems in public housing. Although public housing was initially intended as short-term housing for the working poor, federal preferences that favored the poorest tenants rapidly pushed out most working families during the 1970s and 1980s. Inadequate funds for maintenance, as well as managerial neglect, accelerated the decline of many developments across the country (Meehan 1985; National Commission on Severely Distressed and Troubled Public Housing 1992a).

Evidence began to appear early on that these huge developments were potentially disastrous environments for families. As early as the 1960s, residents of the Pruitt-Igoe development in St. Louis were experiencing high rates of drug use and sales and teen pregnancy. These problems led to high levels of anxiety and helplessness, especially among adult women, and pervasive distrust and fear (Rainwater 1966, 1970).[4]

After thirty years of failed policy and management neglect, the problems first noted in Pruitt-Igoe have become epidemic in troubled public housing communities across the nation. Chicago's public housing is among the worst, but many housing authorities face increasingly serious problems with violent crime in their developments. Disputes are much more likely than in the past to end in a shooting or killing and to involve innocent bystanders (Keyes 1992). These developments are also plagued by high levels of drug trafficking and other types of crime (Dunworth and Saiger 1993; Webster and Conners 1992). In addition, residents must cope every day with darkened hallways, abandoned apartments, graffiti, trash, and street prostitution. Visible disorder—especially among groups of youths hanging out—and antisocial street activity breeds fear, undermines social cohesion, and seems to promote even more serious crime (Skogan 1990).

For residents of the worst public housing, the costs of the violence and community disintegration are profound. Even preschool children in the worst developments learn to hit the ground at the sound of gunfire and to avoid open areas where shootings are common. Children are often victims of or witnesses to the violence. All children who live in these dangerous environments are at risk for psychological trauma and intellectual deficits that result from the chronic fear—much like children living in guerrilla war zones like Cambodia or Mozambique (Garbarino, Kostelny, and Dubrow 1991).

Constant violence also affects adults; it contributes to widespread depression, lack of motivation, and hopelessness. An inherently destructive street culture has developed, which discourages young people, particularly young men, from seeking mainstream employment and actively encourages violent behavior (Bourgois 1995). For all these reasons, the problems faced by residents in the most distressed developments are overwhelming, and the social world is both complex and dangerous.

Crime Prevention in Public Housing

Policymakers agree that controlling crime is a necessary first step to improving conditions (National Commission on Severely Distressed Public Housing 1992a). However, it is not clear how best to address the seemingly intractable problems in troubled public housing developments. The major crime-prevention strategies that have been tried—by the CHA and other housing authorities—include environmental design, situational crime prevention, intensive law enforcement, and community crime-prevention programs.

Environmental Design

In the 1970s, Oscar Newman (1973) developed a prevention strategy primarily to deal with crime in public housing. His approach, Crime Prevention Through Environmental Design, assumes that characteristics of physical environments can either prevent or facilitate criminal activity.[5] Developments offering many places for criminals to hide, easy escape routes, and large public areas that are difficult for individual residents to observe promote crime. According to the Environmental Design model, a major reason that the huge public housing developments of the 1950s and 1960s had such serious problems with crime was the lack of defensible space, defined as public areas clearly associated with a specific apartment (Newman 1972, 1996). Such space might be either a fenced yard or an entryway leading to only one or two apartments or a public area such as a small courtyard shared by only a few households. In a defensible development, tenants who could easily view all public areas from inside their apartments would be more likely to do so. Without clearly defined space, residents had no sense of territoriality to motivate them to keep public areas free of crime and disorder. As a result, public areas, such as the large open spaces around high-rises, were easily taken over by gangs and drug dealers. The public character of public housing was also a fundamental problem: in poorly designed developments such as those in Chicago, buildings lacked the secured lobbies or guarded entryways that could prevent outsiders from entering (Skogan and Annan 1994).

Strategies such as improving the architectural layout of housing developments and controlling physical deterioration have succeeded somewhat in reducing crime in a few public housing properties, although it is not clear how much improvement is owing solely to changes in physical design (Taylor and Harrell 1996). There are also some indications that the overall size of a development has a greater role in determining the level of criminal activity than whether the buildings are high-rise or low-rise (Holzman, Kudrick, and Voytek 1996).

Given the complexity of the problems involved, it is unlikely that design-based crime-prevention strategies can have more than a modest impact on levels of crime. Reducing crime in public housing requires adequate social services, regular activities for youths, and effective management, as well as better architectural designs (Feins, Epstein, and Widom 1997; Rouse and Rubenstein 1978). Further, a safe design may not be enough to overcome the effects of anonymity, distrust, and fear among residents (Merry 1981). Finally, design-based strategies are intended to prevent crime by intruders, but a significant proportion of crimes in public housing are committed by residents or their guests (Keyes 1992; Merry 1981).

Situational Crime Prevention

The CHA's anticrime efforts relied heavily on situational crime-prevention measures. Situational crime prevention encompasses a range of strategies to reduce criminal activity by manipulating the physical environment (Clarke and Mayhew 1980).[6] In the context of public housing, these interventions generally involve attempts to reduce the opportunities for committing crimes in particular locations such as lobbies or hallways. Strategies include screening people as they enter and exit buildings, controlling access to buildings by closing entrances and requiring residents to use keys or security cards, using security guards or video cameras for surveillance, and setting formal visitation policies. These measures appear to be relatively effective in reducing crime (see Clarke 1992, 1995). However, it is possible that target hardening may simply displace criminal activity to other locations; for example, drug dealers forced out of lobbies move into vacant apartments, or drug markets shift from one development to another.[7]

Law Enforcement Strategies

As the war on drugs got underway during the mid-1980s, the focus of crime-prevention efforts in public housing shifted from changes in physical design to aggressive law-enforcement tactics. These strategies included placing mini–police stations in large developments, intensifying police patrols, and conducting undercover investigations (Annan and Skogan 1992; Cuyahoga Metropolitan Housing Authority 1993; Greensboro Housing Authority 1993; Wilkins 1989). However, many of these law-enforcement tactics appear ineffective (Sherman et al. 1997).[8] Likewise, there is little evidence that cracking down on drug offenders reduces crime in public housing or other poor neighborhoods (Kleiman 1988; Kleiman et al. 1988; Pate 1984; Uchida, Forst, and Annan 1992; Annan and Skogan 1993).[9] However, very targeted efforts aimed at preventing crime in specific high-crime hot spots—that is, drug markets and problem buildings—appear to be more successful (Sherman et al. 1997).

Focusing on public nuisances, such as loitering youths, seems to reduce crime (Boydstun 1975; Reiss 1985). For example, much of the huge decline in crime in New York City in the late 1990s is often attributed to the mayor's emphasis on arresting people for offenses like aggressive panhandling or urinating in public. There are serious questions, however, about whether these popular "round-em-up" tactics violate offenders' civil rights or produce long-term effects (Rosenbaum 1993; Rosenbaum, Lurigio, and Davis 1998).

Along the same lines, another strategy that seems to reduce crime in many urban neighborhoods is to focus on maintaining order by making arrests for minor offenses—a strategy based on the broken windows theory (Kelling and Coles 1996; Skogan 1990; Wilson and Kelling 1982), which holds that if visible disorder is left unchecked, more serious problems will follow. For example, one broken window that is not repaired immediately leads to many more broken windows. A massive community policing program in five neighborhoods in Chicago,[10] involving the coordination of other city services to clean up physical blight, appeared to reduce crime and fear, as well as lower the levels of physical and social disorder (Skogan and Hartnett 1997). Although this approach worked in some high-crime communities, the research did not address the question of whether it would be effective in the war zones of Chicago's high-rise public housing developments.[11]

Community Involvement

By the late 1980s, there was consensus that successful anticrime efforts in public housing should involve collaboration among the police, housing authority management, and residents (Weisel 1990). Because residents have the largest stake in keeping developments safe, their active participation in crime prevention through organized programs or other initiatives came to be considered essential.

The community involvement approach (Heinzelman 1981; Lavrakas 1985; Rosenbaum 1988) is based, in part, on the concept of social control. Social disorganization theory suggests that criminal activity is encouraged when a neighborhood is unable to exercise informal social control over its residents or to achieve common goals such as reducing the threat of crime (Bursik and Grasmick 1993; Sampson and Groves 1989; Shaw and McKay 1942). In an organized neighborhood, residents reinforce social norms of acceptable behavior (that is, not vandalizing buildings or cars). These behaviors play a critical role in reducing crime and fear of crime (Greenberg, Rohe, and Williams 1982; Jacobs 1961; Rosenbaum 1988; Sampson, Raudenbush, and Earls 1997). A sense of community, greater social interaction, and clearly delineated neighborhood boundaries and identities also help to control crime (Suttles 1972; Conklin 1975; DuBow and Emmons 1981). For this reason, many community crime-prevention programs seek to strengthen informal social control and encourage residents to closely supervise children and adolescents.

Despite their popular appeal, it is not clear how well these community crime-prevention efforts actually work in poor communities, particularly inner-city neighborhoods like the CHA's developments.[12] Many housing authorities, including the CHA, created tenant patrols and other resident-based initiatives, but, for multiple reasons, such initiatives often fail in public housing (Skogan and Annan 1994). In high-crime developments, residents often fear and resent the police, the police are suspicious of the residents, and the housing authority management is uncooperative.[13]

The failure of community crime-prevention programs to substantially reduce crime and disorder is often attributed to residents' inability or unwillingness to participate. Yet, because many of these communities lack the economic or social resources to mount organized anticrime efforts, this attitude amounts to blaming the victim (Buerger 1994; Halpern 1995). Further, in many low-income and even some higher-income communities, relationships between the criminals and other residents are complex. Drug dealers and gang members are often long-time residents, friends, and relatives of residents who themselves are not involved in criminal activity (Furstenberg 1993). Because of these connections, residents may be willing to tolerate a local gang, comprised of their friends and relatives, in exchange for protection from rival gangs whose members they may not know (Patillo 1998). This complex social world means that few residents will be able, or possibly even willing, to organize effectively to combat crime.

Comprehensive Programs

Less troubled housing authorities have had some success with anticrime programs. The types of programs that seem to work— at least in less extreme circumstances—typically contain elements of all the strategies discussed above, including aggressive law enforcement, security enhancements, tenants' participation, and social services. Most also include improvements in housing authority management. Some housing authorities have experimented with restrictive management policies as a way to promote security and safety among residents. These tactics include screening potential residents through criminal history,[14] requiring credit checks, and limiting access to buildings through the use of resident identification cards (New York City Housing Authority 1993; Webster and Connors 1992; Keyes 1992; Hammett et al. 1994).

Since the mid-1990s, HUD has placed increasing emphasis on comprehensive efforts to address the problems in troubled public housing developments that combine improved architectural design with strategies to reduce crime, increase social cohesion, and promote self-sufficiency. As chairman of the National Commission on Severely Distressed and Troubled Public Housing, Lane had advocated for a long-term strategy of replacing deteriorated housing with either new or rehabilitated developments that mixed higher-income, working tenants with very poor tenants. In response to the recommendations of the National Commission, Congress authorized the HOPE VI/Urban Revitalization Demonstration program in 1993, which allows HUD to provide large grants (up to $50 million per development) to housing authorities to revitalize severely distressed developments (Fosburg, Popkin, and Locke 1996).[15] Under HOPE VI, many housing authorities, including that in Chicago, are replacing their worst developments with newly constructed mixed-income communities that incorporate the latest thinking about designs that will prevent crime as well as provide supportive services for residents.

The CHA's Anti-Drug Initiative

The CHA's Anti-Drug Initiative grew out of former Chairman Lane's efforts to wrest control of CHA's high-rise developments from the gangs. As originally conceived, the Anti-Drug Initiative was a model crime-prevention program that appeared to offer great potential for reducing crime, violence, and disorder. The Anti-Drug Initiative, one of the country's most extensive anticrime programs in public housing, incorporated many elements that researchers felt were essential for a successful program. The initiative involved collaboration among residents, management, and police and included a comprehensive array of services, including law enforcement, tenant patrols, drug prevention and treatment, and situational crime prevention.

The CHA poured resources into the Anti-Drug Initiative to create in-house police and security forces, pay for private security, conduct sweeps, and construct guard booths in lobbies. As described in detail below, four groups were responsible for providing security in CHA housing: the Chicago police, the CHA police, the CHA Security Force, and contract security guards. Police from both agencies participated in sweeps and patrolled buildings; Security Force officers and contract guards monitored building entrances. HUD granted the CHA special dispensation to use its modernization funds (money intended for repairing and refurbishing buildings) to pay for its police and security programs. By 1994, the agency was spending more than $78 million per year on Anti-Drug Initiative programs. Figure 3.1 provides an overview of the Anti-Drug Initiative programs as they existed from 1994 to 1997.[16]

Operation Clean Sweep

Operation Clean Sweep, known locally as the sweeps, began in 1988 and was the first of the CHA's major law-enforcement interventions. CHA and Chicago police both participated in the sweeps, along with staff from CHA's Office of Resident Programs. The first sweeps involved door-to-door inspection of apartment units, undertaking maintenance and repair of common areas (lobbies, halls, elevators, etc.), implementing twenty-four-hour security and strict visitation policies, removing unauthorized residents, and rehabilitating vacant units. Because CHA buildings were not built with exterior doors, crews installed heavy steel security doors on all entrances as well as guard booths and metal detectors. After the initial inspection, residents were sent to a central location to acquire photo identification cards, which they were supposed to present to the guards to gain access to the building. Finally, CHA Resident Programs' staff interviewed residents about maintenance and social service needs, provided service referrals, and generated maintenance work orders.

For various reasons, including an increased demand for service from residents, mounting costs, and the effects of the two class-action lawsuits filed by the ACLU,[17] the sweeps gradually became more limited in scope. When the service and maintenance components were curtailed,

---

Anti-Drug Initiative Programs

Law Enforcement
- Sweeps
- CHA Police Force
- Police Building Walkdowns (BITE patrols and swarms)
- Community policing
- CHA Security Force
- Private security guards

Drug Prevention and Treatment
- CADRE centers

Community Crime Prevention Interventions
- Tenant patrols
- Target hardening

Other Interventions

- Victim services
- Private management
- Resident management
- Redevelopment

Figure 3.1

the sweeps became almost exclusively law-enforcement interventions. Following the decision in *Pratt et al. v. The Chicago Housing Authority* (the second ACLU lawsuit), the agency limited the sweeps to focusing strictly on lease violations (unauthorized tenants, etc.) and eliminated them altogether by the end of 1994.

BITE Patrols and Swarms

The CHA gradually replaced the sweeps with intensive police patrols in individual buildings. The CHA and Chicago police jointly created the Building Interdiction Team Effort (BITE) patrols, or vertical foot patrols, after the sweeps were declared unconstitutional and extreme violence broke out in the Robert Taylor Homes in 1994 (see chapter 2). These patrols involved teams of CHA and Chicago police officers walking through the halls and stairwells of individual buildings looking for evidence of drug trafficking and other criminal activity.

The BITE patrols were an emergency intervention instituted in only a few CHA developments; in early 1995, patrols were assigned to Robert Taylor, Stateway Gardens, Henry Horner, and Rockwell Gardens.[18] But in late 1994, the CHA police began patrolling some buildings on their own, calling these actions swarms. Swarms involved CHA police officers simultaneously walking down (that is, patrolling the halls and stairwells) all the buildings in a development.[19]

In-house Police Force

In 1990 the CHA created its own police force to supplement the activities of the Chicago police, whom Lane felt were failing to provide adequate service for CHA residents. The CHA police, trained at the Chicago Police Academy, could make arrests and respond to calls on CHA property. Some CHA police officers were current or former residents. In 1996 the CHA police force consisted of 450 officers and 50 civilian support persons.[20]

At least in theory, the CHA police worked closely with the Chicago police. Many efforts, including sweeps and building patrols, were conducted jointly; both departments patrolled CHA's developments and responded independently to residents' calls for police service; and both departments participated in their own community policing efforts. CHA police reported incidents to the same computer database as the Chicago police. Although the two police departments were supposed to coordinate their activities, there was often tension between the leadership of the two agencies, which undermined cooperation.[21]

A senior CHA police administrator commented that the agency's officers had probably the most difficult police patrol job in America.

> First of all, the level of ongoing, daily, consistent danger faced by the police officers here is greater than any force in the country, in my opinion. Here, our officers work in environments in certain developments where gunfire is just a routine, regular, all-day occurrence, where gang takeovers of lobbies and buildings is routine, to where you have to battle the gangs hand-to-hand constantly to take back buildings. . . . To where you're seeing people shot, robbed, raped, murdered, I mean, it happens on an ongoing basis . . . Then certain physical issues, such as when you're responding to shots fired . . . the fact that you're running into oftentimes dark buildings, up sixteen-floor buildings where you can't really see, where you're liable to run into anything . . . [22]

In-house Security Force

In 1990, in response to concerns about the performance of its contract security guards (described below), the CHA created its own security force to supplement the police. CHA Security Force officers and private guards served essentially the same function: They were stationed in booths or in the doorways of the high-rise buildings to verify residents' identification and to ensure that all guests were signed in by legitimate tenants. They also prevented people from loitering in the lobbies or entryways and called the CHA police when they saw problems occurring.

CHA Security Force officers did not undergo police academy training, but they received six weeks of training at a local state university. Unlike the contract security guards, CHA Security Force officers were required to have a high school diploma and to pass a drug test.[23] Because of these criteria, the CHA had trouble filling positions, even though the security jobs paid about $15 per hour plus full benefits.

Contract Security Guards

Because of funding constraints and the difficulties in recruiting qualified applicants, the CHA did not have enough Security Force officers to provide security for all of its high-crime developments. Therefore, even after 1990, the agency relied heavily on contract security guards, hiring between eight and nine hundred guards through private companies at a cost of approximately $25 million per year.[24] These guards were paid $5 or $6 per hour, had only twenty hours of training, and were not screened for drug use. One company the CHA hired to provide security during the study period was New Life Self-Development Company, a security company affiliated with the Nation of Islam. The major difference between New Life guards—most of whom were not themselves members of the Nation of Islam—and other contract guards was that they neither carried weapons nor wore uniforms.

In general, all the contract guards were poorly paid, and their jobs were extremely dangerous, often more dangerous than those of police officers. In the context of CHA's high-rise developments, staff recognized that it was nearly impossible for these guards to be effective.

> Obviously, they have a fear factor. . . . I mean, they're getting paid minimum wage to go out there and just deal with armed people all the time, people who are better armed than they are, there's not very much back up for them, residents might give them a hard time about certain things, but there are some real horror stories. . . . Those security officers, contract and CHA, go through an awful lot. I mean, they've been ordered out of buildings, they've had their weapons confiscated by gang members, and several of them have been killed.[25]

Despite recognizing the nearly impossible task the private security guards faced, the CHA continued to use them in its family developments through 1996.

Drug Prevention and Treatment

As part of the Anti-Drug Initiative, the CHA offered drug prevention and treatment referral services in each of its high-rise developments through its CADRE (Combating Alcohol and Drugs through Rehabilitation and Education) centers. The first CADRE centers opened in spring 1991; centers were operating in all three study sites by 1992.

One distinctive feature of the CADRE centers was the personnel: primarily residents staffed them. Each center was supposed to be linked to other agencies that could both provide beds in treatment centers for CHA residents and guide staff members in developing prevention initiatives. The CADRE centers also established partnerships with nearby public schools to conduct prevention workshops and sponsored a variety of other activities, including Project Red Ribbon, which focused on drunk driving prevention. In response to resident need, the centers expanded their services to provide assistance with food, emergency shelter, or other essential needs. Finally, although they were not officially part of CADRE's service package, a number of other programs, such as Alcoholics Anonymous, the Girl and Boy Scouts, and Mama Said (the CHA's parenting program), met in the CADRE offices.[26]

Community Crime Prevention

The CHA's tenant patrols began in 1989, growing out of the volunteer efforts of a group of women in Cabrini-Green who organized a school-escort program. CHA Resident Programs staff worked to coordinate tenant patrols in all swept buildings. Patrol members received six months of training and worked in teams, conducting regular walk-downs through the building and noting any suspicious activity, vandalism, or maintenance needs (CHA 1991). Tenant patrol members received a modest financial incentive (a $50-rent credit) for participating in the program.

A national evaluation of the Public Housing Drug Elimination Program found that the CHA had been remarkably successful in organizing and sustaining tenant patrols, despite very difficult conditions (Hammett et al. 1994). CHA staff noted that residents felt great pride in being part of the patrols.[27] However, despite these initial successes, the CHA encountered difficulty in sustaining patrols in some of its most dangerous developments. Even where patrols were sustained, they often focused on combating vandalism rather than more serious crime.[28]

Related Programs

During the early years of the Anti-Drug Initiative, the CHA installed a number of situational crime-prevention measures: they installed security booths, metal detectors, and steel security doors on lobby entrances and closed off secondary building entrances; the agency also experimented with turnstiles, vandal-proof lighting, and intercom systems in some buildings. By 1996, the emphasis on target hardening had waned, and, in some cases, the metal detectors and security doors had been damaged, left unrepaired, or even simply removed. The CHA also began offering a victim services program in some developments in 1995. This program provided counseling and support to victims of crime as well as encouragement to file charges against the assailants.

Two other significant interventions, ostensibly unrelated to the Anti-Drug Initiative, likely affected crime and disorder in CHA developments between 1994 and 1996. First, the agency began placing some developments into private management or resident management during the early 1990s. In theory, private-property management companies should be able to manage the developments better than the long-troubled housing authority. Two of the developments profiled in the case studies were affected: Rockwell Gardens was put into private management in 1994 and the Henry Horner Homes in 1996. In addition, a Resident Management Corporation took over management of one building in Rockwell Gardens and started a number of social service programs for residents.

Second, the CHA began revitalization efforts in some of its high-rise developments in 1995. The first comprehensive initiative targeted the Henry Horner Homes. Starting in late 1995, the CHA began demolishing buildings in Horner, cleaning up the grounds, and constructing new town homes on site.[29]

In sum, the CHA designed its Anti-Drug Initiative as a two-pronged model crime-prevention effort in public housing. First, the collaborative program involved Chicago police, CHA police and security, CHA management, social service providers, and residents, despite the frequent tension between all these actors. Second, this comprehensive effort included aggressive law enforcement, management improvements, increased security, tenant patrols, drug-prevention services, and target-hardening measures. Early assessments of the program suggested that there had been some positive effects, but there was no systematic information about the long-term impact of the CHA's efforts.[30]

The Anti-Drug Initiative in Rockwell, Horner, and Ickes

The following chapters tell the story of the CHA's battle against crime in selected buildings in three of its high-rise developments: Rockwell Gardens, Henry Horner Homes, and Harold Ickes Homes. CHA attempted to implement its anticrime programs in each of these developments, although each received a somewhat different package of services. All three sites had sweeps and were patrolled by both CHA and Chicago police. However, Rockwell and Horner were swept more often than Ickes and generally had a greater police presence. Ickes primarily had CHA Security Force officers guarding its buildings, while Rockwell and Horner primarily had contract security guards. From 1994 to 1996, Rockwell's guards were from the New Life Self-Development Company. All three sites had CADRE centers, but only Rockwell and Ickes had tenant patrols. The CHA installed metal detectors, security doors, and guard booths in all three developments. Finally, Rockwell and Horner each experienced some unique interventions: Rockwell, put into private management in 1994, featured a resident-managed building, while Horner began undergoing a massive redevelopment in 1995 and experienced the effects of the areawide clean-up for the Democratic National Convention.

Still, all three developments faced similar challenges with crime. Like the rest of CHA's high-rise developments, their residents were extremely poor, the majority of the households were headed by single women, and very few of the adults worked. All were dominated by powerful street gangs, and in all drug trafficking and substance abuse were epidemic. As the case studies show, despite the CHA's costly efforts, none of the agency's interventions had much long-term impact on the lives of individual residents. Indeed, even the massive revitalization effort in Horner seemed unlikely to benefit many original tenants. Together, these three case studies provide an important set of lessons about the challenges of trying to implement community crime-prevention initiatives in such extremely troubled communities.

4 | Rockwell Gardens

The Residents of Rockwell Gardens
Dawn's Story

Dawn is a long-time resident of Rockwell Gardens[1]—
the development widely considered the most dangerous of the Chicago
Housing Authority's (CHA) high-rise projects.[2] She is a thoughtful, articulate woman in her early thirties and has lived in Rockwell since she
was fourteen. Dawn became pregnant as the result of a rape when she was
sixteen; after the birth of her second child two years later, she dropped
out of school to care for her children. Dawn's mother could not help
her with child care because she had young children of her own, and
Dawn could not find another sitter she felt she could trust.

Her children are now teenagers, and she spends most of her time
and energy protecting them from what she calls "the pressure" of the
surrounding environment: young men pressure her daughter for sex, and
gang members try to recruit her son. For years, she has monitored her
children closely by taking them to parks outside the development to play
and keeping them indoors as much as possible. "They mostly sit on the
porch in the building. . . . [They go out] with me. . . . Sometime they go
to the store and back, but I don't really let them hang in front of the
buildings and stuff. If they go to a playground, they go in the Maplewood
Courts playground [an adjacent, low-rise development] because they don't
shoot over there. Or across the [freeway] bridge to the big park." Although

her son sometimes goes to the store or participates in after-school programs, Dawn says her daughter no longer goes outside alone.

Dawn has been on welfare since the birth of her first child. She says she always wanted to be a nurse when she was growing up, but "her children held her back." Although she did eventually get her GED, her only work experience has been an "off-the-books" job as a housekeeper for a few years. She desperately wants a better life for herself and her children, but she lacks practical ideas about how to improve her situation.

Living in CHA housing has taken a toll on Dawn and her family. Everyone she knows lives in public housing: her entire extended family lives in CHA developments all around the city. She says that no one in her family has "made it," that all the developments are "just the same." Three members of her extended family have died because of gang violence, one as a result of a domestic dispute. Several, addicted to drugs, have lost custody of their children. In April 1996, she told us that, since January, she had already been to three funerals for people from Rockwell, which she said was "typical." Dawn is often depressed, but says she has no one to talk to about her feelings because "people in the projects, they don't want to hear your problems. They tell you 'I have problems of my own.'"

Throughout the two years we interviewed her, Dawn offered many insights into the challenges of life in Rockwell. Although her greatest concerns were drug trafficking and violence, the daily problems that she found most frustrating were poor maintenance and unresponsive housing authority management. For example, in 1994, Dawn said she had been coping with severe plumbing problems for two years:

> My tub water don't shut off—the hot water . . . and the kitchen won't shut off. . . . Well, they just fixed my sink not too long ago because they had to take the whole pipe out of the wall because it was full of that greasy, gunky stuff and the water wouldn't flow through and it kept running out, running out. That took them two years to get up and fix that. I had to wash my dishes in my tub every day. . . . [In the bathroom] my walls were white, [now] they yellowish-brownish from the hot water. I have to close the door at night to keep from going crazy hearing that water!. . . . I been waiting six months for them to fix that.

Vandalism compounded the maintenance problems and, Dawn felt, made her building an even more frightening place to live.

> Some people may set their garbage . . . in front of the incinerator, which they not supposed to do that, they supposed to take

it downstairs to the main floor [because the incinerators don't work], but they don't. Either the kids will set it on fire, or the big boys will come and just throw it down the steps, and it's really dark, we can't see! You know . . . I bust my head, bumped into the light room door, it being dark. . . . And then when they do put bulbs in every day, the guys will like take sticks and break the bulbs or take 'em out and make it dark. Seem like they like it dark.

In Dawn's view, drugs, particularly cocaine, have completely devastated the Rockwell community. She spoke poignantly of seeing friends who were once "strong women" wasting away because of their crack addictions. She said she could no longer let some people she knows into her apartment because they would try to steal whatever they could to support their habit.

Man, the rock's [crack] been here seem like forever. Because when I used to come from the grocery store and I be bringing my groceries in, the elevators be broke, and we used to have to carry our stuff up the stairs . . . and there's people in the hallway smoking crack with . . . they was actually using t.v. antennas. . . . People come to your door and—they say, "Can I use your bathroom," I always tell them no, and I know them, but I tell them no because they wanna go in there and break off a piece of your t.v. antenna.

Dawn said she had never used drugs herself, and she stayed away from "project men," whom she described as pressuring their girlfriends to become users so they could use their welfare money to buy drugs.

Dawn was particularly concerned about how the disintegration of the community affected the children of Rockwell. She agonized over the children she saw being abused or neglected by mothers addicted to cocaine, crack, and heroin. She told the following story to illustrate the extremes to which addicts went to feed their addiction: "Them women just go crazy for that stuff, they do anything. . . . Anything. They don't care. One lady sold her baby for some rock. . . . To the man, it was a guy who sold cocaine over there, she . . . gave him her baby, she told him to hold my baby until I come back, I'm gonna go get the money, give me the rocks."

Dawn used to try to intervene when she saw hungry or abandoned children in her building. When she could afford to, she fed them herself. But when she found children who were unsupervised—for example, a five-year-old taking care of a four-month-old—she would sometimes call the Department of Children and Family Services to report the situation. When the social workers came, she would help getting the children dressed and ready to be taken away. She also used to call the police to report shootings or other crimes. Eventually, her family convinced her that it was too dangerous to get involved, a position that causes her much pain. She spoke of her torment over having kept silent after she witnessed a young neighbor using a gun:

> When you in the projects, you do a lot of things, you see a lot of things, but you know you don't wanna say nothing because it can get you hurt . . . but it be on your conscience, and it drives me crazy when I can't say nothing. . . . I see this little boy, he's about twelve years old. He's shooting, I see him shooting at the others [kids]. And I'm looking at this, and I know his mother and everything. Everybody telling me, "No, don't say nothing, don't tell his mother." And now he's dead, the little boy is dead now, and it made me feel if I had a told his mother, maybe he'd still be here.

Dawn said she had high hopes when the CHA first started the sweeps in Rockwell in 1988; she believed they would help to control the gangs and drug trafficking. For a time, she felt that conditions did improve a little, but, by the time we met her in 1994, she told us that all the good effects had disappeared. However, she was hopeful that the CHA's latest effort—hiring a company owned by the Nation of Islam to provide security and manage the development—would help. Also, she reported that things were getting calmer following a gang truce in Rockwell.

But from 1994 to 1996, Dawn became increasingly disillusioned and unhappy. In her view, the "Muslims" proved no better than any other security guards who had patrolled Rockwell over the years. The new management cleaned up the buildings, but she still had serious maintenance problems in her apartment. Drug abuse was still rampant, and the gangs still dominated the development. Sometimes she felt that things had improved for a little while because of a gang truce or the arrest of a particularly powerful gang leader, but the gang war between the Disciples and the Vice Lords always "flared up" again after a month or two.

In spring 1996, Dawn finally moved out of Rockwell Gardens to another, smaller CHA development. A friend of hers had moved there and told her that it was "nice." Dawn was dismayed to find that, although the complex was cleaner than Rockwell and the apartments were better, she still faced many of the same problems: "I only been there not long at all and they been shooting, I been hearing gun shots, one boy done got killed, right out by the building in the back."

Wardell's Story

While most of Rockwell was a place of extreme hardship and social decay, one building in the development was set apart from the rest of the community. In the early 1990s, a group of residents, led by a charismatic man in his early fifties named Wardell Yotaghan,[3] started a resident management corporation in their building.

Wardell's version of life in Rockwell is very different from Dawn's. Unlike many Rockwell residents, he had not spent his whole life in CHA housing; he had moved into the development a decade ago when he married the mother of his three youngest children. He had, however, spent his entire life living on the west side of Chicago and witnessed the devastation that drugs have wrought on his community.

Wardell viewed himself as having been saved from the streets by athletic programs; he said he was inspired by Muhammad Ali's example. He said that most members of his family *have* made it—his mother and sisters worked, and one sister went to college and has her own business. Wardell finished high school and attended college off and on over the years. He worked most of his life as a security guard, but he gave that up when he became a resident activist and president of his building in the early 1990s.

Despite these successes, Wardell had been affected by the same problems that Dawn describes. Over the past two decades, he had lost several friends and relatives to drugs:

> Well, the truth is, most of the people I grew up with, in the area I grew up . . . most of them are dead. . . . It [heroin] took a big toll in the area where I lived. Me and a guy I was talking to a few days ago, he was younger than me, but we come from the same area, we were talking about all the people that were dead that we used to play ball with. When we were young, there were things for us to do. . . . There was basketball, softball, swimming, and those were things that we done. And the guys that we used to do that with, they're all gone.

This destruction had driven Wardell to action; he said his mission in life was to "clean up the mess" that drugs and drug trafficking have created in his community. He had become a full-time community activist: advocating for Rockwell residents, bringing programs and services to his building, and, more recently, fighting to preserve low-income housing in Chicago while the CHA plans to demolish many of its family developments.

Like Dawn, Wardell was particularly concerned about the children of Rockwell. He saw children suffering because their mothers, addicted to drugs, were exposing them to violence: "it ain't no secret that a lot of the people in the building . . . are addicted to drugs. So they go out and these people [the dealers] give them this credit and they don't pay, and here they [the dealers] come up to the apartment and I'm not as much concerned about what they do to that individual as I am about the terror that they bring on the children that she have in the apartment."

Wardell was also concerned about the gangs in Rockwell, but unlike many residents, he was not intimidated by them. In his view, the gangs mostly shot at each other, not at other residents. Wardell said that usually the "gangbangers" warn other residents to get out of the way. He was only upset by the shooting when it put school children in danger:

> They [kids in his building] usually play down in the playground. And, usually if there's gonna be some shooting, the guys that either gonna get shot at or do the shooting tell the kids to go upstairs. . . . So, even when they were shooting on a regular basis . . . we knew what time to go down. The only part that we really was concerned about is that they shoot right at the time the school is taking in and right at the time the school is letting out. I never could understand that.

Wardell had worked with other residents to make his building an oasis from the drugs and violence that pervade Rockwell. The tenants in his building had organized a resident management corporation in 1991 and tried to create a healthy community. According to Wardell, they were helped by the fact that their building sits on the northeast edge of the development, cut off from the other buildings in Rockwell by a major street. Further, the building was being remodeled; because half the units were empty for more than five years, it was easier to form a cohesive group. Despite these advantages, Wardell said the building had had frequent problems with drug dealers; attempts to reduce the problems with crime and drug trafficking bring with them potential risks. "Certainly it takes the tenants' participation to get rid of crime. But if I'm the police, and you call the police, and I come and I say, 'Where's Miss So and So?' Well, that turns people off from calling the police and giving them information. . . . Some tenants will [still] do that. But to me they risk their lives and the lives of their family because these people [drug dealers] are making large sums of money."

Yet, despite his very real concerns about retaliation, Wardell had called the police for help with specific problems, complained to the CHA, and worked with other tenants to push the dealers out of his building. Gradually, he felt this had had an effect, although it remained a constant struggle. "We went to the people that were selling it in our building and said, 'Look, we're trying to do something here. We want you to don't sell drugs here.' And they sort of didn't pay us much attention, but they started looking to see were we really doing something, and when they saw we were really trying to do something, they moved it out."

Wardell's and Dawn's stories offer pictures of the challenges of life in Rockwell Gardens during the mid-1990s—a turbulent era that began with a concerted effort to address crime in the development and ended with the CHA declaring the development "nonviable" and requiring its demolition or redevelopment within a five-year period.[4] Dawn's experience of being overwhelmed by the constant struggle with crime, drugs, and physical decay was typical of many—if not most—adult women in Rockwell. In contrast, Wardell still saw hope for the development; working with his fellow residents he sought to prove that it was possible to build a stronger community—albeit, in a single building—in the midst of one of the CHA's worst developments.

Life in Rockwell

The CHA made many attempts to try to improve conditions in Rockwell during the 1990s before finally declaring the development "nonviable" in 1998. This chapter, focusing on the CHA's battle against crime in the development, tells the story of life in Rockwell during this period. To present this story, we conducted six rounds of surveys with approximately 150 to 200 residents and in-depth interviews with 10 to 12 residents in three of the eight buildings in Rockwell, interviewed CHA staff, and directed ethnographic observations in the development (for a detailed description of research methods, see Appendix).

Vincent Lane, former executive director and chairman of the CHA, used these words to describe Rockwell in 1994: "Rockwell, per capita, is the worst, most dangerous place in the country."[5] He made this comment six years after he initiated Operation Clean Sweep in Rockwell, in the first round of his battle with the gangs over control of the buildings. CHA's own figures had long indicated that Rockwell was its highest-crime development (CHA 1994). Even CHA officials agreed that none of their attempts to control the gangs or the drug trade in Rockwell had any lasting impact.[6]

When it was built in 1961, the CHA intended Rockwell Gardens to be an experiment, a change from the agency's practice of building high-rise developments on "superblocks" cut off from the surrounding community. Some original housing on the Rockwell site was left intact, interspersed with the eight thirteen-story buildings that make up the development (Bowly 1978). However, the original community consisted of two- and three-story flats; by constructing high-rises, the CHA doomed to failure the attempt to integrate the development into the neighborhood. Because the buildings were simply too large and too different to be easily absorbed, Rockwell ended up looking like any other high-rise development.

As with its other high-rise developments, Rockwell suffered from serious management problems almost from the start; the poorly maintained buildings deteriorated rapidly. As an indication of the severity of the problems, by 1991 a judge ordered CHA to vacate the development because of city fire code violations (*Chicago Tribune*, July 25, 1991). The CHA corrected some of the worst violations and kept the development open, but the agency had still not fully complied with the judge's orders by 1995 (Popkin et al. 1995). In 1991 a consultant reported it would cost nearly $50 million to repair the development's basic systems—plumbing, heating, electricity, and elevators;[7] these costs have only increased in the ensuing years. Rockwell's extraordinarily high vacancy rates also indicated serious management problems; by July 1995, the average vacancy rate had climbed to nearly 45 percent.[8]

Rockwell's population is predominantly female and very young: more than 60 percent of the residents are nineteen or younger. Officially, less than 10 percent of the residents are adult males; unofficially, many adult men live in the development with their mothers or girlfriends. Most residents live in dire poverty; CHA figures indicate that less than 10 percent are employed and that the average income is only about $6,000 per year.[9]

Located on the west side of Chicago, about four miles from downtown, Rockwell is extremely isolated. It is bordered by the Congress Expressway on the south, major thoroughfares on the north and east, and railroad tracks on the west. The food and liquor stores that serve the development are located within these borders, and the development has little foot or automobile traffic. Nearly everyone who enters Rockwell either lives or works there or in one of the remaining three-flat apartment buildings within the developments' boundaries. However, residents do have good access to public transportation; an elevated line stops a few blocks away, and a major bus route runs through the development.

May 1994: Bleak Conditions in Rockwell

In May 1994, Rockwell Gardens was a bleak and forbidding place. The eight high-rises all had exterior, gallery-type hallways

Photo 1. Jackson Street Building, Rockwell Gardens. *Photo by Jean Amendolia.*

Photo 2. "Playground" at Rockwell Gardens. *Photo by Jean Amendolia.*

that the residents referred to as "ramps" or "porches." The grim ramps were covered with metal grates—to prevent residents from either falling or throwing things over the edge. Because of safety concerns, parents preferred their children to play on these porches rather than risk being caught in shootouts on the playgrounds below.

Despite its name, there was nothing remotely gardenlike about Rockwell; the grounds were barren, with only a few trees and patchy grass. There was a playground with some intact equipment and a basketball court. However, because the basketball court was located between two buildings occupied by rival gangs, it was often too dangerous to use. A senior building—that is, a building exclusively for elderly and disabled residents—located in the middle of the development, had a small lawn and green benches in front of it, which constituted the only real green space in the development.

In May 1994, the development was littered with trash, and the buildings were covered with graffiti. Not surprisingly, residents were concerned about maintenance and vandalism. The outside hallways allowed some light during the day; but gang members frequently stole or broke the hallway light bulbs, which left them completely dark at night. As Dawn described, in general the dimly lit stairwells were dark and forbidding. Because of this problem, 74 percent of the residents cited broken light bulbs as a "big problem."

Photo 3. Graffiti—Rockwell Gardens. *Photo by Nina Taluc.*

Gang members frequently "tagged" both the exterior and interior walls. The elevator doors were usually covered with layers and layers of graffiti. More than 80 percent of the residents in May 1994 considered graffiti to be a big problem in their building.

The incinerators in Rockwell's buildings stopped functioning in the early 1990s. Rather than dispose of their trash in dumpsters, some residents simply tossed it into the halls or stairwells. In addition, the dumpsters were not always emptied promptly; overflows allowed trash to blow around the ramps and public areas. In May 1994, 70 percent of Rockwell residents saw trash and junk inside their buildings as a big problem; more than 60 percent said that it was a major problem outside as well. Adding to the squalor, the hallways reeked of human waste and garbage, and the buildings were infested with rats, mice, and roaches. Cora, a woman in her thirties who had lived in Rockwell for most of her life, described the miserable conditions in her building in May 1994: "It seems like someone just takes them [light bulbs] out or bust the bulbs. So the hallways are dark. . . . Dirty. Because they go in the hallway, and there's urine in there. . . . They know someone, and they can go and use their washroom. They'd rather use it in the hallway. That's not right. Have the whole hallway stinking and . . . make the whole building nasty."

Years of management neglect had caused many basic building systems at Rockwell to fail. By 1994, there were continuous problems with broken elevators—a result of both vandalism and poor maintenance—and, as Dawn described, heating and plumbing problems were common. As in all CHA high-rise developments, the apartment interiors were bleak: black linoleum floors, rusty metal kitchen cabinets, unpainted cinder block walls, exposed light fixtures, baths without showers, toilets without lids, and closets without doors. Interior infestations of cockroaches, mice, and rats were epidemic.

The extraordinary number of vacant units invited management problems: people threw trash in them; squatters took them over; children played in them, exposing themselves to dangers from the debris and broken windows; and vandals stripped them of pipes, sometimes flooding the apartments below. Gangs occasionally used the vacant units as meeting places, and drug users turned them into shooting galleries and crack houses.

The Monroe Street Building Resident Management Corporation

Of the three buildings we tracked, one followed a different trajectory than the other buildings in Rockwell. Wardell Yotaghan and his fellow tenants in the Monroe Street building took steps to create their Resident Management Corporation in 1991, after the building was slated for major renovation.[10] This renovation included "modernizing" all apartment units—that is, installing new kitchen cabinets, closet doors, updating bathrooms, and adding new tile—and upgrading the building systems, including boilers, plumbing, and elevators. According to Wardell, Monroe Street residents were afraid they would have to move and initially organized the Resident Management Corporation to resist relocation.

> We wouldn't move, so that's what sort of brought us together as a group. We felt as long as we was paying our rent, we should be able to enjoy the rehab of our building. And . . . how we really got into resident management is we saw an article in the . . . paper [about a building in Cabrini-Green], who was in full resident management. . . . We sat down and read it as a group, and

we come to the conclusion that they wasn't no geniuses over at Cabrini. They wasn't no smarter than the residents at Rockwell, and that we should give it a try, so we did. And we've been steadily moving ahead.

Although much of the actual repair work was delayed for several years, the renovation had a profound impact on the quality of life in the building. Because of residents' protests against relocation, the CHA agreed to complete the renovation in stages by working on half of the units at a time. These units had to be vacated for work to begin, and, according to Wardell and other building residents, many problem tenants moved out. By 1994, the residents were mostly older people committed to the goals of the Resident Management Corporation.

In May 1994, the Resident Management Corporation was "in training"; that is, they had only minimal control over building management, and conditions in the Monroe Street building were not yet much different from those in the other two sample buildings. After the Department of Housing and Urban Development (HUD) took control of the CHA in May 1995, the building was placed in "dual management"; the Resident Management Corporation received much more day-to-day responsibility and acquired the ability to screen new tenants. In August 1995, residents moved into the newly renovated units, and the CHA began work on the second half of the building.

The Resident Management Corporation's board consisted of eleven residents. Other residents volunteered for the group's programs for children and youth. In 1995, the Resident Management Corporation secured enough outside funding from foundations to hire an executive director and to support several programs designed to promote economic self-sufficiency, including resident-owned businesses, activities for children and teens, and a computer lab with internet access.

Crime in Rockwell

Gangs and gang violence were part of ordinary life in Rockwell Gardens in May 1994. According to residents, few families in Rockwell were not affiliated with the gangs in some way. Three gangs vied for control of the development, including some of the most violent gangs in Chicago. The Gangster Disciples (GDs) controlled two buildings; the Traveling Vice Lords controlled three, and the 4 Corner Hustlers controlled one and shared turf with the GDs in another. Complicating the situation, different factions of the same gang often fought with each other over turf or drug sales. The Monroe Street building was neutral, a highly unusual phenomenon in such a heavily gang-dominated area. This unique status was probably owing to both the work of the Resident Management Corporation and the building's relative isolation from the rest of the development.

In May 1994, Rockwell residents indicated a high degree of concern about the gang presence in their buildings. Overall, about 65 percent said they felt that "groups of people hanging out in the lobby and stairwells" and "young people controlling the building"—that is, blocking doors, challenging any nonresidents who came in and out, and intimidating other residents—were big problems inside their buildings; 74 percent reported that "groups of people hanging out" were a big problem outside as well.[11] The situation in the Monroe Street building was somewhat better, but even there, a majority of residents (57 percent) reported major problems with people hanging out near their building.[12]

As Dawn and Wardell described, drug use and drug trafficking had devastated the Rockwell community. The heroin epidemic that began to sweep through the west side of Chicago in the late 1960s marked the beginning of a trend that grew steadily worse over the next three decades. The cocaine and crack epidemics of the late 1980s and early 1990s had particularly disastrous consequences for the community.[13] Dawn described a typical scenario: "God, everybody was on that stuff. All the women. One lady used to live in our building, she had a real pretty house, she had everything, she sold everything for cocaine. Sold her kids' beds and everything. Kids were crying, they came home . . . she had sold everything to the dope man."

Like Dawn and Wardell, most Rockwell residents were very concerned about the effect of the drug epidemic. In May 1994, 75 percent of Rockwell residents said that drug sales were a big problem inside their building; even more (82 percent) said drug sales were a big problem outside. Nearly 80 percent reported that drug use was a big problem both inside and outside. Again, the situation was somewhat better in the Monroe Street building, but more than half of the residents there still perceived drug sales and use as major problems.

The War Zone

Having three powerful gangs battling for power in such a small community—Rockwell was only eight high-rise buildings—created a highly volatile situation; residents were living in the midst of what was essentially an urban guerilla war zone. In May 1994, more than two-thirds of the residents reported that "shootings and violence" were big problems both inside and outside their buildings. About 35 percent reported "big problems" with people being attacked or robbed inside, and 44 percent reported this was a serious problem outside; 19 percent said that rape or other sexual attacks were big problems inside their buildings, and 26 percent said rape was a big problem outside; and 40 percent reported that burglary was a big problem.

Residents reported numerous incidents of extreme violence. Cora's sister, Thelma, said that she had heard gunshots every night for the past twelve months. Ivy, another long-time resident, told of her son's friend being fatally shot in the head while getting off the elevator. "[My son's] friend came back because he had a phone call on the pay phone. Then he went back in the building and he was on the elevator with some guys. When he got off the elevator, they shot him in the back, and they shot him in the head. He died right there by the elevator."

It seemed nearly impossible to live in Rockwell and not be personally touched by violence. Almost every Rockwell resident seemed to have been affected: some had relatives or friends who had been killed or injured; and many more had been caught in or witnessed gang shootouts. In May 1994, nearly 30 percent of the residents reported that a bullet had been shot into their home in the past twelve months. Other violent crimes reported by significant proportions of residents (15 percent or more) included being beaten or assaulted, being caught in a shootout, and being stabbed or shot. Just less than 20 percent said they had experienced a burglary.

High as these figures were, they most likely *underestimated* the actual level of victimization that occurred in Rockwell. Obtaining an accurate measure of victimization is always difficult. In Rockwell, the problem was exacerbated by the fact that residents had become accustomed to the violence. Some residents discussed their own victimization experiences in a seemingly casual and off-hand way. For example, Jackie, a lively woman with a flippant attitude, said casually in the middle of an interview that her brother had been killed just a few months earlier and added that the gangs "don't bother me. I'm just ready to leave."

One possible reason for this apparent casualness may have been that, as a survival tool, residents were coping by denying the impact of violence. Dawn and several other residents indicated that talking about their own experiences was generally frowned on; they felt that no one else wanted to listen because everyone was overwhelmed by individual problems. Finally, most crimes residents experienced were not committed by unknown assailants, but rather by other Rockwell residents—even family members or friends. For this reason, residents rarely reported crimes to police, both because they faced a legitimate threat of retaliation and because they were reluctant to report people they knew. This situation may also have reduced their willingness to discuss their experiences with "outsiders," in this case, researchers whom they did not know well enough to trust entirely.

Still, residents' descriptions of the many incidents that they or their families had experienced made the horror of the violence very clear. For example, in May 1994 Cora told of being brutally beaten within the previous twelve months by a group of young men from another building.

> [My son and I] had to go to . . . see his grandmother [in another building] . . . and some gang members hollered out—he's [my son] staying in 2514 [Van Buren St.], so it's like there's this group between one building and the other. They jumped on my son. And I was there, and I wasn't going to let them jump my son, so they jumped on both of us. . . . Both of us had to go to the hospital because they had two-by-fours. They kept him overnight for observation, and I wound up going in later for my leg.

Cora said that she and her son received no help from the security guards (or other residents) who witnessed the event. The principal of the elementary school located in the development eventually called the police for her, but Cora said that the police did little because the boys were juveniles. The boys who attacked her were from Rockwell; Cora continued to see them around the development. As far as she could tell, the only consequence her assailants suffered was that they were suspended from school and reprimanded.

This apparent lack of consequences for the attackers likely contributed to the victims' fear and reluctance to report crimes to the police. In May 1994, only 30 percent of the residents said they had reported a crime. As another long-time resident said, they were clearly very concerned about the possibility of retaliation: "You can't just tell on them boys like that. You go out there and bring the police to one of them boys. If they take him to jail, the rest of them boys is going to get you. That's just the way it is."

Many residents described getting caught in gang shootouts and bullets being shot into their apartments. One resident described her terror during a three-day period of shooting. After one bullet entered her apartment, she and her children moved their beds away from the windows and crawled on the floor, under the windows, when they had to go to the bathroom. Even so, a second bullet narrowly missed her head the next day.

Property crimes might not be as dangerous as the shootings and assaults, but they, too, clearly contributed to residents' level of fear, particularly when the CHA seemed unresponsive to their plight. Dawn told of her experience after her apartment was broken into and her lock broken: "I had a break-in. . . . They had tore the whole lock completely out and messed up the door with a crowbar. . . . They broke in on a Friday, [CHA] didn't come repair my lock until Tuesday. My door couldn't lock, I had to put a chair underneath it, and then tie a string around the knob and stay in my house."

Not surprisingly, Rockwell residents had high levels of fear of crime. In May 1994, 63 percent said they felt unsafe "being out alone in the area right outside (their) building at night." Residents felt much safer inside their apartments than outside, but still approximately one-third said they felt unsafe "alone inside (their) apartments at night."

In addition to the intense gang violence, domestic abuse was a constant factor in Rockwell; many women were not safe even in their own apartments. Rhonda described a routine she and her neighbor had worked out for "check day," that is, the day welfare checks are delivered: "Well, I have a next door neighbor, and we have codes in case she get into it with her old man in her apartment, and he won't let her out the door. We have a knock on the wall, our walls being so close, she'll knock on the wall and I'll know the code and I'll know what to do and I can call the police."

Coping with the Violence

Rockwell residents experienced extraordinarily high levels of violence, and many had developed strategies to help them cope with the constant anxiety and fear. One strategy was to downplay the impact of victimization experiences: residents either did not discuss them, or, if they did, they discussed them offhandedly as Jackie had done. Clearly, many residents also assuaged their pain and anxiety with alcohol or illegal drugs. But the most common strategy seemed to be for residents to "mind their own business." They mostly did not report crimes when they saw them (or they did so anonymously), and they generally did not report their own victimization except to CHA management or other residents. Indeed, even the tenant patrols were instructed to report only vandalism or maintenance problems, for fear of gang retaliation if they reported any drug-related activity. As Jackie said, "Because somebody is always some kin to somebody around here, so you gotta watch what you say. So it's best that you don't say anything." Residents also coped by keeping to themselves, avoiding making many close friends and associating with only a small, trusted circle. They avoided going out of the building after dark or even in the late afternoon when gang activity escalated. When they did have to go out, they stayed in groups.

Residents' biggest concern was protecting their children; like Dawn, many residents spoke of restricting their children to their apartments or porches and monitoring their activities very closely. Residents also described keeping their children indoors during major gang wars and feared even to risk taking them to school during these periods of heavy shooting. Although these strategies kept children safe, they paid a high price by missing school and other activities and lacking freedom to run and play outside.

Social Ties

In Rockwell's dangerous social world, everybody knew everybody else, yet trusted only an inner circle of friends and relatives. In May 1994, about half the residents said they felt that "people in their building generally go their own way," while just 27 percent thought that they generally helped each other out (25 percent said both).

Residents generally indicated that they knew most of their neighbors and sometimes relied on them for help with things such as babysitting, carrying in groceries, and helping to keep the porches in front of their apartments clean. Even the gang members sometimes carried residents' groceries upstairs, when they were not fighting. Thelma cited "helping with funerals" as an example of how neighbors help each other: "Well, maybe a death might come, and we might go around, take up a collection. . . . Some people don't have all the insurance money to bury people. Might cook some food, and stuff like that, try and help them out."

However, while they might know each other, most residents, particularly in the two buildings on the west side of Rockwell, had only a small circle of people that they trusted. Even Cora, who had lived in Rockwell most of her life, said she had only a few real friends in the development: "I know quite a few, but I only have a good five, six people that I would call my friends around here."

Residents' tendency to "keep to themselves" undermined any attempt to organize community crime-prevention activities. The CHA hoped to encourage Rockwell residents to work together to make a safer community. Many of its interventions, particularly the tenant patrols and CADRE centers, were intended to organize residents to help themselves; in theory, if the policing efforts increased safety, then residents would feel safer and be more willing to get involved.

Indeed, the majority of residents also saw themselves as at least partially responsible for the goal of improving conditions in Rockwell. Most (57 percent) believed that both the CHA management and tenants should be responsible for stopping crime and drugs in their development. Surprisingly, despite their fears, the majority of Rockwell residents were optimistic about their ability to improve conditions: 76 percent said that they thought that if tenants worked together, they could do "a lot" to solve the problems of crime and drugs in their development. However, while residents thought it was *possible* to improve conditions, they did not think it was *likely* because of residents' fears. As Jackie said, "If we stick together—but everybody is not going to stick together. . . . If we be together, we can get a lot of things done like clean up together. . . . But we can't get everybody. We can only get maybe about two people."

Residents of the Monroe Street building were the only tenants who seemed to feel that they could realistically work together to bring about change. Indeed, they felt that through the Resident Management Corporation, they were already working together successfully to reduce crime and other problems in their building. Samuel, a Resident Management Corporation board member, described the building: "Well, it's safer now simply because . . . the people who are in the building are concerned about the welfare of the building. We have a very serious building president. . . . So what we are striving for is people who want to live a productive life. Live in a better environment. So like I said, 2450's [West Monroe] a little different from other buildings because we are under renovation, and we are in the process of tenant management." Wardell found that the residents in his building regarded themselves as a "family" and tried to help each other out. "We, we're one big family. And we look out for each other, whatever needs to be done, somebody in that building will do it. Somebody need to go grocery shopping, everybody might be busy, but somebody will end up taking them. If they need to go to the hospital . . . whatever need to be done, if they got legal problems or whatever, we try to get it done. As a family."

In sum, in the mid-1990s, Rockwell Gardens was an extremely troubled community. The CHA had invested millions of dollars in sweeping the development of crime in the late 1980s, but by 1994 any effects of that expense had long since disappeared. The filthy development reflected years of vandalism and managerial neglect. The social world was dominated by three powerful street gangs, who had turned Rockwell into an urban war zone. Drug trafficking was pervasive; dealers occupied common areas in every building. Heroin and cocaine use had devastated the development and many of its single mothers; an epidemic of abused and neglected children raged. Many residents had lived in Rockwell for years and knew each other well, but they generally distrusted each other and felt that mere survival required them to keep to themselves.

The CHA's Battle against Crime in Rockwell

Because Rockwell was historically so troubled, Vincent Lane chose the development as the place to launch his widely publicized war on crime. Three months after taking control of the CHA, Lane ordered the first sweeps in Rockwell in response to several shootings, two murders, and a bombing in the development within a three-week period (*Chicago Tribune*, September 21, 1988). The sweeps received intense media scrutiny, and, despite the first ACLU lawsuit, most outside observers initially viewed the sweeps as a success. A year later, all buildings in the development had been swept twice, and the *Chicago Tribune* described the sweeps in Rockwell as Lane's first step in turning around Chicago's public housing (*Chicago Tribune*, September 17, 1989).

However, after the initial enthusiasm, it was clear that the first sweeps did not bring about lasting changes; by the mid-1990s, Rockwell was as violent as ever, and Lane still considered it to be the most dangerous place in the country. The CHA continued to try various law-enforcement strategies to control the crime, including periodic sweeps of individual buildings, as well as another sweep of the entire development in 1992. In May 1994, residents still felt that Rockwell was extremely dangerous.

In the early 1990s, Lane expanded his war on crime from Operation Clean Sweep to create the more comprehensive Anti-Drug Initiative. Rockwell was among the first sites to receive Anti-Drug Initiative services, but none of these efforts was ever very successful. Rockwell had one of the first CADRE (CHA drug-prevention) centers;[14] it opened in 1989, but it never developed the range of services and level of community involvement achieved by centers in other developments. CHA staff began recruiting residents for tenant patrols in 1990; however, according to the program director, the patrols in Rockwell were at their peak in 1991 and functioned only sporadically thereafter.[15] Both the Chicago and CHA police forces patrolled Rockwell and participated in sweeps and other law enforcement initiatives, but the CHA Police Department had a smaller presence in Rockwell than in other CHA high-rise developments; for example, the CHA police never opened a substation in Rockwell.

Moorehead/New Life in Rockwell

Entering into a contract with Moorehead/New Life Self-Development Company was one of the CHA's more radical steps to address the problems of crime and poor management in Rockwell. Providing security in public housing was one of the Nation of Islam's major enterprises; the group owned four security companies nationwide and had reportedly achieved some widely publicized successes in other cities (*Washington Post*, September 2, 1996). New Life's main role in Rockwell Gardens was to provide security, but Lane said he also hoped that residents would benefit from the Nation's philosophy of self-reliance.[16] For this reason, New Life was also involved in helping Moorehead develop initiatives to hire residents—many of them gang members—to paint hallways and stairwells and renovate apartments.[17]

Moorehead/New Life took over management of Rockwell in May 1994. First, the new management company cleaned up the grounds and painted the hallways bright red, covering up the layers of graffiti. Residents, cautiously optimistic about the new management team, hoped they might finally improve conditions in the development. The Resident Management Corporation in the Monroe Street building maintained primary responsibility for their building but received security and basic maintenance services from Moorehead/New Life.

To improve conditions in Rockwell, Moorehead/New Life hired more janitors and required that on a daily basis they remove trash, clean all halls and stairwells, and check for broken light bulbs. They improved grounds maintenance by keeping the lawns mowed and removing trash and other debris. As part of a "Unity Day" in 1995, the company also hired residents to pick up trash, paint hallways, and perform repairs in individual units.

Residents clearly perceived an improvement in maintenance after Moorehead/New Life began managing the development. Residents reported that the new management was more responsive and kept the buildings cleaner, although vandalism remained a serious problem. In May 1995 Dawn reported: "Well, it got a little better. 'Cause they keep the building, they mops every day. They put bulbs in every day. But then when they leave, the guys break the bulbs out, and urinate all in the hallways, and throw garbage cans, they just turn 'em over. So, they doing that now."

Conditions in the Monroe Street building improved even more than in the other two buildings. Its Resident Management Corporation used its clout with the CHA management to obtain better services for the building, which was undergoing renovation and objectively improving. Finally, because the Resident Management Corporation had strengthened community ties, residents felt empowered to stop the vandalism in their building. Evelyn, a board member, explained why conditions improved in February 1996: "Well, like I said, they renovating, you know, that building so there used to be a lot of trash and light bulbs broken and graffiti . . . on the walls. We don't have that anymore, 'cause we talk to the kids and tell 'em that's not right."

However, while physical conditions improved superficially, Moorehead managers themselves acknowledged that their ability to make more substantial improvements was limited. First, their budget did not allow them to hire enough skilled tradesmen (for example, plumbers, electricians, and so on); thus, apartment maintenance never improved as much as building maintenance. Second, the CHA failed to allocate the funds for major system repairs (for example, replacing incinerators or elevators) because the agency had been allocating its modernization funding for security. Finally, the property had been mismanaged for so long and was so deteriorated that they could make only cosmetic improvements. One site management staff person commented on the situation: "There's a lot of waste that's been cut out by us being here to watch the stuff. . . . The bottom line is that if they don't put the resources in, you can only do what you can do with the resources at hand."[18]

New Life Security

New Life Self-Development Company, Moorehead's partner in managing Rockwell, was put in charge of security for the development. Before the CHA contracted with Moorehead/New Life, Rockwell had security guards from a variety of private companies who sat in booths in the lobbies of the buildings. Residents regarded these guards as ineffective: in May 1994, the majority said that the guards were doing a "poor" job of preventing crime (60 percent) and reducing fear of crime (59 percent). Residents complained that most contract security guards failed to enforce entrance procedures, harassed female residents, and did nothing to protect residents from violence.

At the beginning of June 1994, the New Life guards moved into Rockwell with much fanfare. These men, presumably members of the Nation of Islam, did not live in the development. However, as with the maintenance plan, part of Moorehead/New Life's program for Rockwell was to hire young men from the community as a way of providing them with a positive alternative to the drug trade.[19] The first guards were extremely polite and wore the unofficial uniform of bowties and white shirts associated with the Nation of Islam. Most significant, from the residents' perspective, was the fact that they did not carry weapons.

Residents called the new guards "the Muslims." Initially residents reacted very positively. Several, including Cora, who had been a guard herself, spoke well about the New Life guards' apparent rapport with the gangs and their plan to hire gang members for "real" jobs. "It's different because the gangbangers give them more respect. Because I guess them being out there and communicating and everything. They talks to them. Besides, they'll hire some of the boys off the street to work. . . . That's lifting them up more. Taking them off the street. Making them do something good for themselves." Many residents were struck by how polite and helpful the new guards had been in their first week. New Life guards were carrying residents' groceries from their cars, stopping visitors to ask for identification, holding doors open, and generally interacting politely with residents. However, a few residents were more skeptical, concerned that, however good their intentions, the New Life guards would be unable to control the gangs without using weapons.

Although the New Life guards got off to a good start, like so many other of CHA's anticrime efforts, the experiment quickly turned into a failure. During the company's first six months of providing security in Rockwell, several shootings involved the New Life guards and the gangs. Despite these problems, CHA officials remained relatively sanguine about the success of their experiment. They were optimistic that, given enough time, the New Life guards would be able to have a positive influence on the young men in the development. Lane was hopeful:

> It has been up and down. . . . The big difference is that the gangs have never shot at or injured a Nation of Islam guard. . . . The main types of complaints we get from tenants about the [other contract security] guards is that they disrespect the women. . . . They disrespect the kids. But I've had no complaints like that about the Muslim guards. They talk to the kids, try to get them into positive programs. I've had to go in with guns several times to support them. This is not a short-term process. I have been impressed with what I've seen the Muslims do with those guys in prison—they get them out there in the street selling newspapers when it's 100 degrees. I know that takes time, so I didn't expect the changes to come fast. Gangs are about drugs and money. They respect Farrakhan and all that, but this is about money. . . . I'm satisfied with detente in the interim.[20]

Results of the follow-up surveys in January, May, and December 1995 show that, while some fluctuated in their views over time, Rockwell residents did not share Lane's optimism. Ultimately, they evaluated the New Life guards as harshly as they had rated their previous security guards.[21]

Residents became disillusioned with the New Life guards for several reasons. First, the original New Life guards were too quickly replaced with untrained young men who lived in the development; many were reputed to be gang members, and whether they were legal residents was a subject of some dispute.[22] As Samuel put it, he knew that New Life's intent was to help the community, but residents felt the company had been naive in thinking that they could get gang members to function effectively as security guards: "When they first came in, they had older guys. They also consider themselves helping the community, so they hire the guys who live around here. Well, they have good intentions, but a lot of the guys they hired were or are gang members. So, now if you want to be realistic, if you hire a gang member—he's still in a gang—his buddies come in, you think he's gonna stop it? Make them sign in and stuff like that?"

Second, although the New Life guards treated tenants very politely, they were just as ineffective as their predecessors in preventing drug trafficking. These resident concerns, already evident in the second round of interviews in the winter of 1995, became more serious over time. Many residents expressed disappointment and a sense of betrayal. They had hoped that the "Muslims" would finally be the answer to Rockwell's problems. Instead, the New Life guards had turned out to be polite, well-meaning, and ineffective.

Finally, given their lack of training and supervision and the fact that most were reputed to be gang-affiliated themselves, the New Life guards had some serious conflicts with the local gangs. In July 1994, shortly after New Life took over security for Rockwell, local newspapers reported that the gangs ran some guards out of the development and held them at gunpoint (*Chicago Tribune*, July 22, 1994). Because of this incident, the CHA conducted a swarm (the intensive police patrol that replaced the sweeps) and temporarily put CHA Security Force officers into Rockwell.[23] The tension between the New Life guards and gangs apparently escalated; by January 1995, residents were clearly distressed about an incident in which one of the supposedly unarmed New Life guards had allegedly shot and killed a gang member (*Chicago Tribune*, October 20, 1994).

After this episode, the problems between the guards and gangs seemed to abate for a time, and residents reported no further violent conflicts. However, while the gangs may have stopped trying to use violence to intimidate the guards, it became clear that the gangs gradually regained control of the buildings. Residents began to complain that the guards were "too friendly" with the gangs and that gang members were hanging out with them in the guard booths. In describing the relationship between the guards and the gangs in Rockwell, Samuel explained that the gangs simply never respected the New Life guards.

The gangs' theory was this, they looked at the Muslims just like they did some of the contract security: "Stay out of our way, we got no problems with you." And they virtually told the Muslims when they came here, "We understand you all Muslims and, to be blunt with you, you may be black, but that don't mean nothing. What we're saying is we're going to run our own business. You stay out of our way." So by them [the Nation of Islam guards] being unarmed, what could they do?

By February 1996, residents reported that the guards had completely ceded control of the buildings to the gangs. Our own observations supported residents' comments: when we arrived in the development to conduct the interviews, gang members carrying large sticks were walking up and down in front of the buildings, periodically swinging their sticks around and slapping them against their hands. They had locked the front doors, and other young men were standing in front and behind the doors, asking everyone who came in or out to explain why they were visiting or leaving the building. We had to tell them that we wanted to go to the CADRE center and then wait while they decided whether to let us in; the guards had disappeared. When we visited the development during the summer of 1996, New Life security had all but given up monitoring the entryways. On one visit, we found a building where gang members had taken over the guard booth and were using it to hold a meeting; five other young men were guarding the building entrance.

Residents, who had been promised great improvements, felt disappointed and betrayed by the failure of the New Life guards. Tina, a longtime resident, summed up the tenant feelings: People were excited about the New Life guards when they first arrived, "'cause they thought it was gonna be different. . . . The boys wasn't gonna be downstairs on the first floor no more. Probably hanging out and then less gangs and stuff. . . . Because they said it was gonna be a big difference." When, in February 1996, we asked why residents were so disappointed with the New Life guards just nine months after their arrival, Tina replied bluntly, "'Cause they lied. They told us things that they supposed to did and it didn't happen."

Ultimately, the CHA decided that the New Life experiment had been a failure. In addition to residents' complaints about the guards' poor performance—which even made the press because of the connection to the Nation of Islam[24]—the company had become very controversial. New Life was already under federal investigation because of its relationship to the Nation of Islam; then Senator Robert Dole of Kansas, the Senate majority leader, had questioned the appropriateness of awarding government contracts to the Nation because of Minister Louis Farrakhan's controversial statements about Jews and whites (*Washington Post*, January 21, 1995). Further, HUD was investigating whether Lane had offered New

Life the Rockwell security contract as a quid pro quo for the Nation of Islam's agreement to lease space in a shopping center that he had developed. After the HUD takeover in the spring of 1995, Wardell and the other leaders of the Resident Management Corporation in the Monroe Street building convinced the new CHA administration to provide them with CHA Security Force officers to prevent vandalism in the newly renovated units. In February 1996 the CHA decided not to renew Moorehead/New Life's contract for the rest of the development (*Chicago Tribune*, February 17, 1996).[25] When the CHA hired a different private firm to manage Rockwell, CHA left only the CHA Security Force officers in the Monroe Street building and CHA police patrols to secure the development.

Police in Rockwell

The sweeps were by far the most controversial element of the CHA's anticrime programs, and residents held strong opinions about them years after the initial actions had taken place. Residents' attitudes about the sweeps were contradictory. In May 1994, just after the CHA lost its legal fight to continue emergency sweeps (see chapter 2), only 33 percent of Rockwell residents thought the CHA should be able to search apartments without residents' permission. Despite this concern about illegal searches, the majority (75 percent) wanted their buildings swept again.[26]

Residents' comments helped to illuminate their apparently contradictory attitudes about the sweeps. Some raised concerns about the sweeps' violating their civil liberties, and a number objected to the way the police treated them or their families during the sweep. However, most thought that the sweeps had been at least somewhat effective in reducing crime, which suggested that they felt that it had been worth enduring the searches to improve conditions in the development. Kim, a resident of the Monroe Street building, expressed both concern about residents being mistreated and the desperate need for relief from crime:

> I think CHA should do the sweeps . . . but the only thing about the sweep is that they treat everybody like criminals. Not all of us are criminals, you know. . . . I'm sure they know which apartments sell the drugs and which one are the bad tenants. . . . Sometimes my sister may come to visit and they doin' a sweep. They put them out with no shoes on. They treat them like criminals and that's something—I think that's wrong for them to do. . . . But the sweeps—we need the sweep.

Over time, the sweeps became a less salient issue; however, in later interviews, some residents periodically mentioned that they would like the CHA to bring back the sweeps to help control the crime and disorder.

In addition to the sweeps and other major police actions, both the CHA and Chicago police regularly served Rockwell by responding to emergency calls and patrolling the development. Further, both departments initiated community policing programs in Rockwell in the summer and fall of 1995.[27] One senior CHA official acknowledged that because of the extreme problems with gangs in Rockwell, none of these law enforcement efforts had been very effective.

> I'd say at this point, the police have probably been most effective [in] reference to controlling the situation in Ickes. Within Rockwell and Horner, you have a hard core, large-scale gang element there. And, like I said . . . though I feel that we've stabilized it, the statistics would seem to indicate that, and there's far less shooting that goes on over there in those developments than there used to be, but there's still a large amount of crime. And that's because it's like a stronghold of some of the major gangs.[28]

In general, Rockwell residents held very negative views of the CHA police and infrequently relied on their assistance. Each year only about 30 percent said they had reported a problem to the police in spite of the high levels of violence.[29] Some residents did say that they had reported crimes, particularly property crimes, to police during the two years that we interviewed them, despite their well-founded fear of retaliation. However, even those who said they did report crime were fearful of the consequences and tried to remain anonymous.

These negative views were more serious than simply regarding the police as ineffective; Rockwell residents also complained that the CHA police mistreated tenants and were less effective than the Chicago police. Given that the CHA police force was one of the most expensive elements of the Anti-Drug Initiative, these concerns indicated a serious problem. April, an elderly resident who was active in her building, gave an example where the CHA police "disrespected" her and other tenants: "I'm on the tenant patrol. And they came in, they was supposed to have been doing a small sweep one night. And when they came in, they tore all the locks off of the laundry room and off of the meter rooms and things. So I was sitting in the tenant patrol room. One CHA police come in there and just totally disrespect me. . . . I don't deal with calling them, I always call the Chicago police."

Tenant Patrols

CHA initiated its tenant patrol program in 1990 to supplement its own police and security forces. CHA staff began trying to recruit Rockwell residents during the early days of the program. In spite of this early start, the staff felt that Rockwell had one of the least effective tenant patrol programs. Initially, the patrols were quite active, particularly during the period when Rockwell was in danger of being shut down for code violations in 1991. However, because of the problems with gangs, the CHA had a great deal of difficulty sustaining these patrols.[30] One program manager summarized the problem:

> Rockwell is a strain, the gangs are just real special at Rockwell. At one point, we had every building but one in Rockwell that was definitely under gang control, and [the gang leaders] advised us and anybody who came down to the [tenant patrol] meetings not to bother to come down anymore. We tried it though, we went three years straight. We went back to back and every year we go back and make an attempt, but it wasn't happening . . . right now, it's a war, it's an out-and-out war for survival. And who's going to just control the turf.[31]

She added that the resident programs staff had relocated a number of tenant patrol participants because they had been threatened with retaliation.

Despite the potential dangers, tenant patrols continued to function sporadically in Rockwell, although the Monroe Street group was by far the most active. They generally limited their activities to monitoring vandalism and problems in vacant apartments, and walking down the hallways of their buildings twice a day. The dangers from the gangs in Rockwell were too serious for the tenant patrols to engage in much active crime prevention; if they took action, they risked retaliation.

The Monroe Street group was stronger: the Resident Management Corporation provided a higher level of social cohesion, and the gangs were less active there. Tenant patrol members at Monroe Street spoke about their work as a type of mission; they clearly felt empowered by the experience. They took their work seriously, seeking to make their community stronger and advocating personal responsibility. But, as Wardell reported in May 1995, even the Monroe Street building patrol became less active over time because of likely retaliation and poor security.

> They do tenant patrol less now than they were a year ago. . . . As more and more strange people came in the building, the tenant

patrol became less and less effective. You know, they don't have arrest power, they don't have police power, they don't have a weapon. . . . So, they were very effective before the change, because they interacted with the CHA security. . . . And they felt proud at . . . what they were doing, and they felt like they were really helping. But when the security changed . . . if you went and told them something, didn't nothing happen, so the tenant patrol, they still do tenant patrol, but they mainly just write things down and bring it back, give it to . . . whoever they're supposed to send it to . . . but they're more afraid now.

Residents generally thought highly of the tenant patrols; about half of Rockwell residents consistently said that the tenant patrols were doing a "very good" or "good" job of reporting crime (49 percent) and preventing fear of crime (42 percent).[32] Given the patrols did not attempt to engage directly in crime prevention, these relatively favorable ratings may suggest support for fellow residents willing to try to take action to improve conditions, rather than a true assessment of their impact. In the dangerous world of Rockwell where the gangs had more power than the police, it was simply unrealistic to think that a community crime-prevention effort like this one could have much effect on this level of crime and violence.

CADRE Center

In addition to its security and policing efforts, the CHA had a drug-prevention program, primarily aimed at children. Rockwell was one of the first developments to have a CADRE center, which opened in late 1989. The CADRE center in Rockwell was never very successful, in part because of the extreme problems with gang violence and, according to staff, the large number of young leaseholders in the development who were not interested in the services the center offered.[33]

The Rockwell CADRE center offered the basic set of services and programs described in chapter 3, including the help of resident staff who had received substance-abuse prevention training; they, in turn, trained other residents. Hiring and training residents was one main goal of the CADRE programs. In addition, the center had a Student Assistance Program at two elementary schools, with components such as in-school workshops on substance abuse. Finally, the Rockwell CADRE had a "Just Say Know" program, a CHA initiative to provide positive after-school activities, such as field trips, sports, and recreation.

Generally, the residents were familiar with only a few of the CADRE center's programs; most knew of it as a place that provided programs for children. Relatively few had actually used any CADRE center services, except for the after-school activities. Yet, the majority of the residents who had used CADRE services gave positive reports about them. Those residents seemed to value having a place to go—or a place their friends could go to in a time of need—and their children having a constructive alternative to drugs. Residents appreciated the staff's willingness to help. As Dawn said (May 1994), "If it wasn't for these people here . . . it wouldn't be none, no type of activities for the kids, but, see, they take the kids on trips here, and I sign my kids up for everything."

Impact on Conditions

Early 1994 marked the beginning of the CHA's second major attempt to reduce crime and violence in Rockwell Gardens. In May 1994, Rockwell was an urban war zone, with filthy, decaying buildings dominated by violent gangs, overrun with drug trafficking, and cut off from the surrounding community. Between May 1994 and December 1997, the CHA spent millions of dollars trying to improve the situation in Rockwell. But the crime was overwhelming, and the agency's programs were plagued with problems, undermining their effectiveness.

According to the residents, despite the shortcomings of the CHA's efforts, conditions in Rockwell improved dramatically between the spring of 1994 and the winter of 1995. The changes were most striking in the Monroe Street building, where residents reported that serious problems with drugs and crime had all but disappeared. However, even with the improvement, residents continued to report substantial problems with vandalism and drug-related crime in 1996 and 1997. Exacerbating the situation, tensions among the gangs in Rockwell grew after the collapse of a CHA-wide gang truce in early 1996, which led to a vicious gang war. Finally, problems in the Monroe Street building began to increase again in late 1997 as a wave of tenants from other buildings moved into the rehabilitated units.

The previous section described the programs the CHA implemented to try to control crime in Rockwell during this period; here we describe the impact of these efforts, using scales to summarize the patterns of change over time in residents' perceptions of major problems in Rockwell.[34] In addition, we discuss the reasons for these changes and the ongoing problems that culminated in the CHA beginning to plan for demolishing much of the development in 1998.

The Effect of Private Management: Physical Conditions Improve

Private management was one reason that physical conditions in Rockwell got better between May 1994 and the end of 1995. One of the CHA's goals in hiring Moorehead/New Life to manage Rockwell was to combat Rockwell's serious problems with vandalism, that is, to ensure that broken light bulbs were promptly replaced, graffiti painted over, and trash not allowed to accumulate in hallways and stairwells. As described earlier, when Moorehead/New Life took over management of Rockwell, staff made improving janitorial service a priority and to involve gang members in painting hallways and preventing graffiti "tagging."

Rockwell residents felt that the new management was generally successful in addressing problems with vandalism. As figure 4.1 shows, the proportion of residents who reported that broken light bulbs, trash and junk, and graffiti were big problems inside their building declined by half from 1994 to the end of 1995, falling from 91 percent in May 1994 to 55 percent in December 1995. Likewise, the proportion who said that trash and graffiti were big problems outside their buildings dropped from 86 percent in May 1994 to 43 percent in December 1995.[35] While conditions improved in all three buildings, the Monroe Street building experienced much more change than the rest of Rockwell. Figure 4.2 presents the Monroe Street building without the other buildings on the west side of the development (on Jackson and Van Buren streets) and shows that conditions at Monroe Street were substantially better by December 1995. Residents, although pleased with the improved conditions, were not optimistic that the changes would last. As Dawn said (August 1995), "Yeah, it is cleaner. They clean up every day, they mop every day. You don't smell urine . . . you don't smell that all day, too. It's changed. I wonder how it's gonna be three more months from now?"

Conditions remained relatively good throughout 1995, but in early 1996 an especially vicious gang war erupted. As gang activity increased in the development during 1996, residents in the two buildings on the west side of the development reported some increase in vandalism, especially graffiti and broken light bulbs. The situation grew worse between 1996 and 1997, with nearly two-thirds of the residents of these buildings reporting increasing problems with graffiti and broken light bulbs and more than half reporting serious problems with trash.[36] As figure 4.2 shows, after the CHA removed its Security Force officers, even the Monroe Street building was affected; residents there reported a sharp increase in problems. For example, in December 1996, just 24 percent of Monroe Street residents said they had big problems with graffiti in

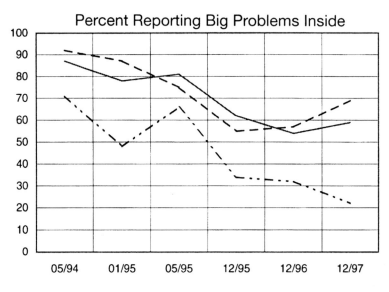

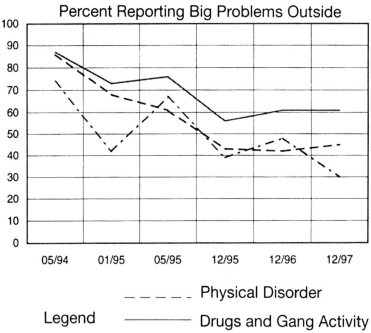

Figure 4.1. Rockwell Residents' Perceptions of Crime, 1994–1997

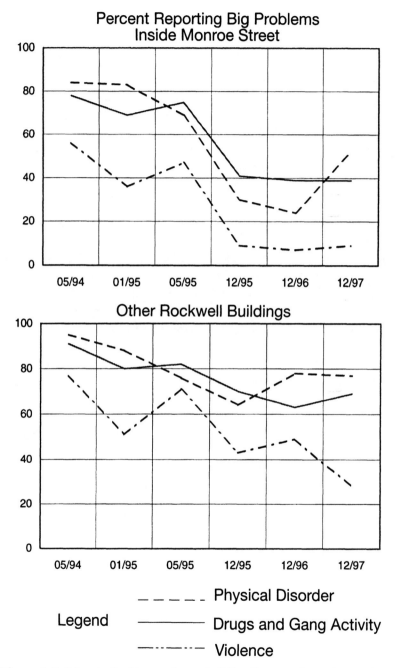

Figure 4.2. Crime in the Monroe Street Building Compared to Other Rockwell Buildings

their building; in December 1997, nearly twice as many (43 percent) reported big problems.

The private managers—both Moorehead/New Life and the companies that succeeded them—seemed to have more success controlling trash and graffiti outside the buildings on the west side of the development. From December 1995 to December 1997, just over a third of the residents of these buildings consistently reported big problems with graffiti and trash.[37] In contrast, Monroe Street residents reported almost no problems in 1996, but an increase in problems with trash and junk outside their building in 1997 (see figure 4.2).

Drug Sales and Gang Activity: Modest Improvement

Virtually all of the CHA's efforts in Rockwell were intended to attack the pervasive problems of drug sales and use. Despite the evident shortcomings of the CHA's programs—the New Life security guards, police actions, tenant patrols, and CADRE center—Rockwell residents perceived a substantial reduction in drug trafficking, drug use, and visible gang activity both inside and outside their buildings between May 1994 and December 1995. However, even with this improvement, problems with drug-related crime remained severe.

Figure 4.1 shows the drop in the proportion of residents reporting "big problems" with social disorder—drug sales, drug use, "young people" (gangs) controlling the building, and groups of people hanging out both inside and outside their buildings—over time. The percentage of residents reporting big problems inside their buildings dropped from about 87 percent in May 1994 to about 62 percent in December 1995; the figures for social disorder outside were similar.[38]

Although problems decreased in all three buildings, most improvement occurred in the Monroe Street building (figure 4.2). After the Resident Management Corporation took more control of the building and CHA Security Force officers replaced the New Life guards, the building apparently improved even more dramatically. For example, the percentage of residents who reported big problems with "young people controlling their building" was just 12 percent in December 1995, as compared to 59 percent for the other two buildings; likewise, the percentage who reported big problems with drug sales was just 21 percent, as compared to 56 percent for the other buildings in our survey.

It is important to be careful in interpreting these results because Rockwell residents were accustomed to living with an extraordinarily high level of drug-related crime. A seemingly improved situation to them would likely still appear to be an extreme problem to most outside observers; substance abuse clearly remained a serious problem. It was not unusual to see large numbers of young men openly smoking "blunts" (cigars filled with marijuana and sometimes laced with other drugs). Still, residents in all three buildings seemed to feel that *visible* drug dealing had decreased somewhat over time. As Thelma said (May 1995): "Than in the past, I've seen less. . . . Not really too many people been standing around because the police have been over here every day. So it's less people, well lesser guys outside."

There are several possible explanations for the reduction in residents' perceptions of problems with visible drug trafficking and gang activity. First, the Monroe Street Resident Management Corporation made concerted efforts to reduce drug dealing in their building; by late 1995, the CHA's Security Force was helping to keep the gangs and drug dealers away. The incredible improvement in conditions in Monroe Street certainly affected the overall results. Second, the CHA's sweeps and patrols likely had some impact on the rest of the development, driving the drug dealers out at least temporarily. Third, the gang truce, effective during most of 1995, may have affected the general level of gang activity.

Vacant Units

The enormous loss of population in the development between 1994 and 1997 may have also reduced the amount of active drug trafficking in the development; according to the CHA, the number of occupied units in Rockwell dropped from more than 1,000 in 1991 to just 479 in 1997. The official vacancy rate climbed to about 45 percent by the summer of 1995. This figure actually *underestimated* the number of vacant units because units that needed major renovations or were in buildings slated to be closed were not counted as part of the total. The Monroe Street building was half empty until 1997 because of the renovation there, but the number of vacancies in other buildings grew because of evictions and the failure of Moorehead/New Life management to turn over the units quickly to new tenants.

With so many vacant units and the corresponding decrease in the number of residents, there were likely to be fewer dealers overall, and those that stayed in the development could easily move their business indoors, thereby becoming gradually less visible. Indeed, residents themselves seemed to think that the drug dealers had simply moved inside. Thelma explained this phenomenon (December 1995), "I guess they're going somewhere where people can knock on their door or something. I guess they . . . using somebody's apartment to sell it out of there, but I don't see 'em that much."

While the loss of population may have allowed the drug dealers to move indoors, the vacant units created new problems for the remaining residents. In addition to drug dealers using the units for hideouts, vandals removed plumbing to sell to support their drug habits and caused floods in the apartments below. Drug users made the units into crack houses and "shooting galleries," that is, places where people go to use intravenous drugs.

Wardell spoke of the problems with vacant units in his building in December 1995, "People just using it [the building], more or less as a clubhouse. . . . Some of those places [vacant units] are dangerous places. We find condoms, beer cans, syringes, you name it, and some of them rooms, we find they have their little cots or whatever."

By far the vacant units presented the most serious problem to unsupervised children who wandered into unsecured apartments to play and encountered hazards such as drug paraphernalia, used needles, exposed pipes, and peeling paint. The greatest danger was unprotected windows, and at least one small child fell to his death from a vacant unit during the mid-1990s. Dawn told the story in January 1995,[39]

> This was last year [1994]. . . . He fell from the thirteenth floor. Little baby. . . . They was playing in a vacant apartment and didn't have those guard rails [on the window]. The people had just moved out. And there was little kids in there playing, and one little boy fell. . . . He died. That was a sad day for everybody. Everybody was crying. I thought it was a blanket falling from the window. [Interviewer: "You saw it?"] Coming from the store. . . . You look up and you see something falling down. You think somebody's thrown their covers out the window or something. When it hit the ground and the guy that was standing up against the fence, he looked and said, "Oh, my God," and fell to his knees. I looked over there, and it was a baby.

Violent Crime

Despite the ongoing and severe problems with gang intimidation, Rockwell residents' complaints about most types of violent crime dropped between mid-1994 and late 1995. The development remained an extremely dangerous place, but again, primarily because of the improvements in the Monroe Street building as well as the CHA's efforts, the gang truce, and the dramatic loss of population, residents generally reported fewer problems with assaults and sexual attacks both inside and outside their buildings (see figures 4.1 and 4.2).

Although complaints about most types of violent crime declined more or less steadily from mid-1994 to late 1995, residents' reports of major problems with shootings and violence tended to vary considerably: an increase during periods when there was more gang conflict, and a decline again afterwards. In general, the majority of Rockwell residents reported severe problems with shootings during the warmer months (about 70 percent in both May 1994 and May 1995), and less in the winter (about 40 percent in January 1995 and December 1995).[40] However, the Monroe Street building again showed much more substantial improvements; in fact, the proportion reporting major problems in December 1995 fell to only about 10 percent (see figure 4.2).

Reflecting the seasonal changes in gang violence, Cora (January 1995) described a brief period of peace during the colder months, an interval she attributed to the effect of CHA's patrols rather than the weather: "They [the gangs] haven't been shooting, and the kids can walk around. It's a little safer because CHA security be riding around. The CHA police, they've been riding around more." However, by May 1995, the violence had escalated again and Cora was very distressed. "'Cause the way they be shooting from one building to the other building, if the kids be on the basketball court, they outside, they have to watch they back. 'Cause they don't know if they'll be shooting or whatnot, and it's sad. It's sad. That's how much shooting they be doing."

Gang Peace—Summer 1995

After the period of intense violence that Cora described in the spring of 1995, Rockwell experienced an unusually peaceful summer, something residents had not seen in years. This was the summer when Dawn really felt the development might turn around, that things might finally have really improved. Residents were particularly surprised by the peaceful summer because, as noted above, gang violence tended to be worse in warmer weather and that year the weather was unusually hot. One factor that may have helped to reduce the violence in the summer of 1995 was the fact that the HUD takeover of the CHA at the end of May had allowed Moorehead/New Life to sponsor a development clean-up and hire gang members to paint the buildings and carry out other maintenance activities.

More likely, given that the gangs dominated life in Rockwell, a more powerful factor was that the major gangs in the development had agreed to a truce, or "peace," which essentially constituted a cease-fire. Cora spoke about how happy she was to be able to sit out on the porch in the summer and not worry about getting shot. "There's nothing going on bad. There's nothing bad been happening, you can sit on the porch more now. 'Cause I know I sat on the porch yesterday until . . . about one o'clock, and just quiet." Thelma said that the gangs were "partying together" and had even put on a rap show for the other residents: "The gang members, they like, they trying to unite. It's like . . . well, the only two gangs over here that I've really known about is the Vice Lords and Disciples. And they've been trying to combine lately, so they've been throwing little community parties together, and they been getting along just fine."

Thelma thought the truce might be the result of the efforts by the New Life staff to keep the gang members busy. However, other residents pointed out that although the summer truce was unusual, the gangs had had truces off and on since 1993 because they were "good for business"; that is, drug dealers could sell their goods more freely if they did not have to worry about getting shot. Whatever the reason, the gang truce during the summer of 1995 was apparently different enough for residents to hope that it might signal a more profound change.

The Gang War Returns—Winter 1996

The "peace" in Rockwell held only for a few months, quickly undermined by the conflict within one of Rockwell's major gangs, the Gangster Disciples. The failure of the gang truce was part of a CHA-wide phenomenon. In the summer of 1996, the *Chicago Tribune* (August 9, 1996) reported that a long-standing truce in Cabrini-Green had failed; the subsequent gang war affected many other CHA developments.[41] One factor leading to the collapse of the truce was the turmoil in the Gangster Disciples. More than thirty top Gangster Disciple "warlords" had been convicted of federal conspiracy charges related to drug sales since 1995; the gang was weak and factionalized (see, for example, *Chicago Tribune*, July 3, 1997). Another factor was the CHA's closure and demolition of buildings in many developments, which disrupted long-held gang territories (*Chicago Tribune*, July 4, 1997). But regardless of what caused the collapse of the truce, CHA residents in all developments were left to cope with the violent aftermath.

In Rockwell, a key leader, likely a Gangster Disciple warlord, was arrested in late 1995, thereby creating turmoil among the different factions of the gangs that controlled the development. By December of 1995, residents indicated that although the violence was not yet as bad as it had been the previous spring, there had been some shooting or what several referred to as a "brief gang war." Dawn's hopes for a real peace were dashed. As she said, "they still fighting. A boy just got shot a couple of days ago, about four or five times, so they gangbanging again outside the building."

Drug Trafficking

Although the gang war intensified, residents' reports of problems with drug sales and use changed little between 1996 and 1997. Conditions remained better than they were at the outset, but the majority of residents (just over half) in the Jackson and Van Buren Street buildings continued to report serious problems. Monroe Street residents reported fewer problems inside their building, but, in both 1996 and 1997, just under half reported serious problems outside.

Residents in all three buildings spoke of the hopelessness of trying to control the problem of illegal drugs. In addition to fear of retaliation, several pointed out that many Rockwell residents used illegal drugs so they were not likely to be interested in trying to reduce the problem. As Ida put it, "Well, a lot of residents buy the drugs, too, so that's a problem. I don't know. I guess we just, we should . . . have meetings and just try to talk about it to do something, everybody put their heads together and try to come up with some type of solution."

Gangs Control the Buildings

When we visited Rockwell in February 1996, we could see obvious signs of the increased gang tension. As mentioned earlier, young men armed with sticks were patrolling in front of the doors; they went inside and waited as we approached. Gang members—not guards—were screening visitors to the buildings. Residents we interviewed confirmed that the gangs had taken over the two buildings on the west side; they were controlling access and intimidating residents. Jackie described how the gangs dominated the lobby and security booth in her building: "Well, they don't really be outside, they be inside. Like I said before, they stay inside like in the lobby. That's where they be. And sometime it's in the booth with the security." Thelma said that the gangs had even locked the police out of her building: "But in order for the police to come in, they have to get into the building because they [the gangs] had locked them out of the building. It's like they [the gangs] got they own security. . . . That's what they be doing now, they'll lock the door."

In addition to gang control of access to the buildings, residents also reported that the level of gang intimidation had increased. Several described a problem that they said had not plagued Rockwell since the second set of sweeps in the early 1990s: gangs and drug dealers took over apartments from legal tenants and forced the women and their families to flee or be held captive. Wardell described how the gangs intimidated female residents: "Some guy that knows that, either two things, the girl got on drugs and get in debt to him, and they take over her unit. Or it may be some girl that moved here from Tennessee or wherever, no relatives or friends, they take over her unit. . . . And there was nothing basically they [the women] could do. They were kept there during the daytime while their kids at school, then if they go somewhere, the kids are there, so it's a Catch-22, especially if you're afraid anyway."

The gangs, intimidating residents in many ways, created an atmosphere of fear.[42] Ida told of coming home to find members of the gang that controlled her building beating up a boy outside her door: "they was beating up a boy on my porch a month ago. . . . I come up the stairs, and they had just blocked where I couldn't even go in my door, they told me I couldn't come in until they get through."

While the residents we interviewed spoke of worsening problems with gang intimidation in February, the 1996 and 1997 surveys did not show much change in their perceptions of the severity of problems with drug-related crime and gang activity. About 60 percent of residents consistently report major problems. Indeed, residents of the two buildings on the west side of the development actually reported some reduction in "gang control" and "groups of people" hanging out between December 1995 and December 1996. This finding may reflect the fact that the gang war that was so intense in February had eased somewhat by the end of the year. But even with the improvement, about half of the residents reported serious problems.[43]

In the Monroe Street building, which was still insulated from the worst of the violence in 1996 by the CHA Security Force officers who were stationed there, residents reported almost no problems with gang activity (figure 4.2). However, the officers had been removed by December 1997, and conditions began to get worse. For example, in December 1996, just 9 percent of the residents from Monroe Street said that gang control was a big problem, but in December 1997 this figure had doubled to 21 percent.

Violent Crime

The 1996 gang war was unusually vicious. In February 1996, a shooting occurred on the street next to the management office, and residents were very disturbed. Several reported picking their children up at school at 1:00 p.m. in order to bring them home before things got worse later in the day. Dawn said that the shooting was surprisingly brutal:

They shot somebody on the streets yesterday, and they shot at the policeman and the fireman because they didn't want them to help the boy. They wanted the boy to lay there and die. And if anybody tried to help him, they said they was gonna shoot. So, he laid out there a long time. And finally the police came. They was gangbanging, they say. I don't know. [Interviewer: "Is that typical, that they won't let anyone come to help?"] No, that was the first time something like that happened. [Interviewer: "How do people here feel about that?"] People didn't like it, you know, people . . . didn't like that at all. 'Cause they had beat him up and then shot him in the back, so you know.

The young man who was shot died shortly thereafter; in April, residents reported that the shooter was still living in Rockwell. Although the shooting occurred literally on their doorstep, management staff downplayed the violence; in an interview the next day one actually said that things were "very safe in Rockwell."[44]

In contrast, Dawn described residents' terror in the face of the escalating gang violence. "Everybody's scared and the one's that not scared, they leave, and they move out. The gangs, they coming from all over the place now. I mean, there's some boys over here that I done saw today that I ain't never even saw. They hanging all out. I'm like, every year it's more and more of them coming. New faces, and they just coming. And it seem like they come right to here." Indeed, this incident—coupled with the increasing gang tensions—drove Dawn to apply for housing in a different development.

Ten months later, in December 1996, while the gang war may have eased somewhat, residents' concerns about violence continued. Although violence usually decreased during the winter months, about half the residents overall reported that shootings and violence outside were a big problem in Rockwell that December (figure 4.1). Again, Monroe Street residents reported relatively few problems, but 60 percent of the residents of the Jackson and Van Buren Street buildings reported extreme violence outside their buildings.[45] Further, after dropping in 1995, the proportion of residents reporting bullets coming into their apartments rose to more than 20 percent; 12 percent reported being caught in a shootout. Several residents spoke of being caught in shootouts owing to the escalating gang war. Rhonda knew two people who had been shot: "Well, one person got shot five times, but he's still in the hospital. My sister got shot in a crossfire on her way back this way. She doing okay." Not until the winter of 1997 did the development again experience a spell of relative peace; the proportion of residents reporting major problems with shootings and violence dropped again to about 30 percent in 1997.[46]

The Last Days of Rockwell Gardens

Rockwell Gardens underwent an incredible series of changes between our first visit in May 1994 and our last in December 1997. In May 1994, after years of sweeps and other attempts to reduce the crime and violence, Rockwell was regarded as the CHA's most dangerous development. Drug trafficking occurred openly, and drug use, particularly by women, had devastated the community. Rockwell also had a long history of serious management problems. In the face of overwhelming odds the buildings' physical deterioration and poor maintenance rendered the possibility that any major improvements could occur remote.

Yet, for a time, conditions in Rockwell did improve. Private management cleaned up the development, at least superficially. CHA's Anti-Drug Initiative efforts appeared to have some effect; drug trafficking became less visible, and, most significantly, the gangs held to a truce that lasted—with some exceptions—for more than a year. Although residents still thought Rockwell was far from a good place to live, it was indisputably better than it had been in the early 1990s.

Monroe Street Success

The biggest changes occurred in the Monroe Street building, where the Resident Management Corporation succeeded in creating a healthy, functioning community that was relatively unaffected by the surrounding violence. Given that their building was located in one of the CHA's worst developments, the accomplishments of the Monroe Street Resident Management Corporation were truly impressive. The group started after-school programs and obtained foundation funding to support its efforts. The Resident Management Corporation had even challenged the drug dealers and asked them to leave the building on at least one occasion. When it encountered problems with management or poor security, the group challenged the CHA to demand better services. Not surprisingly, when we analyze our survey findings, it is clear that the Monroe Street building showed more substantial improvements than either of the other sample buildings. Monroe Street residents were justifiably proud of their efforts, and in February 1996 Wardell still saw his building's future as being very bright.

> If we're not hindered. If they [CHA] don't hinder us, I think we can become a model, not only for Rockwell, but probably throughout the CHA . . . because we're no more intelligent or educated than, we're probably your average public housing residents. It's just a desire for change, a desire to do better, a desire

for the kids to do better. And to work hard at it. And the understanding that nobody's gonna come here and make the change for you, you've got to change in your heart and your mind first, and then the other comes about.

As inspiring as the Monroe Street story was, a number of special circumstances had made it possible. It was not at all clear that this effort could be duplicated elsewhere, almost certainly not in other parts of Rockwell Gardens. First, the Monroe Street building was somewhat isolated from the rest of the development; it was not possible to shoot from the building into other Rockwell buildings, so it was less valuable to the gangs. Second, the building was undergoing renovation, which meant that physical conditions were objectively improving and most problem tenants had been evicted. Third, because of the Resident Management Corporation, the building received extra resources from the CHA, particularly after the HUD takeover in the spring of 1995. Because of this special attention, the building had better janitors and, after a series of problems with vandalism, had CHA Security Force officers posted at the entryways.

What really made the Resident Management Corporation so unusually effective (more successful, according to staff, than almost any other Resident Management Corporation in the CHA) was its strong social structure—the leadership of a core of older, long-time residents. Wardell, the Resident Management Corporation president, was a charismatic and creative man whose optimism and sense of purpose were clearly inspiring to the other residents. Several other residents mentioned how Wardell had managed to keep them organized and on track in their efforts to build a stable community. The core group of resident leaders created an atmosphere in which other residents set aside their habitual distrust and came together to work for the collective good.

Subsequent events documented just how fragile—and vulnerable to gang influence—these changes really were. Despite the impressive successes of private management and the Resident Management Corporation in the Monroe Street building, conditions were still bad at the end of 1997; majorities of residents reported serious problems with drug dealing, gang activity, and vandalism. The gangs were so powerful in Rockwell that their behavior had much more impact on life in the development than did CHA's interventions. When they made peace, the development experienced periods of calm; when tensions increased for any reason—because a gang leader got out of jail, or two rival gang members fought over a woman, or because of a fight over drug turf—Rockwell again became a war zone. Once the truce was broken, neither the CHA's

interventions nor police efforts could prevent the situation from deteriorating. Ultimately, despite a brief victory, the CHA lost the battle to
control Rockwell Gardens.

CHA Defeat

The collapse of the fragile peace finally forced Dawn
to give up on Rockwell. When we saw her in February 1996, she announced her intention to move out of the development that had been
her home for seventeen years. "I've been here too long, I guess, and then
I'm tired of gangs, you know, stuff like that. I'm just tired of it. I'd like
to walk out of my building sometime, and it's nice and peaceful, it ain't
no bunch of n——s just standing there, and you constantly saying excuse
me and they don't hear you, won't move out of your way. You actually
have to detour and walk the other way to get out. I just, I'm tired now. I
had enough." When we asked if she thought there was some chance that
things might get better, Dawn said: "Yeah, I used to give it a lot of credit.
And then when it do start turning around and getting a little better, then
somebody just mess it up, they just start shooting or . . . it's gonna be
terrible over here this summer, watch. They gonna be shooting all the
time over here this summer. They gonna be gangbanging very tough. I'm
not planning on being around."

Many other residents also gave up on Rockwell, and, by the end of
1997 parts of the development resembled a ghost town. Both CHA and
federal policies had changed. The CHA was no longer spending its resources trying to control crime in unworkable developments.[47] Instead,
following new federal regulations, the CHA was assessing its properties
and determining which were no longer viable, that is, which were more
costly to rehabilitate than to replace with Section 8 vouchers. Because
the CHA expected that Rockwell would fail the viability requirement,
the agency stopped filling vacant units and began closing buildings.

As these changes in policy became clear, the CHA's relationship with
Wardell Yotaghan and the Monroe Street building Resident Management
Corporation became more adversarial. Wardell became the head of a group
called the Coalition to Protect Public Housing, which challenged the
CHA's plans for demolishing and rehabilitating its family developments,
particularly Cabrini-Green.[48] At the same time, federal policy seemed
to be shifting away from supporting the concept of resident management
corporations. In 1997 and 1998, highly publicized scandals affected
Chicago's LeClaire Courts and Boston's Bromley-Heath Resident Management Corporations, two of the oldest and most well-respected resident management corporations in the nation.[49] These scandals further

undermined support for the resident management concept in public housing.

With these tensions, the Monroe Street Resident Management Corporation seemed to lose its special status. In 1998, when the CHA closed down two other buildings in Rockwell, the agency simply moved the tenants into the Monroe Street building without allowing the Resident Management Corporation to screen them. Whether this move was the result of increased tensions between the Resident Management Corporation and the CHA or simply of the agency's need to quickly rehouse the other tenants was unclear, but the consequences for the Monroe Street building were devastating. Wardell described the situation:

> [Conditions are] very bad. They [the CHA] moved tenants from 2501 and 117 into 2450 without them being screened. The CHA closed those buildings down. It has had a pretty bad impact on the RMC [Resident Management Corporation] . Before they came people were basically—85 percent of them tried to abide by the rules here. But the people from those buildings didn't have any rules. They came here with a different kind of mentality. The tenant patrollers and floor captains are having all kinds of problems with them. It's not all the people who came; it's not even half; I'd say its 15 percent of the people who came are people who don't care for rules and regulations and they're making all the trouble.

Conditions throughout the rest of the development were no better. The gang war continued unabated, and, with the uncertainty of the redevelopment looming, tensions were high. Wardell commented, "Today is a perfect day; there's been no shooting. There has been a lot of shooting lately, every day for the past ten days to two weeks. It's been very terrible."

Joseph Shuldiner, the CHA's executive director, acknowledged that conditions around the Monroe Street building had deteriorated as a result of the building closings: "Vacating the other buildings hasn't been enough. People have been congregating around 2450 [Monroe Street]. They're clearly using that alley as a thoroughfare."[50]

In April 1998, Rockwell, along with eight other CHA high-rise developments was officially declared "nonviable."[51] The plan for Rockwell calls for the demolition of 708 units and the rehabilitation of 346 existing units, including the ones already completed in the Monroe Street building. The CHA plans to replace 304 of the demolished units with new housing; the resulting development is less than half the size of the original. The official plan calls for offering a new mixed-income development, with only half of the remaining units for current tenants.

Tragically, Wardell Yotaghan, who had struggled so hard to save his community, died of a heart attack in June 1999. His final days were spent trying to ensure that the CHA's plans for its developments would not displace large numbers of current residents, but without his leadership, the odds have become even more unfavorable. Because his vision was so central to the success of the Monroe Street Resident Management Corporation, the group now faces an uncertain future. The planned redevelopment and consequent massive relocation and public expenditure may eventually lead to a better quality of life in Rockwell Gardens. The question is whether many of the residents who suffered through life in the development during the 1990s will be there to benefit from its rehabilitation.

5 | Henry Horner Homes

The Residents of Henry Horner
Clarice's View

For more than thirty years, Clarice has witnessed Henry Horner Homes' harsh transition from temporary housing for the working poor to a dead-end for some of the nation's poorest families.[1] She fondly remembers when Horner was a decent place to live, a step up from the crowded basement apartment where she and her family had lived before. In the early 1960s, she says life in Horner was "beautiful":

> We lived on the eleventh floor. And the elevator was always working. Once in a blue moon, it might not work . . . but it was lovely when we first moved there. It was like going from this small apartment to this beautiful place, and you see flowers, you see grass and whatnot, and everything was clean, and like on the eleventh floor where I was living at . . . the porch always stayed clean, people always helped everybody out. I mean it was beautiful.

However, even then, she says the development had serious problems with crime. The leader of the Vice Lords, one of Chicago's oldest and toughest street gangs, lived in Clarice's building. While his presence brought crime, she says it also provided residents with a measure of protection from other gangs. Further, she says that residents tried to protect each other from the violence.

If somebody was trying to get raped and the guys hear it, people gonna be coming from everywhere and coming and stop it, and if you was raped, that was because nobody didn't hear you or something, you know, people did get raped in the building. But if somebody heard . . . a woman screaming or something, if someone heard a man jumping on a woman, they would come out there and stop it . . . everybody, even the people that you thought you didn't like, they would come out there and help you.

Clarice says that conditions in Horner grew worse during the 1970s as the CHA stopped screening new residents, and problems with vandalism, drugs, and crime increased rapidly. She still remembers the first time someone she knew was murdered in Horner; more than twenty years later, she vividly recalls the incident:

I remember when this boy got killed in our building; that was the first funeral I really went to, he used to live on the thirteenth floor . . . he was like a year older than me, but we all used to hang together, and his mother was at work and their next door neighbor . . . he was going in [the boy's] house through the window to rape his sister . . . And he [the boy] was running after him [the neighbor], and he slipped in the hallway, and the guy stabbed him and shot him.

While she remembers Horner as having been a comparatively good place when she was growing up, Clarice's childhood was far from easy. She had serious problems with asthma that left her hospitalized for much of her adolescence, but she still managed to graduate from high school. She was sexually assaulted by a man she was dating when she was a teenager. As she grew older, she worked for a few years, had two children, and eventually moved into her own apartment in the development. Since then, Clarice has worked off and on, but, because of her asthma and more recently multiple sclerosis, she has had to rely periodically on public assistance to support her family. Her illnesses have been exacerbated by the stress of coping with drug-addicted relatives who live in the development. These relatives routinely rely on Clarice to care for their neglected children.

According to Clarice, by the 1990s, the once "beautiful" grounds were filthy and barren, and gangs and drug trafficking dominated life in the development. Individual murders now failed to shock residents, unless they involved young children or were unusually brutal. Along with the deteriorating conditions, Clarice feels that the community where residents cooperated and helped each other in times of need has disappeared.

She describes young gang members who have become increasingly preda-
tory: many have reached the point where it brings them pleasure to watch
someone else in pain. They no longer honor the community's values.

> People don't have no respect . . . as they used to have sometimes
> for their own parents. And there used to be a time, you could
> not say anything about nobody's mama. Sometimes I seen this
> same young man I'm talking about, I seen him jump on his
> mother. . . . And then I see a lot of young guys lately be beating
> up these girls and hitting on these girls. I can't deal with
> that. . . . And like one of the guys in the gang . . . he had sex with
> a thirteen-year-old, and I know he's twenty or twenty-one. . . . You
> used to do that, everybody would be on you. Now he, yeah, he
> had sex with her . . . that's what I'm saying changed. The mo-
> rality of people done had changed.

Clarice has little hope that anything can improve the dynamics of
life in Horner. Although the development is now in the midst of a major revitalization effort and many residents are hoping for a brighter future, Clarice feels nothing can really undo the years of community decay.
Rather than gamble on the redevelopment, Clarice, believing it is the
only way to ensure her daughters' safety, has opted to leave her home
of thirty years and start again in a new community.

LaKeisha's Perspective

LaKeisha lives on the opposite end of the develop-
ment from Clarice, separated by a major thoroughfare and by gang turf
divisions. She, too, has little hope that conditions in Horner will improve but, unlike Clarice, has no plans to move in the near future.
LaKeisha was born in Horner in the early 1970s and has never lived any-
where else. She is a troubled young woman, who dropped out of school,
became pregnant, and moved into her own apartment with her gang-
affiliated boyfriend when she was only eighteen years old. Her boyfriend
was a drug addict, and their relationship became increasingly abusive.
After three years of escalating violence, she finally forced him to move
out. Since then, LaKeisha, working at a series of low-wage jobs and
dreaming of moving to a better neighborhood, has struggled to maintain
a decent life for herself and her daughter.

LaKeisha grew up in an unhappy, violent family. Her father, who
deserted the family when she was twelve, had serious problems with
drugs and alcohol. At age fifteen, LaKeisha was brutally raped by an older
acquaintance; she believes that this experience damaged her profoundly.
Although the rest of her family still lives in Horner, she says they are

not close. She also says she keeps to herself and has few people she considers friends.

Difficult as her life has been, LaKeisha believes that life in Horner is even worse now than when she was growing up. She complains about the pervasive drug dealing, the constant noise and disruption in the hallways, and people knocking on doors and shouting at all hours of the night. She is very worried about the impact of this environment on her young daughter and does not allow her to play outside within the development. Her goal is to move away so her daughter can attend school in a safer neighborhood: "I managed not to get into all the drugs and violence and everything. My whole family never got into it, but I don't want her to take up with it also because it's getting worser now than it was when I was growing up. It's much worse. So I don't want her to go [to the school] where I went."

Although LaKeisha hopes that the redevelopment effort that began in 1995 might finally improve conditions in Horner, she also fears that it will not really benefit her or other current Horner residents.

> Because it's always a lot of false promises made especially over here with Chicago Housing Authority, it's like you get what you're getting and it's like you either accept it or you don't, you have no choice in the matter. We're gonna say this to make it sound good, so you won't give us all this back talking and complaining, and once they tear 'em down, what can we say then, we have to accept it then, because the buildings are down. But it's like we're gonna tell you this now to make you happy so you can agree with us until it happens, we're gonna let only certain people move over here, and it's not fair.

Barbara's Vision

Barbara's vision of the future of Horner is very different than either Clarice's or LaKeisha's. She lives in the same building as Clarice and still believes their community has a great deal of potential. Barbara did not grow up in public housing, but she moved to Horner in the early 1980s after the building she was living in was suddenly closed for code violations. She was born in the South, and her family moved to the West Side of Chicago when she was just a small child. She describes her large family as close-knit and supportive. Many of them still live nearby, both inside and outside Horner.

Barbara graduated from high school in the late 1970s and had her first child when she was just eighteen. She has worked off and on at various jobs since she was a teenager, using public aid only for short periods of time. She has five children by three different fathers. She says she has essentially raised her children alone and views herself as having succeeded at being "both mother and father."

Despite the fact that the father of her youngest child is a drug addict, Barbara feels that she and her family have been relatively unscathed by the drugs and gang violence that surround them. Although she says that she and her children have not been directly affected, she acknowledges that they have been hurt by the violence. She described (in May 1994) how the death of a family friend affected her children:

> My kids were very close to a young man that was murdered. . . .
> He died on Christmas. He was really, really close to my family
> and it affected all of us a lot. . . . The young man, he was in a
> gang, but we knew him and knew what type of person he was
> and it affected my son so bad that I had to sign him into a men-
> tal health center. . . . When something like this happens, they just
> don't know how bad they're affecting people. . . . My little girl
> cried forever, seemed like. Still today—this is four months later—
> and she's still asking questions about where is he, will he ever
> come back. Things I can't answer.

Barbara went on to say that this incident upset her teenage son so much that he became suicidal, literally paralyzed with fear that he, too, would die violently. As she said, "He don't want someone to just snuff his life out like he never existed."

Barbara believes that her fellow tenants contribute to the problems in their community. Many are drug addicts or alcoholics and do not adequately supervise their children. Others allow gang members to live in their apartments illegally.

> Some of 'em [the people causing trouble] are long-time former
> residents, some of 'em are friends of former residents, gang af-
> filiates, associates, from out of prison or another area that their
> affiliates are in, you know. They come here, they stay with
> people. Then, too, I guess you could say half of it . . . in a sense
> is the people of Horner because you have a lot of these females
> who allow these guys to stay in their apartments. Even though
> [these residents] are not out there physically doing the violence,
> you're promoting it when you let them stay in your house . . . you
> give them a place to hide.

While Barbara is concerned about the violence in the development—and the impact on her children's lives—she views the problems within her own building as manageable. She even says that the gangs, by protecting their drug business, provide a measure of security for the building. As she says, "I know it sounds so ironic, but you think about these young mens that people fear, they're so notorious, and you know them when they were kids, and they respect you, they look out for you, they look out for everyone in the building." Indeed, she claims that the CHA's attempt to control the drug trafficking and gang activity has actually made conditions in her building worse, that the police harass the residents and fail to keep rival gangs out.

Barbara says she has prevented her own children from getting into serious trouble by keeping them under tight supervision; she has allowed them only to play on the porch outside her door or where she can see them. Even her twenty-one-year-old son is required to be home by 10:30 p.m. and to let her know where he is going to be. As she says, "there's so much going on out there in the streets, it's not that I wanna know every little thing you do, but I do need to know where you are."

In addition to closely monitoring her own children, Barbara is very active in the Horner community. She is a long-time volunteer at the local elementary school and is very involved in the Local Advisory Council (LAC) that represents Horner tenants.[2] Indeed, Barbara believes she has a mission to try to save her community:

> I started getting the feeling [when I took care of children in the neighborhood] that I could be of some assistance, so I made it in my mind that I didn't want to go. That nothing would ever change . . . everybody that moves in the projects, if they ever got a chance to get out, they would get out and wouldn't look back, you know what I'm saying? They're running from the problems. But if they had stayed and worked to find a solution to the problems, then nobody would have to run away from the problems. So . . . they moved to a neighborhood where you know it's infested with the same [gang and drug] problems instead of staying there and letting the kids know it's somebody that they could talk to or somebody that care about them, it's somebody that really is willing to go the extra mile with them, so I decided to stay.

Barbara, who has been very involved in the redevelopment effort in Horner, is cautiously optimistic about the future of the development. She hopes that the redevelopment will lead to a healthy, mixed-income community with enough housing for most former Horner residents. However, she sees clear threats to this dream: the CHA's failure to provide adequate security and rumors about possible changes in federal housing policy, which might increase tenant rents or limit the number of units for very low-income tenants.[3]

These women's stories provide three perspectives on life in Horner during a period of rapid transition. In 1994, Horner was even more deteriorated and just as dangerous as neighboring Rockwell Gardens, and residents had little hope that conditions would ever improve. Only two years later, the development was in the early stages of a massive revitalization effort; buildings were being demolished, new townhouses constructed, and there was tremendous uncertainty about what would happen to the tenants. Like many other residents, Clarice chose to leave in search of a better life elsewhere. LaKeisha, overwhelmed by the problems and fearful about the coming changes, saw no good options for her and her fellow residents. In contrast, Barbara chose to join a small group of activist tenants and gamble on the possibility of working with the CHA to create a new, healthy community that would include the original Horner tenants.

Life in Horner

In this chapter, from the perspective of the residents of three of the development's high-rise buildings, we tell the story of life in the Henry Horner Homes from 1994 through the beginning of 1999. The mid-1990s brought tremendous change to Horner and the surrounding community. As in Rockwell, we conducted six rounds of surveys with approximately 150 to 200 residents,[4] and we held in-depth interviews with 10 to 12 residents in three of the nineteen buildings in Horner; we also interviewed CHA staff and conducted ethnographic observations in the development (for a detailed description of research methods, see the Appendix). By describing the development as it was when we first visited it in 1994, we can comment on the CHA's various attempts to combat crime in Horner and their impact on conditions. The revitalization effort that began in Horner in late 1995 ultimately had a much greater effect on life in the development than any CHA anticrime efforts; we discuss the early phases of this effort and the potential impact on residents.

Like Rockwell Gardens, Horner, a notorious CHA high-rise development, was, in 1994, clearly in the worst physical condition of the three case study sites. It was also extremely violent; as in Rockwell, several gangs vied for control of the development, and major gang wars and frequent gunfire rendered a constant atmosphere of fear and intimidation.

The Horner development lies just west of Chicago's booming downtown and sits incongruously next to the United Center, home of the Chicago Bulls and an entertainment mecca for the city's wealthy and influential. Although the entire development is often referred to as the "Henry Horner Homes," the development is actually divided into three sections: the

Horner Homes, the Horner Extension, and the Horner Annex. The development is long and narrow; the main section—the Homes and Extension—is only two blocks wide, running from Lake Street to Washington Street, but approximately one mile long, extending west from Ashland Avenue to Western Avenue. The Annex is located several blocks south of the Homes on Warren Street. When originally constructed, the three sections had a total of 1,777 units.

Horner Homes, the oldest section of the development which opened in 1954, mixed fifteen-story high-rise and seven-story mid-rise buildings. The buildings used interior hallways and thus lacked the "porches" and metal grates that characterize the buildings in Rockwell Gardens, but their bleak, concrete exteriors and small windows nonetheless gave the buildings the same grim, prisonlike appearance. The Horner Extension consisted of four large high-rise (thirteen-story) and three mid-rise (eight-story) buildings. The Extension, opened in 1961, featured a unique apartment layout: the buildings contained duplex apartments. The Extension buildings had exterior hallways and porches that were covered with metal grates, as in Rockwell Gardens. By 1994, some Extension buildings had already been closed for a number of years, and so many windows in the occupied buildings were boarded up that it looked like the entire area had been abandoned. The Annex consisted of three relatively small buildings—one seven-story mid-rise and two low-rise buildings—adjacent to the United Center.[5] We specifically focused on three buildings in the development: two buildings in the Homes section, and one building in the Extension, which we refer to as the Lake Street building.

According to CHA figures, Horner had a population of 3,057 in 1991. By 1997, the official population had fallen to 2,158 residents living in 682 occupied units. The actual population was undoubtedly higher as many adult males (boyfriends, adult children, and other relatives of leaseholders) lived in the development illegally. Resident characteristics changed little from 1991 to 1997. In both years, the households were almost exclusively African-American, female-headed households. Only about two of ten heads of household were employed. The population was relatively young; nearly six of ten residents were under age twenty-one.[6]

In 1991, the Henry Horner development gained notoriety as the setting for Alex Kotlowitz's best-selling book, *There Are No Children Here*. The nonfiction book, focusing on the lives of two boys growing up in Horner, documented their painful struggles to cope with the overwhelming decay, crime, drug sales, drug use, and personal trauma that pervaded their everyday lives. It is somewhat surprising that, despite the public attention generated by Kotlowitz's book and the subsequent television movie, the CHA was slow to devote resources to Horner; by 1993 little had changed from the deplorable conditions Kotlowitz found when he finished his work in 1989. Indeed, the situation in Horner did not begin to improve until the CHA and the Department of Housing and Urban Development (HUD) agreed to a lawsuit settlement in 1995 requiring the CHA to undertake a major, $200-million revitalization of the development.[7]

Horner had a long history of management problems, as Kotlowitz vividly documented. He described the CHA inspection in the spring of 1989 when the staff discovered basements in Horner filled with pools of fetid water, "scurrying rats and dead cats and dogs," human and animal excrement, and drug paraphernalia. In the middle of this horrible mess—so bad that the CHA inspectors became instantly sick and quickly abandoned their job—thousands of new kitchen appliances and cabinets sat rotting away in these basements, while many Horner residents were waiting for new appliances (Kotlowitz 1991: 240–241). Although these basements were eventually cleaned, overall conditions improved little by the early 1990s. In fact, by 1994 some buildings had become so deteriorated that the CHA declared them uninhabitable and closed them completely.

In the late 1980s, there were two hospitals nearby, and a supermarket was located an easy ten-minute bus ride away, near the University of Illinois-Chicago campus. Because all these neighborhood amenities closed by the early 1990s, residents had to travel outside the area for medical care or groceries. The only major institution in the area in 1994 was the new United Center, set apart from the surrounding area with wide swaths of parking lots. Besides liquor stores, there were almost no businesses nearby, despite the close proximity to the Chicago Loop. A number of churches and schools existed in the community, but few social services or other cultural institutions were available. A notable exception was the Major Adams Boys and Girls Club located in the middle of the Horner Homes. A second club, the James Jordan Boys and Girls Club, named in honor of Chicago Bulls star Michael Jordan's late father, was built just outside Horner in 1996. The economic isolation in Horner in May 1994 was extreme. One CHA official described the environment: "I mean, you can't have this great program in place at Horner . . . and expect anything to work at Horner . . . if you're surrounded by an economic wasteland. And that's what Horner is, there's nothing there."[8]

Plans for Revitalization

The revitalization of Henry Horner, announced in the summer of 1995, changed substantially the eventual fate of the housing development and the surrounding community. The plan includes five incremental phases of redevelopment, which continue in late 1999. Other events also brought new attention and resources to the area. In 1995, the city of Chicago designated the Near West Side, which includes both Horner and Rockwell, as one of its three Empowerment Zones, a HUD initiative to promote economic development in distressed neighborhoods. The area also benefited from the investments the city made to host the 1996 Democratic National Convention at the United Center. In preparation for the convention, the city launched a massive effort to clean up Horner and the surrounding neighborhood. In the wake of all this attention, the area even received a new name, Westhaven, in an attempt to distance association from the stigma that shadowed Horner.

Unlike CHA's other redevelopment efforts, the Horner Revitalization Initiative was prompted by not only changes in federal regulations but also resident initiative: the Henry Horner Mothers Guild, a small group of Horner residents, in 1991 filed a lawsuit against the CHA and HUD.[9] The suit alleged that the CHA's failure to maintain the development constituted "de facto demolition." Under federal regulations then in place, housing authorities were required to replace every unit of public housing that they demolished, a policy called "one-for-one replacement."[10] The *Mothers Guild* case argued that the CHA's neglect had rendered their units uninhabitable; thus, the units needed to be either rehabilitated or replaced. The case was settled in March 1995 by a consent decree detailing extremely ambitious goals:

> This Horner Revitalization Program shall convert the Horner development from a densely-populated, dilapidated and exclusively very low-income project characterized by high vacancies and dangerous and hazardous conditions to a mixed-income neighborhood consisting of new and renovated mid-rise and low-rise, low-density homes that are fully occupied and maintained in a decent, safe, and sanitary manner.[11]

To meet these goals, HUD committed $200 million to a five-year plan of demolition, rehabilitation, and new construction.[12] The Horner Revitalization Initiative, officially begun in August 1995, became the first and most ambitious of the CHA's efforts to redevelop its properties.

Deplorable Conditions

By 1993, the effects of years of poverty and neglect were visibly etched on the physical space in Horner.[13] Bleak high-rises stood among patches of dirt and battered concrete; the few pieces of playground equipment sat rusting, broken, and unused. Only scattered forlorn trees and aged or abandoned cars marked the landscape. Boarded

Photo 4. Graffiti in First Floor Hallway, Hermitage Street Building, Henry Horner Homes. *Photo by Elise Martel.*

up and broken windows and graffiti scarred the exterior faces of the buildings, while the streets and parking lots were pockmarked with potholes.

In 1994, most residents felt that the physical state of their buildings was dreadful: 80 percent said that graffiti was a big problem both inside and outside, 67 percent said that trash and junk in the outside areas was a big problem, and 62 percent complained of trash and junk littering the building interiors as a major problem. It was not unusual for the incinerators to back up—on at least one occasion, all the way to the seventh floor—creating an almost unbearable stench. As in Rockwell, the hallways often reeked of human waste as well as garbage. Further, the buildings—particularly those in the Homes section—were infested with rats, mice, roaches, and even feral cats who roamed the hallways.

Perhaps the most terrifying problem was the nearly total darkness of windowless interior hallways and stairways. Without working light bulbs, simply getting home meant long and harrowing hallway walks. Nearly everyone living in these buildings (82 percent) reported that broken light bulbs constituted a big problem. Residents were disheartened by the awful conditions. Regina, a CHA resident of nearly twenty years and a community activist, complained the CHA too often made only half-hearted attempts at providing service: "I observed the maintenance people mopping, and they use dirty water. . . . You just can't wipe dirty water

Photo 5. Rear Entrance, Washington Boulevard Building, Henry Horner Homes. *Photo by Elise Martel.*

on the floor and leave it there and wipe it up and think you've done your job. It's half done. They're half doing their job."

In May 1995 we witnessed a stunning example of poor maintenance in these buildings: A janitor was pushing a dumpster with a huge hole in the bottom out of a building in the Homes. As the janitor pushed it, he scattered trash over the grounds, but, during the time we watched, he made no effort to clean up the mess he was creating.

Residents complained about the janitors' failings, but they also blamed their fellow residents for breaking light bulbs, tampering with light fixtures, dumping trash in the stairways, and immobilizing the elevators. Tina described the problem: "They [CHA janitors], you know, try to replace [the lights] during the day. You'll see 'em walking around with two crates full of nothin' but light bulbs, and I . . . see 'em screwing 'em in, but before the day is over with, either they been busted, or taken out, and like . . . some of the apartments in the long hallway, you know, it's . . . pitch black."

Although litter and graffiti were unsightly and compounded the sense of an environment out of control, malfunctioning elevators had traumatic consequences for health and safety. LaKeisha lived on the tenth floor of her building, and both she and her daughter suffered from acute asthma. She described carrying her daughter up the ten flights of stairs on many occasions, a dangerous situation for both of them. In addition, several women, like Janelle, noted that broken elevators compounded the maintenance problems on the uppermost floors:

> Sometimes peoples on this first floor lobby stops the elevator. I
> don't know how they do it, but they can fix it so where it can
> only go where they want it to go, or you can only catch it on
> some floors. And they know how to work their—I call them their
> elevators. . . . So that's why the janitors can't use the elevators
> to come up, and . . . [since there] ain't no light [in the stairways]
> we hardly ever see a maintenance man. We do see him down-
> stairs in the lobby, but we never see him upstairs.

At Horner, low-quality building maintenance was matched by low-quality apartment repairs. Residents we spoke to reported a wide range of problems, many long-standing. Leaking pipes and faucets, broken windows, and exposed light sockets with faulty wiring were just some of the chronic and dangerous problems that had been left unrepaired in Horner for some time.

The hazards created by years of neglected maintenance to the buildings' infrastructure were especially troubling, given that many small children lived in the development. For example, as in Rockwell Gardens, some Horner residents reported that their faucets could not be turned off, resulting in a constant stream of scalding hot water. After years of complaining, Regina said she had little expectation of ever getting her requested repairs completed properly: "So I just gave up on it. So then when the ceiling falls in, then I'll see them in court because I told them about it [the leaking] and they didn't do anything about it. Didn't ever say anything about it. I'm not going to say anything else about it."

Residents described trying to cope with the miserable conditions in Horner by keeping their own apartments as clean as possible and mopping the areas in front of their doors. However, there was little they could do to overcome the terrible smells, the dirt and dust that blew in windows, and the infestations of rats and roaches.

Living on the Front Line

As in neighboring Rockwell Gardens, it was unlikely that you could live in Henry Horner and not be touched by the constant violence. Residents reported a world that at times turned into a literal war zone, where their lives were caught on the front lines as gangs fought for control. Clarice described her terror the day her daughter was caught in a shoot-out and a boy walking just behind her was killed: "She was coming home from school. They [gang members] told her to go in. They'd wait till she go in, and the boy behind her—they shot him. He died. But she was right there, and she was real scared." Laverne, a mother of two who lived in the Lake Street building, described her thankfulness for a brief period of relative calm when we spoke with her in May 1994: "[The gunfire] might have been about a month ago or so—since they quieted down there. But before then it was like every day, all day long. But they go through their little periods of time. It might last for two or three weeks, and then they'll quiet down. . . . . They just calmed down last month. . . . They really just calming down when one of our boys had been shot. . . . And now that they've calmed down, I don't know how long the shooting going to stop."

As in Rockwell, gangs permeated nearly every aspect of Horner life— economic, physical, and social. In 1994, three of Chicago's most powerful gangs were fighting for control of drug sales and the development. The Gangster Stones, a faction of the Black Peace Stone Nation, controlled most buildings in the Horner Homes section and the most lucrative drug market. The Gangster Disciples, Chicago's largest and most lethal street gang, controlled the buildings in the Extension.[14] Finally, the Conservative Vice Lords controlled the mid-rise buildings along Damen Avenue, which divides the Homes from the Extension.

In May 1994, Horner residents were very worried about the presence of gangs and drug trafficking. About 76 percent reported "big problems" with groups of people "hanging out" both inside and outside their buildings. Further, 72 percent said that "young people controlling their building" was a big problem; that is, young gang members monitored, and sometimes blocked, the doors, screened visitors, and challenged outsiders. Finally, more than 80 percent of Horner residents reported drug sales and drug use were major problems, both inside their own apartment building and in the surrounding area.

Many Horner residents were distressed about crime and violence in their community. About 51 percent of the residents said that "shootings and violence" were big problems inside; 61 percent reported major problems outside their buildings. People being attacked or robbed, both inside and outside, were "big problems," according to 43 percent of the residents and 28 percent said rape or other sexual attacks were big problems. Finally, about one-third reported that burglary was a big problem in their building.

Reflecting the high level of crime in Horner, residents reported being victims of a number of different types of crimes in the past year. Property crimes, such as burglaries (reported by 17 percent of the residents in the survey) appeared to be relatively common. However, the high level of violent crime was most striking. Of Horner residents, 11 percent reported that they or a member of their household had been

Photo 5. Lake Street Building, Henry Horner Homes. *Photo by Jean Amendolia.*

stabbed or shot, and 16 percent said they had been caught in a shoot-out; 15 percent said someone in their household had been beaten or assaulted during the preceding year.

In May 1994, clear differences emerged in reports of violent activity among the three buildings we specifically studied—the Lake Street building and the two buildings in the Homes section. More than 70 percent of Lake Street residents reported that shootings and violence were big problems both inside and outside their building in May 1994. In contrast, 44 percent of the residents from the Homes section reported that shootings and violence were big problems inside their buildings, and 55 percent reported major problems outside. Similarly, a shocking 40 percent of the Lake Street residents reported bullets had been shot into their apartment in the last year, compared to 11 percent of those from the Homes. Charles, a life-long Horner resident in his mid-thirties, came home one day to find a bullet in his apartment in the Lake Street building: "[I] came home from work, and my wife, she was hollering and said they had been shooting, and they shot from [the adjacent building], and I was living on the front, on the Lake Street side, and they was shooting from that building down. I was living on the front side, and that bullet went in my bedroom."

A gang war between the Black Gangster Disciples and the Conservative Vice Lords over territory in the Extension section of Horner precipitated the extreme violence in the Lake Street building. The Lake Street building faced a building controlled by a rival gang, and residents were living on the front lines of the war. The gangs apparently shot at each other across the open space between buildings, sometimes standing on the porches and firing directly across into the upper floors. In May 1994, Barbara reported that a number of people in her building had recently been shot, and several had died: "[One resident's son] got killed. They walked him in the building. Shot him in front of her, and . . . he died. So it's gang-on-gang activity. . . . Everybody wants this territory." Her neighbor, Inez, also described the intense violence: "One boy got shot three times. He's still in the hospital, and that's been about two months ago. He's going to be paralyzed. He was just standing there at that particular time. He just was standing outside, and they decided to open fire."

Although problems with violence in the Homes section of the development were severe, they were not nearly as extreme because the Gangster Stones controlled most buildings east of Damen Avenue and, in May 1994, appeared to have no rivals within their territory. This stability in the Homes section of the development undoubtedly was responsible for the comparatively low level of gunfire during this period.

As in Rockwell, the amount of crime that residents said they had experienced probably substantially underestimated the actual level of violence. Residents tended to underreport crime to the police—and probably to our interviewers and even their friends and family—because they both feared retaliation and hesitated to report people they knew.

Given the high levels of shootings and violence in Horner, relatively few residents appeared to have reported incidents to the police or guards. As in Rockwell, just 31 percent of the residents in May 1994 said that they had reported a crime to the police or guards in the past year. Several residents said they had called the police on occasion, but they felt the police had either not done enough or failed to respond at all. Several echoed the sentiment that "the police only come out when there's a tragedy" (that is, a shooting or a killing). However, the primary cause of residents' reluctance to report may well be the complexity of the relationships between victims and perpetrators: people they knew or recognized, not unknown assailants, committed many crimes. Understandably, many feared retaliation if they reported a crime to police. Brenda, who had lived in the Homes section for only a few years, was convinced people would find out if she reported crime to the police: "Because if you report something to them [CHA or police], then you have to worry about it getting back over here. Someone over here will find out."

Janelle described the terror her fiancé experienced when some "boys" who lived in his sister's building attacked him. Despite their fears, neither of them reported the crime to police.

> I guess I can say this, to me it was a crime, but it wasn't reported. My fiancé, he was going to visit his sister, and going to pick up his income tax check, and it was in [another building]. He went up in there to his sister's house, and he stayed there for a while, and he never made it upstairs. I think he said when he got to the third floor, some boys jumped him and robbed him, the money out of his coat pocket. They came out and took his coat, injured his arms. He had to go to the doctor and everything, and now he's been afraid to come outside. Been afraid to go to work, and he work nights. But he do go to work, but I have to watch him in and out, like he say if it take him more than ten minutes to get to his car, call the police. And I have to do that every night.

Tina's story illustrates some dilemmas of a world where violence is an everyday occurrence. Just twenty-seven years old, she already had five children, including two sons aged twelve and thirteen. Over the past year, other boys in the development—some of whom were now their friends—had repeatedly assaulted them: "They [my kids] heads have been busted, that's my oldest two kids, they heads have been busted, my second son have been stabbed in his back, they just been actually jumped on! . . . When they got their heads busted they was on their way home from school . . . and the kids attacked them. And one, the one boy that actually lives in the building, now knocks on my door and wants to play with them!" Tina described a particular incident in which one of her sons was stabbed. She confronted the assailant's mother directly rather than involve the police: "And I go in the bathroom, sink full of blood, a towel full of blood. I'm like time to check bodies. So I go cut on the lights and everything, and he was like, 'Mom, they stabbed me in my back' . . . and he told me who did it. I took him over there to the boy's mother and everything and showed her what he did. 'Well, I'll help pay his hospital bill,' [she said]. I'm still waiting on payment."

Given these common experiences with violence, it was not surprising that a majority of residents (63 percent) we surveyed said they felt unsafe if they were outside alone at night, and some (33 percent) felt unsafe even inside their own apartment. However, as bad as the violence seemed in May 1994, some residents felt things might be starting to improve. They believed a recent gang truce was beginning to bring down the level of crime. The truce apparently was even affecting the besieged Lake Street building, where Barbara lived. She noted the change: "Now they have a peace treaty so I can just walk out and go. . . . Back when the peace treaty wasn't on . . . sometimes you can't go out in the morning because they're shooting when the kids going to school. Just terrible."

The public crimes committed by gangs and drugs dealers were not the only sources of violence in the community. Private, domestic violence was also rampant, and, as in Rockwell, many women did not feel safe even in their own homes. For example, LaKeisha spoke at length about her violent relationships with her siblings and her former boyfriend. Janelle, another young mother, said that she was forced to move from one end of the development to the other to avoid a former boyfriend: "I moved in this building because I was forced to move here. . . . I was stalked and being battered by my kids' father. . . . I don't know how he used to get in there so much. Because, every night, when I'm getting off work or whatever, this man would walk in my house or stand in my hallways or something."

Coping with the Stress of Constant Violence

The threat of violence took a painful toll on the families living in Horner. Residents often adopted a fatalistic attitude about the constant violence. Barbara described the realities of living in the war zone:

> I'm going to be perfectly honest with you—and this may help the survey a little bit. By me living in it so long, I've become conditioned to the situation which it stands. It's an everyday thing for me. I don't fear it because it's reality to me. It's everyday reality to me. But I would imagine someone who hadn't lived in it—which we do have new residents coming into the CHA

all the time . . . it would be considered fearful for them, but I'm speaking for myself. I'm conditioned for it. It's everyday. It's like, if they're going to shoot, they're going to shoot. If they're not, they're not. That's just the way that stands.

Most residents we met were parents or grandparents. Their greatest worry about living in Horner was raising children in an environment where violence was commonplace and crime readily visible. It was nearly impossible to always protect their children in such a place, and the neighborhood offered little positive distraction. As LaKeisha explained, "There's nothing out there anyway, there's no type of slide. . . . It's dangerous to play in the playground. No swings, nothing out there." Janelle described her efforts to keep her three young children off the streets and in their home: "I don't let my kids out to play around . . . only because I stay fifteen stories high, and if something happened I just can't get to 'em in time. . . . I never let them play. No. I never, I'm here three years, I can't even count the time I let them come down here and play. They don't come down to the lobby, the playground. I just don't do it. I don't know nobody down here, and my kids don't know nobody." Others coped by taking their children out of the neighborhood as much as possible. Inez, a mother in her thirties and a relatively new resident, was particularly committed to exposing her children to enriching activities in the city. "The majority of the time my kids aren't even at home. I take them to the museums or—my kids are always gone because I want them to know that there are other things to do with yourselves besides sit out there and play and hang out and do whatever. So I figure if I give them a chance, by taking them places, maybe that'll keep them occupied. And they won't even think about stuff like that."

No one said Horner was the kind of environment they would select for their children if they had a choice. But, as one resident said, "It's all I can afford." In the meantime, they coped as best they could and hoped that their children would avoid being swept into the world of gang violence and the drug economy. As Inez explained, "I don't think I really have a problem. But you never know until your child is at that age. But the same thing can happen somewhere else. So the only thing I can do is try to teach them the best that I know and hope."

Strained Social Connections

In Horner, most residents had lived there for years and knew many other tenants well; often they had long-term friends and family who also lived in the development. Because privacy was lacking in Horner, residents could easily observe each other's activities from their windows and were familiar with most people who lived in the development. But often these social links were not sufficiently protective against the dangers in the community. Residents we interviewed spoke of an ever-present wariness in an environment that could become dangerous at any time: "You don't know who you can trust," or "You have to look out for yourself," or "People are scared." As Inez explained, social ties were usually closely circumscribed; residents took care of their "own" and regarded those outside their inner circle with great suspicion: "I don't know. I know the few people that I talk to, you know. If you need something or they need a favor, we look out for each other. But the rest of the people, I don't know how they go about helping each other." Wanda echoed this sentiment: "They basically go their own way. They communicate, but, it's like everybody mind his own garbage. Everybody fighting and drugs and guns. And you know, nobody cares if the kids don't have a place to play."

The majority of Horner residents (58 percent) in May 1994 felt that both the CHA management and residents were responsible for stopping crime and drugs in the development. Only 24 percent of the residents said tenants alone were most responsible. Some residents stressed their inability to handle the dangers presented by gangs and the power of the drug market. According to Inez, "Well, I don't think the tenants could do it. So I think the CHA management should do whatever they have to do to try and get those people out of here." Some, such as LaKeisha, felt that residents should shoulder more of the responsibility for crime and drugs: "I think the tenants. We have to stay here. I think a lot of the tenants are the ones who's out there doing the loitering and stuff. And their kids, you know, are in the hallways doing something. It's a lot of parenting control, I think, plays a big part in it. Not enforcing curfew, being in the house—that can make a big difference."

Despite their concerns, most residents were relatively optimistic about their ability to improve conditions: 66 percent said they thought that if residents worked together, they could do "a lot" to solve the problems of crime and drugs in their development. Very few (10 percent) said they thought they could do nothing at all. However, as in Rockwell, these results may have been more of a measure of "hopefulness" than what residents thought would actually happen. Given the opportunity to discuss the issue in the interviews, many residents expressed resignation that collective action was unlikely, given residential wariness about their neighbors. As one man explained: "If they stick together and keep the police on them, it would help a lot. But a lot of these people are scared, you know. Scared of anything."

The biggest obstacle noted was that the perpetrators were also the sons, brothers, daughters, nephews, boyfriends, and long-time friends of those who were complaining. Laverne explained how difficult, given these social and economic complexities, it was for residents to take action: "Well, most of tenants in the building, it's their children. . . . We have the meetings. But like I was saying, the problem is not going to go away because half the parents who come to the meeting that are complaining, it's about their child. So how can you stop something when it's your child."

Differences were apparent among the three buildings we studied. The Lake Street building on the west side of the development, which had experienced such high levels of violence, appeared to be more cohesive; those residents were more likely to report they worked together on problems. This building had a number of older, long-term tenants who seemed to have formed a strong community. Residents in that building, like Barbara, were more likely to describe neighbors helping one another, particularly with child care:

> A lot of us do try and help one another out. I try to work with the kids myself. They always know that my house has an open-door policy. . . . I believe in the way I was brought up, that it takes more than the mother and father to raise children. It takes other people, and sometimes maybe I can't see things the way my children want to see, but they can go to my neighbor and talk to her. And maybe they will understand her more than they do me. So yeah, we work things out for the most part—a lot of us.

Although Horner in some ways was a tightly-knit community, with residents who knew each other well, the overwhelming violence meant that residents treated each other warily and were reluctant to work together to improve conditions.

The CHA's Battle against Crime in Horner

Rockwell Gardens was where the CHA began its battle against crime in its developments in the late 1980s. The CHA did not turn its attention to Horner until 1991. As in most of its high-rise developments, the CHA's Anti-Drug Initiative—the sweeps, security guards, in-house police, tenant patrols, and CADRE (CHA drug-prevention) center[15]—faced daunting challenges: years of neglect, intense violence, powerful gangs, and beleaguered residents skeptical of the CHA's ability to effect change. Even a well-designed, expertly implemented program would have faced difficult odds. For various reasons, the CHA was never able to fully implement its Anti-Drug Initiative interventions in

Horner. However, in 1995, the CHA began implementing the court-ordered Horner Revitalization Initiative, which holds the promise of bringing bigger, more substantial change to the community.

CHA staff cited the extreme level of gang violence and physical isolation as factors that undermined the agency's efforts in Horner during the mid-1990s.[16] They also believed that resident leadership in Horner was generally weaker than in many other CHA developments. Comparatively few effective resident organizations and vocal activists rallied to protest CHA's decisions. One senior CHA manager commented, "The [Local Advisory Council] president at Horner is a strong leader, but there's nobody there to really back her up. She's really operated on her own out there."[17] In 1994, Vincent Lane, then the chairman of the CHA board, admitted that the agency regarded Horner as being in such poor physical condition that it was simply not worth any significant investment: "Horner is a unique case. It was the worst development CHA had when I got here. I'll be honest, I want to put the money where it will have the most benefit. I saw no point in investing in buildings that had already become so deteriorated. They should be vacated, and people consolidated in other buildings."[18]

A more cynical view—one widely held among residents—was that CHA had allowed the buildings to deteriorate. Tearing them down would then be justified, and the land underneath, which had growing market value with its proximity to the United Center, could be sold or redeveloped for more affluent households. More likely, Lane, who was also the chairman of the National Commission on Severely Distressed and Troubled Public Housing during the early 1990s, anticipated changes in federal laws that would ease the demolition of public housing and permit the creation of mixed-income developments. However, the *Mothers Guild* decision, which mandated the revitalization of Horner, meant that the CHA and HUD had to invest hundreds of millions of dollars in redeveloping the site by replacing any units they demolished with new construction.[19] In the meantime the Anti-Drug Initiative was underway, fighting against years of neglect and decay.

Sweeps in Horner

The CHA conducted the first Operation Clean Sweep action in Horner in June 1991. The entire development was swept again in November 1992 and for the last time in November 1993 in response to an increase in gang violence (*Chicago Tribune*, November 17, 1993). In addition, as in Rockwell Gardens, a number of large-scale police actions responded to specific violent incidents. Operation Clean Sweep, however, involved a much larger range of services, including issuing resi-

dents' identification cards and surveying tenants about their social service and maintenance needs; the CHA also installed "target-hardening"
measures such as metal detectors, steel exterior doors, and guard booths
at the main entries. During the 1993 sweep, the agency installed turnstiles at Horner, which were meant to prevent drug dealers from running through the buildings.

Our first visit to Horner—part of a preliminary assessment of the
CHA's anticrime efforts—occurred shortly after the second set of sweeps
in November 1992. At that time, the residents we interviewed felt the
sweeps had improved conditions, albeit only temporarily (Popkin et al.
1993, 1995). The sweeps became more controversial in the spring of 1994,
following a judge's ruling that the CHA's actions violated residents' civil
rights.[20] As in Rockwell, Horner residents' attitudes about the sweeps
were contradictory and remained so throughout. In May 1994, only 37
percent of the residents said that they thought the CHA should be able
to search apartments without tenants' permission; yet, the large majority (78 percent) of residents also said they wanted their buildings swept
again.

As Shanita's comments exemplify, some residents objected to the
sweeps as an invasion of privacy. "[Sweeps should not be done again] . . .
because that's invading your privacy. When they come in you house they
want to look around. . . . When I was here they just came in, checked
the stove and refrigerator—made sure that it was the one they gave me
when I first moved in. They went in my bedrooms and came right back
out." However, others, like LaKeisha, viewed the sweeps as one of the
only ways to control the crime and violence in their community: "So,
you know, I don't think anyone likes them to look through their stuff,
but where I live I think it's necessary." Indeed, given continuing problems with crime and drugs in their buildings, some residents we interviewed said that they actually wanted more frequent sweeps. Anita
explained, "Well, like I said, our building's not too good, but I know
they still have guns and drugs in that building. They need to sweep more
often than they do."

Although most residents we interviewed felt the sweeps helped reduce crime and disorder, they also complained that these improvements
were short-lived. Some, like Regina, questioned whether it was worth
enduring the indignities of the sweeps. "We know that when they done
the sweep it'll be quiet and peaceful for a while, and normally they'll
be real strict on security that be downstairs. But after a day or so you
know, it's pretty near right back to the same thing, and you go through
all of this—for what?"

After the legal controversy in the spring of 1994, the CHA gradually

phased out the sweeps and replaced them with swarms, increased police patrols and building walkdowns, which involved the CHA and Chicago police patrolling the halls and stairwells of high-rise buildings.[21]
In time, the sweeps became a less salient issue, although the proportion of Horner residents who wanted their buildings swept again remained unchanged.[22] The fact that such a large proportion of residents
still wanted their buildings swept, despite the controversy, spoke to their
level of desperation about the problems with crime and violence in their
buildings.

Security Guards
Following the sweeps, guard booths were constructed
at the main entry, behind the newly installed metal detectors. Guards
were to be there twenty-four hours a day to screen people entering the
building and allow only leaseholders and their invited guests to enter.
The implementation of the security guards clearly failed at Horner; residents consistently perceived the guards as useless at preventing crime
in their buildings. The program, which, except for brief periods after the
first sweeps and during the revitalization effort, was staffed entirely by
low-paid private contractors, started poorly and disintegrated swiftly.

Tina's response to a question about what the guards did to provide
security was scathing: "Besides sleep? And get high? That's it! . . . One
guard slept from when I walked . . . my youngest three kids to school . . . at
about 8:30 [until] I came home. He was still laying on the desk, and then
I came back downstairs around 12, and he was still in the same position!" Clarice was equally frustrated: "They [the guards] don't care who
comes in the building. . . . If the police be around, they might try to pretend like they doing something, but if the police not there, they don't
care who come in. It's up to the, well, the gangbangers is the ones who
let people in the building . . . instead of the guards. The guards be in their
booth just sitting down."

Even when we first interviewed Horner residents in the winter of
1993, they complained that the guards were inconsistent about enforcing entrance procedures (for example, screening visitors or checking identification) and were ineffective in keeping people from hanging out in
the entryways (Popkin et al. 1993, 1995). When we returned to the development in May 1994, the majority of residents complained that the
guards did a poor job of preventing crime (69 percent) and reducing fear
(71 percent). These dismal ratings only grew worse over time; nine
months later in January 1995, nearly 100 percent of the residents we
surveyed rated the guards' performance as "poor."[23]

Although residents always thought the guards were ineffective, in

1993 and 1994, Horner guards were generally at their posts. But by January 1995, residents reported that the guards were only showing up sporadically, and by May 1995, the situation had deteriorated so completely that those hired to "guard the building" did so by *sitting in their cars on the street.* Barbara described the situation in the spring of 1995: "I guess [they show up] when they feel like it. You may have one set of guys that can come on, they'll stay for their entire eight hours, but then again . . . the next set may not show up, or if they do come, they'll stay a while and leave."

Following the HUD takeover of the CHA in May 1995, the new administration attempted to remove the guards from Horner altogether. Acknowledging the guards' ineffectiveness, the CHA argued that increased police patrols, particularly bicycle patrols, would provide adequate security. As conditions deteriorated, lawyers representing Horner tenants in the *Mothers Guild* case filed a complaint about the guards' removal and alleged that the CHA was violating the terms of the consent decree that required the CHA to maintain safe conditions during the renovation.[24] After a few weeks, the CHA agreed to reassign private guards to Horner on a limited basis, although most continued to guard the building from cars or vans on the street (*Chicago Tribune,* September 19, 1995). However, considering the guards' performance, residents seemed to think their return made little difference. Inez described the guards sitting in cars or around fires they had built in garbage cans to keep warm: "But the only reason we have security right now is because of a court order. But they sit in their cars or they sit across the street where the [store] is, and build their fires and do whatever it is they wanna do, but they're not in the building at all."

In addition to the problems with guards failing to appear at their posts, residents consistently complained that the security guards often treated them disrespectfully. As in the other developments, many, such as Laverne, complained that the guards were flirting with and harassing female residents: "Some of [them] are respectful. But the other ones, they just seem like they just try to talk to you. What I mean by that— they flirt . . . they let young girls go in and use the telephone. . . . It's like, well you can't use the phone if you don't want to talk to me, if you don't let me touch you. . . . You have security guards, they get off work or during their lunch hour, they go upstairs to the [woman's] apartment." However, the most troubling complaints from residents were allegations that security guards not only failed to protect people from crime but also in some cases endangered them. Barbara said that the guards in her building locked residents out during shoot-outs, leaving them exposed to the gunfire: "We don't really have a problem with security except when they're [the gangs] shooting. Then they [the guards] try to keep the doors locked. . . . They're looking out more so for their safety than ours. The security is rotten."

Considering the forces at work, it is not difficult to understand why the security guards failed so miserably in Horner. The guards, all employees of contract security firms, were armed, but they were paid only $5 or $6 per hour and received only twenty hours of training. CHA staff acknowledged that in the dangerous Horner situation it was virtually impossible for these poorly trained guards to do their job effectively.[25] For near poverty-level wages, inexperienced guards were not likely to stand up to the gangs. They received training and wages that might have been appropriate to patrolling suburban parking lots but not manning the front lines of an inner-city war zone. Residents like Laverne understood the dynamics of the situation: "The security guards are scared. . . . They don't want to stop and ask, 'Do you live in this building?'"

In February 1996, LaKeisha summarized how the security guards had lost control of the buildings in the Homes section:

A lot of things are out of control. The buildings themselves, like it's gone, no guards, nothing. It's back the way it used to be. They [the CHA] did that with the guards, put them over here to change it, maybe this will help them out, and for a while it did, but the guards slackened up some. . . . They [the gangs] started disrespecting the guards. When they first came over here, people were scared of that; "Oh, they gonna have guards over here. Now you can't even go in this side," and this and that, and they couldn't. But once they [the gangs] start . . . breaking those guards down, you know, "Well, you gonna let us in," or this and that. A lot of the guards were on drugs themselves—they buy drugs from the drug dealers—so they let them stand out there, so they [the gangs] took advantage of that. That's how they pushed them [the guards] out of the building.

The dangers in Horner undermined the guards' effectiveness, but poor fiscal management also clearly contributed to the failure of the security program. As discussed in chapter 2, in 1994, the CHA determined that all six of the private security firms it contracted with to provide security in its high-rises had billed for services not rendered (*Chicago Tribune*, June 24, 1994). One firm, which provided security for most of CHA's high-rise developments, was accused of failing to adequately staff guard stations, shuffling staff from one station to the next to try to cover up the shortage.[26] Thus, in part, the guards seemed to disappear from Horner because the contract security firms simply stopped sending them there but continued to bill the CHA for their services.

Problems with security in Horner continued as the revitalization initiative got underway in 1996 and 1997. In December 1996, only a small proportion of Horner residents reported having guards in their building; these were primarily residents from the Lake Street building that received extra security under court order. A year later, no guards were stationed in any buildings. HUD required the CHA to spend its funds on major improvements to its developments and reduce significantly the amount of money the agency had available to spend on security services. In 1996, the agency stopped hiring contract guards, and in May 1998, the CHA's Security Force laid off 152 security officers due to budgetary constraints.[27] What remained of the CHA's Security Force patrolled the development on a regular basis by foot and car, but inadequate security remained a major concern.

Police

As in Rockwell, police from both the CHA and the city of Chicago were assigned to patrol Horner on a regular basis. The two departments participated in joint activities such as the sweeps, swarms, building walkdowns, and emergency inspections, and both departments initiated community policing programs in 1995.[28] As discussed in chapter 2, the Chicago police expanded their citywide community policing program (called the Chicago Alternative Policing Strategy, or CAPS) to include CHA housing in the fall of 1995, and some residents, particularly those from the Lake Street building, reported attending CAPS meetings.[29] The CHA also began implementing its own community policing program, although it was less well defined. As part of this effort, CHA police officers patrolled Horner on mountain bikes for several months and increased foot patrols (*Chicago Tribune*, September 1, 1995). Residents seemed to feel that the main effect of these increased patrols was to shift drug dealing from one building to another. Tonisha commented, "If the police come, they'll try to chase them [the drug dealers] back out. But when they leave, they start all over again."

And Janelle added, "I think those bikes, the police on the bikes, chased them [the drug dealers] away. . . . And so they—they call it shop—open shop and closing shop. So what they did was they closed shop in one area and opened it up in another."

In addition to the patrols, the CHA police had a small office at Horner, which they used as a holding cell. Senior CHA administrators felt that the agency's efforts in Horner had been somewhat more successful than those in Rockwell, although they were well aware that serious problems with crime remained. In both Rockwell and Horner, CHA personnel felt that the police were doing the best they could, but were fighting an uphill battle against the entrenched gangs.

> We're doing an effective job, quite frankly. A very effective job. But in reference to doing an even better job, the problem is not enough people combined with a huge gang problem. . . . There are no street gangs like Chicago street gangs. This is gang central right here. This [CHA housing] is where it's all focused in on, where all the major gangs conduct a good amount of their activity, where the soldiers live, where the generals come and go, it's just such a huge problem. And when you take into account that we're operating in an environment where 98, 99 percent of the people are unemployed, wherein about 80 percent or more of the families are single-family household situations, wherein 80 percent, probably more, of the people are under twenty-five, this is like a hunting ground for the gangs. So what it basically boils down to are huge numbers of gangs coupled with unbelievable armament and relatively few CHAPD [police department] and Chicago police officers to deal with the situation.[30]

Despite efforts of the CHA and Chicago police to cope with crime in Horner, residents remained reluctant to report crime to police; in fact, the proportion that admitted reporting a crime to police or guards declined significantly over time.[31] As Barbara said in December 1995, this reluctance stemmed from the very real threat of retaliation: "They [residents] too afraid [to report crime]. . . . I try to tell [the police] like I tell the lawyers . . . they don't have to raise their kids here. They don't have to worry about, 'Well, can I go out to the store, and will I come back in safe?' you know. Because you can get killed any time, and nobody may never find out who done it. . . . Why would they even think to ask somebody to testify about what they have seen?"

Conflicts with Residents
As in Rockwell, many Horner residents we interviewed had negative attitudes toward the CHA police and viewed them as less effective than the Chicago police and disrespectful to tenants. However, in Horner, perhaps because of the greater police presence, the complaints were more serious, with many residents—particularly those from the Lake Street building—reporting that the CHA police were violent and abusive. In January 1995, Clarice complained the police were harassing the residents in her building: "Oh, I did call on one of the . . .

CHA policeman, because . . . my daughter was bending down, and he put the stick between her legs and whatnot. . . . Like the nightstick. And she was bending down, and he put it like that and stuff. She said he act like it was an accident, but she didn't think it was. Because it was another young man there, and he arrested him, and he's not a gangbanger, and he wasn't doing anything, so they were just harassing people that day."

Six months later in May 1995, Regina complained that the officers were being abusive to residents and searching apartments without cause: "Basically they . . . knock on people's doors, [and will] break doors down if don't nobody answer the door, they kicks it in. . . . They goes into the apartments, ransack the apartments . . . the vacant apartments [that CHA had secured]. They take hatchets with them and chop those doors open. . . . Then you ask them, 'Why was you tearing that door up, you gonna leave it like that?' They [reply], 'B—— this and m——f—— that, you can't tell me what to do!' . . . They don't care what they say to you and how they say it." The situation continued to deteriorate: when we returned to the development in August 1995, almost all the residents we interviewed from the Lake Street building reported incidents of CHA police officers forcibly entering apartments, opening previously secured vacant apartments, and verbally abusing residents.

In February 1996, Barbara reported that the CHA police were beating up gang members regularly:

> They're [the police] beating the gang members. They are really beating the gang members, but even though those guys are gang members, they still have rights. And . . . to me, that's unnecessary force. If they catch them with something, they ought to take 'em to jail. Unless they're physically trying to harm them, they shouldn't beat them, those are somebody's kids, you know. All of 'em aren't bad kids, they're just starving for attention, some of 'em for love, some of 'em for all the things that they were never able to have, and that selling drugs afford them to have these things. And . . . they're still human beings, and they still should be treated as such. If we sit back and let them take their civil rights from them, then they're going to do the same thing to us.

Continuing Police Presence

The police apparently continued their heavy presence in Horner through 1996. In October, CHA and Chicago police conducted a sting dubbed "Operation Blue Tornado." The operation resulted in the drug-related indictments of ninety-five people, including fifty-two residents, for drug activities at Horner. Police claimed that this sting shut down a $100,000-per-week drug-selling business (*Chicago Tribune*, October 8, 1996) in one high-rise in the Homes section, but residents said the raid resulted in the arrests of many innocent tenants. Moreover, these heavy-handed tactics did not significantly improve safety in the development.

Tenant Patrols

Despite repeated attempts, the CHA was unable to organize effective tenant patrols in Horner. Occasionally a group of residents took the training offered by the CHA's Office of Resident Programs, but these groups apparently collapsed quickly. As one administrator put it, "Horner is the one development, every time we think we've got 'em, they're gone."[32] The CHA's resident programs staff believed the lack of participation at Horner was due, in part, to the high proportion of young leaseholders—also a factor in Rockwell Gardens. CHA staff felt that the strong gang presence in Horner had effectively intimidated residents, who were highly skeptical that tenant patrols really could improve conditions in their buildings. "So we've got some [Horner residents] in training, and we've got to do some special things with them. I think that the pessimism is so strong there, that if things don't happen immediately, they give up. It's such a sense of hopelessness."[33]

Our interviews with residents confirmed CHA staff's analysis.[34] Most residents said they would not be willing to participate in the tenant patrols. Their main objection was fear for their personal safety. Like Barbara, they were concerned that the police would not protect their anonymity, and they would be vulnerable to gang retaliation. "I saw something once. I called the police—I figure I'm being protected. Police come right back to my door and let it be known that I was the one who seen it. So therefore people will not do this tenant patrol because the police do not have respect for their privacy. This is why they don't get any information." Residents also said they were not willing to participate in tenant patrols because they did not have child care or because it was safer to "mind their own business." Others explained that they were focused on leaving Horner altogether, rather than trying to improve conditions there. Finally, a few residents, like Clarice, said that some resident volunteers for the tenant patrols were themselves connected to the gangs in their buildings: "We had a tenant patrol [meeting] to help us combat the gang and everything, and the people that wanted to be in it, their kids was in it [the gang] or they was helping the gang out in the first place, so why you gonna have the devil taking care of the devil? It's stupid, you know. So we said we wasn't gonna have one."

Janelle, who lived in the Homes section, said that the tenant patrol in her building quickly failed because the gangs intimidated the participants, spying on their meetings and threatening retaliation.

> They [the gang] run everything. That's why, you know, everybody act like they scared. Everybody scared to call the police. We had a tenant patrol. We used to have meetings and everything, . . . but people scared to come out. Then we had people that was coming to the meetings, then going back telling the guys what we were saying at the meetings. We had a couple of people that threatened our lives. . . . It was like everybody just started dropping off, you know, one by one. And we had got down to where it was just me and one other lady. . . . Because everybody else, you know, chickened out.

Thus, the tenant patrol program failed in Horner because of residents' very real fears that becoming involved would expose them to retaliation from the gangs and drug dealers. With gang members attending meetings and threatening those who were brave enough to attend the meetings, it is no wonder that residents quickly "chickened out" and decided it was safer to keep to themselves.[35]

CADRE Center

The Combating Alcohol and Drugs through Rehabilitation and Education (CADRE) center opened in Horner in June 1992 in a first-floor apartment of one high-rise building in the Homes section of the development. CHA staff viewed the Horner CADRE center as more successful than the one in Rockwell.[36]

The Horner center offered the standard set of services and programs, including drug-prevention programs and help in getting access to drug treatment. However, the Horner CADRE initiated a much wider and more creative range of prevention programs for youth than the center in Rockwell Gardens. Staff established relationships with the three schools adjacent to the development. The CADRE center had a Student Assistance Program and periodically presented workshops and all day retreats (called "Snowflakes") on substance abuse, conflict resolution, and gang avoidance. Staff also ran a "Just Say Know" program. The center invited Chicago police and state's attorney's office representatives to participate in school visits, in an attempt to build better rapport between young Horner residents and law enforcement officials.

In addition, CADRE staff developed a relationship with the Chicago

Academy of Sciences, where they took twenty-five young people every other Saturday for tutoring. The staff took middle school children on college tours and camping trips to expose them to life outside of CHA housing. CADRE staff attempted to involve parents in these activities, to help to strengthen families and thus decrease the likelihood of adolescent involvement with drugs and gangs.[37] According to one CADRE staffer, "The whole concept is, we're trying to promote family unity and assist in every way we can to build family structure. Make it more sound, more strong."[38] CADRE staff believed that the fact that most staff and volunteers were Horner residents helped the programs' effectiveness: "So we're hiring right directly from the community. They're always in touch with people after 4:30. The people now know what they're doing, what CADRE provides . . . so when they're going home people are coming and needing services and needing questions answered, and they would take care of them even then. But there's a trust factor, by them being residents. So they're very effective."

CADRE center staff were less successful in getting residents into drug treatment. In part, this failure reflected a shortage of beds in local drug treatment centers. However, CADRE staff felt they had not been able to reach most substance abusers to convince them to give up their drug habits. They conducted regular door-to-door outreach efforts, yet were disappointed with the turnout for drug treatment referrals.

> The drug problem is the same too. It hasn't changed because people have drug habits. The demand outweighs the supply. As long as the demand outweighs the supply, we will have a drug problem. This is a people problem, not just a drug dealer problem. Residents can go to CADRE, but they are not. Only two or three people a month are placed in detox. I don't know if you can call that successful. It is good for them, but as a percentage of the population being served, the program has not been successful.[39]

Another factor that limited the success of the Horner CADRE was the center's location on the east side of the Homes and the ongoing fight for turf among the gangs. Because Damen Avenue divided territory between the Gangster Disciples in the Extension and the Conservative Vice Lords and Gangster Stones in the Homes, residents, even adult women, were reluctant to cross that line.

Residents that we interviewed generally had very positive views of the CADRE center. Although most had not used the services, they trusted that the CADRE staff would help them if they needed it. Those, such as Tina, who had used the services, were very pleased with their experiences. "They went around knocking on everyone's door, 'Hey we're down here, we'll help you with this, and you know, we got this program and that program,' and then I got to know the workers that work here, and everything, and when I got stuck up they was more than willing to help me." In addition, several residents with children were particularly pleased with the youth programs and viewing them as one of the few positive things in the development.

The Horner Revitalization Initiative

The biggest force for change at Henry Horner in the 1990s would become not the Anti-Drug Initiative, but the Horner Revitalization Initiative.[40] The *Mothers Guild* suit was first settled by consent decree in the spring of 1995; however, HUD took over the CHA in May 1995, and the terms of the settlement were then renegotiated. A new consent decree with a full redevelopment plan was issued in August 1995. The settlement of the *Mothers Guild* case coincided with the implementation of the federal HOPE VI program (see chapters 2 and 3), which provided funds for public housing demolition and revitalization. The Horner Revitalization Initiative thus became the first of the CHA's efforts to revitalize its worst public housing properties.[41]

To meet the ambitious goals of the *Mothers Guild* decree, the CHA was required to demolish all high-rise and some mid-rise buildings in Horner, rehabilitate the remaining mid-rises, and construct new townhouses in the community. More units were to be built than destroyed, although half of these new units were to be rented to working-class families not currently living in CHA housing.[42] Horner tenants were to be given a choice of a Section 8 voucher, scattered-site housing, or a new or rehabilitated unit in or around Horner. To ensure a viable, mixed-income community, the consent decree also mandated that security measures be put in place, the site be landscaped, and parks and play areas be constructed; in addition, the development management was to be private rather than handled by the CHA. Finally, although the consent decree required that the CHA carry out a needs assessment of current Horner residents to determine their needs for social services, it did not provide any funding for these services.

Two days after the final decree was signed, demolition of a long-vacant building in the Horner Extension began; four more of the seven buildings in that section of the development were demolished within the next few months. Before any more buildings could be demolished, all the Extension units had to be replaced; this requirement stalled the demolition for several years, even as the CHA moved ahead with constructing new townhouses on the site.[43] The revitalization slowed following the Democratic National Convention in the summer of 1996, and the pace did not increase again until late 1997.

The first phase of the redevelopment called for the construction of 466 units: 200 on the Horner site, and 266 in the surrounding area.[44] The remaining high-rises in the Homes section were to be demolished; residents voted to rehabilitate the three buildings in the Annex and the mid-rises in the Homes. Half of the new and rehabilitated units were to be set aside for current Horner residents, and half were to be used for "low-income" tenants (that is, tenants with incomes between 50 and 80 percent of the local median income). Although a few Horner residents, who as a whole were considered "very low-income" tenants, qualified for low-income housing, most low-income tenants were working families recruited from around Chicago.[45] This first phase of the redevelopment was initially to be completed in April 1997, but it was still incomplete in early 1999 (*Chicago Tribune,* February 28, 1999).

The effects of the revitalization initiative could be seen by mid-1996. The first fifty-six new townhomes were constructed on the Horner site in time for the Democratic National Convention that was held in the neighboring United Center in July of that year, and Pinnacle Realty Management Company took over the day-to-day management of the development. The city cleaned up the surrounding neighborhood by spreading wood chips and planting shrubs in the vacant lots. The Lake Street elevated train line was reopened, and all the major roads were resurfaced. The CHA cleaned up the development grounds and even built a new playground across from the Homes buildings.

As the revitalization effort began, Horner residents had mixed feelings about the proposed changes. Many residents we interviewed were unsure what the future would hold for them and whether they would be allowed back into the revitalized development. Like LaKeisha, many said they feared losing the only home they had ever known: "I think a lot of us was born over here or raised over here. We feel comfortable over here, everyone knows each other. No one wants to like move away or be put somewhere else where they don't wanna go. I think everyone wants something better, but they don't wanna have to leave their own neighborhood to get something better."

Inez, a Lake Street resident, was particularly concerned about the implications of the proposed screening process, which could prevent any residents who had poor rental histories—failure to pay back rent, damage reports, or other lease violations—from returning to the revitalized development.[46] Furthermore, under the federal "one-strike" provision, households with a member having a criminal record would no longer be allowed in Horner, or any other CHA development. "If you don't [make it through the screening], then I guess you have to take one of the other options, like scattered sites, Section 8, or something like that."

The Extension, where the Lake Street residents lived, was affected first. By early 1996, these residents had already noticed some reduction in crime. Several, like Barbara, said that the demolition of buildings had reduced gang tensions and forced gang members to realize the agency was serious about moving ahead with the redevelopment.

> I think that what happened was once they saw those buildings torn down, it was a reality. You know, it just hit them, bam they really gonna do this. And I think that people now realize that they're really gonna lose what they know as home. So I think that it's making a change in them . . . because not only are we losing what we call home, they're fixing to lose what they call home. So the area that they staked out as their territory is not fixing to be their territory anymore. So therefore, in order to try to hold on a little bit, the gangs have been . . . [more or less] getting along.

Some Lake Street residents became actively involved in creating the new Westhaven community. Two building leaders were appointed to the Horner Residents Council, which was created by the consent decree to represent the Horner residents in decree-related issues. Barbara and other tenants also became involved with a community organizing effort to try to bring social services and economic development to Horner.

In contrast, residents from the Homes Section were much less positive about the revitalization. With the exception of the new playground, the revitalization effort did not have much effect on their section of the development during the early stages. The development was put into private management in 1996, which may have improved janitorial service, but did little to address the major problems of failing building systems, including incinerators, plumbing, elevators, and heat. Further, they had not yet been offered the relocation services that Extension residents received and were uncertain about their future. Tonisha's comments reflected this confusion: "I think they was talking about moving. See we done heard so many stories, they was talking about moving everybody over there. Then they talk, turn around, talking about they gonna remodel, rehab them [the buildings]. So you just hearing too many different stories."

Janelle, like many Homes residents, was suspicious that the new housing would be turned over to middle-class people who wanted to move into the gentrifying neighborhood:

I think they wanna give it to the, well, the more fortunate peoples; they say the middle class and some low-income. I think they wanna give it to all these people that already got a good life, but complaining about they live too far. And they tired of catching the Metra [commuter train], so they just want one transportation, they want a place where they don't have to drive their own car to park, 'cause they spend too much money parking, they wanna be able to save all that money parking and just catch one ride to their job and that's what they gonna get.

By the spring of 1998, 160 new townhomes had been constructed on and around the Horner site. The new townhomes were attractive, with significantly more "curb appeal" than the high-rises they replaced. In the surrounding community, off-site units filled in vacant lots and replaced abandoned buildings, giving the area a less desolate look. The mid-rise buildings in the Homes section had been cleaned-up: sandblasted, tuckpointed, given new windows and accessible entrances. In the Annex—those three buildings across from the United Center—one building had been completely rehabilitated and renamed "the Village of Westhaven," and rehabilitation of the other two was underway. Only a few families remained in the Lake Street building, all awaiting new townhomes. However, the two buildings in the Homes section were still occupied, and conditions remained miserable.

Impact on Conditions

In the early 1990s, conditions in Horner were deplorable: filth, vermin, graffiti, trash, and junk were everywhere; drug use and sales were rampant; three rival gangs vied for control of the development. The CHA spent millions of dollars on sweeps and security enhancements in the development in 1992 and 1993, with few tangible results. Residents noted short-term improvements, but no longer-term effects. Indeed, residents noted that at least one "target-hardening" measure—turnstiles installed in the building entryways—did little but protect the drug dealers from the police. Dealers could stand inside the lobby and sell drugs through the turnstiles to buyers standing outside; to catch them, police had to go around the building and enter through the front entrance, by which time the dealers could easily disappear. Several residents commented that the only advantage for residents was that this system kept the customers out of the lobby. Inez described the typical scene: "They [the dealers] made them [the customers] go out and around through the turnstile. So they just handing them [the drugs] to them so they're not necessarily in the lobby. They did change that after they [the CHA] locked the building down and put the turnstiles in."

Between May 1994 and December 1997, the CHA continued to spend millions of dollars on security in Horner for guards, police, tenant patrols, and the CADRE center. In the summer of 1995, the agency began implementing the Horner Revitalization Initiative, which slowly brought profound changes to the development: By 1998, demolitions, closings, decreased population, and townhome construction altered the development considerably. However, conditions in the high-rise buildings slated for demolition remained much the same, and drug trafficking and violent crime remained serious concerns. Moreover, the extent to which the original tenants had benefited from the changes in Horner remained unclear.

According to residents, some problems in Horner improved gradually over time, particularly after the revitalization initiative got underway in late 1995. However, as shown in figure 5.1, although the situation seemed to have improved, residents' concerns about crime and drug trafficking remained high even in 1996, a year after the revitalization began, and in 1997, with revitalization well underway. Budget shortfalls forced the CHA to reduce its spending on security; the agency increasingly shifted resources to new and rehabilitated sections of the development and away from the high-rise buildings. Horner did, in fact, change over time; improvements and increased residential concern became apparent as the revitalization effort picked up steam. We use scales to summarize the patterns of change in residents' perceptions of major problems with vandalism, drug trafficking, and violent crime in Horner.[47] Finally, using data from a follow-up study conducted in 1998,[48] we discuss the early impacts of the revitalization initiative.

Physical Conditions

Horner residents' reports of physical problems inside their buildings remained very high throughout the mid-1990s, even as the revitalization initiative got underway. The three high-rise buildings that we followed were all targeted for eventual demolition. By the winter of 1996, the Lake Street building was the last building left open in the Extension, and the overall tenant population had dropped precipitously as many residents elected to leave Horner for scattered-site or Section 8 units. However, even as the revitalization was beginning to change the look of the overall development, conditions in the remaining high-rise buildings were bleak. In May 1994, the overwhelming majority (more than 90 percent) of residents had noted major problems with graffiti, trash

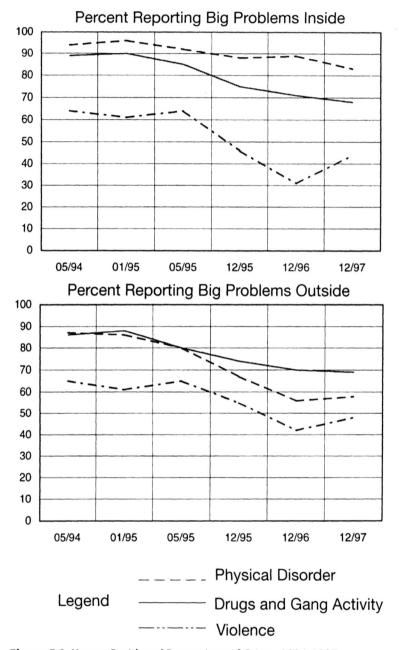

Figure 5.1. Horner Residents' Perceptions of Crime, 1994–1997

and junk, and broken light bulbs in their buildings. As figure 5.1 shows, after the revitalization initiative began, this figure dropped to 88 percent in December 1995 and remained at about that level in subsequent years. Residents did note some changes as private managers took over maintenance. For example, in December 1997, residents reported a dramatic improvement in problems with broken light bulbs.[49]

Not surprisingly, residents consistently complained about the terrible conditions in their buildings. Those from the two Homes buildings described ongoing problems with trash piling up—probably resulting from both vandalism and the buildings' faulty incinerators. And, as in 1994, especially troubling to them were the dark hallways and stairways resulting from broken light bulbs and fixtures. As Anita commented in May 1995: "Trash is always in the hallways. No light bulbs, it's just always nasty in the hallways now." Although residents complained about the janitors, much of their frustration was aimed at their neighbors and CHA management. Wanda summed up the situation in February 1996:

> The same thing—broken lights, trash everywhere outside. The janitors—they can't really blame it on the janitors because they do come in the morning, and they do clean up. But over the weekends, the janitors don't do anything on weekends. Then everything is a mess on Mondays, and it might be Wednesday by the time they get everything cleaned up and fixed up. They never got the supplies they need from Housing, no light bulbs, never. It's just basically the same.

Residents of the Lake Street building generally had fewer complaints about the physical conditions in their building. With a smaller tenant population, particularly as the revitalization effort progressed, resident leadership asserted some influence to get better janitors and encourage residents to work together to keep the building relatively clean. As Barbara explained in September 1995, "We don't really have that much [graffiti], just a little bit. In the elevators, a couple of residents and myself, we usually keep the elevators scrubbed down and cleaned. So we don't really have a problem with graffiti." Barbara went on to say that even the gang members who lived in the building kept a trash can out front for their garbage.

Although conditions in the two buildings in the Homes section remained grim and the Lake Street building improved slightly, the situation outside improved substantially after the revitalization initiative began at the end of 1995. Residents' complaints about major problems with graffiti and trash outside declined from 80 percent in May 1995 to 67 percent in December 1995 and just over 50 percent in 1996 and 1997 (see figure 5.1).[50] The first clean-up occurred in September 1995, coinciding with a formal ceremony marking the demolition of the first buildings in the Extension. According to Regina, the mayor and other officials attended the ceremony: "I think they cleaned it up because Mayor Daley was coming to the ceremony of knocking down the buildings. So that's when they did the cleaning up."

Lake Street residents had consistently reported less severe problems with graffiti and trash outside than residents of the two buildings in the Homes. Furthermore, the improvement in physical conditions was much greater in the Lake Street building. For example, the proportion of Lake Street residents reporting "big problems" with trash and junk piling up on the lawns and parking lots fell from 61 percent in May 1994 to just 24 percent in December 1995; the comparable figures for the Homes buildings fell from 70 to 60 percent. These differences reflect the impact of the redevelopment effort, particularly the drastic loss of population. In the early phases of revitalization, following demolition and closings, the Lake Street building was the last occupied building in the Extension. The population of the Lake Street building itself shrank as residents opted for relocation rather than remaining in the development. Fewer residents—and fewer buildings for the gangs and drug dealers to occupy—undoubtedly led to fewer problems with vandalism.

By 1998, at least on the exterior, Horner was much cleaner than in May 1994. Indeed, given all the changes, it is surprising that residents' complaints about trash and graffiti outside did not decline more—even in December 1997, nearly half the residents (about 45 percent) still reported major problems with graffiti and with trash in the parking lots and lawns. This finding suggests that despite the reduced disorder, vandalism remained a serious problem.

Powerful and Persistent Drug Market

The CHA's Anti-Drug Initiative interventions were primarily intended to reduce the use and the sale of illegal drugs. The security guards were supposed to prevent dealers from selling in lobbies or in front of buildings, and the CADRE center's main purpose was to prevent young people from using drugs. The Anti-Drug Initiative programs faced formidable challenges in Horner: the drug market, which pervaded the development, was controlled by powerful, warring gangs. The security guards were poorly trained, poorly supervised, and had little ability—or incentive—to challenge the gangs.

In May 1994, Horner residents reported overwhelming problems with drug trafficking, substance abuse, and gang activity. As figure 5.1 indicates, residents' complaints about drugs and gang activity declined over time, with the proportion of residents reporting major problems declining from about 90 percent in May 1994 to about 75 percent in December 1995 both inside and outside their buildings.[51] Despite the improvements, concern about drugs and gangs remained high, with about 70 percent of the residents in 1996 and 1997 reporting serious problems.

Clearly, levels of drug- and gang-related crime in Horner remained extreme. Even as the revitalization brought marked changes and the population declined in 1996 and 1997, more than half the residents continued to report serious problems with drugs and gangs, indicating that Horner remained a troubled community. Further, it is important to be careful in interpreting reports of "improved conditions" when such extraordinarily high levels of crime exist.

Residents' comments described the pervasive drug dealing. Inez said that drug dealing was common in her building, like "going in and out of a gas station." "They come from everywhere. Taxicabs. You'll see people coming, getting out of their trucks, and semi-trucks and everything. Just to go get drugs. You'd be surprised." These residents seemed to view drug dealing as a fact of life in Horner. Lake Street residents' comments often suggested they had reached a practical accommodation with the dealers: residents like Barbara would tolerate dealers as long as they left other residents alone: "We do have drug dealing going on in the building, but we don't have a problem with the gang members who's dealing in drugs, and we don't have a problem with the people who are buying it. You know, the guys, they show respect for the people that's in the building. They do what they do for whatever reasons they do it, but they don't involve the people that's in the building."

Moreover, it was clear that at least some Lake Street residents were in some ways grateful for the gang presence—"the boys" who provided protection from unknown outsiders. These residents had endured a fierce gang war with a neighboring building; recall that in May 1994, 40 percent had experienced bullets shot into their apartment. Because the security guards were either absent or ineffective, the gang substituted as the only real security system. Inez explained: "The only security you have is actually the boys [gang members] themselves. . . . You know, they'll make sure that you get in the building safe, or if something's gonna happen they'll tell you. . . . They say that they there to protect the building, along with, I guess, make their money. But they pretty much look out for us." Clarice agreed, saying that said she had to rely on gang members to protect her and her family: "I got in contact with the CHA police, and they was supposed to watch my door, and since nobody did I got in contact with the gangbangers. And I told them what was going on, and then they talked to the guy, and I didn't have the problem anymore."

Until the Lake Street building was vacated in 1997, and only tenants who had qualified for the new townhomes remained, residents' views seemed to fit the old adage, "Better the devil you know than the one you don't." The boys, the gangbangers, the drug dealers—these were not strangers, but young men known to many residents. Experience might have suggested to residents that these young men, not the CHA security or the police, could provide the best day-to-day protection from the fearsome threat of gunfire and gang war. Thus, drug dealing and other gang activity was tacitly accepted as a trade-off for peace and respect. Yet it was, of course, the gang members from Lake Street and their counterparts in neighboring buildings who wielded the guns and knives and could disrupt the peace at any time.

Residents from the Homes section also sometimes described an interdependency between the drug dealers and other residents. For example, Janelle was grateful for the presents her children received from the drug dealers, the only residents in the development with money for luxuries: "This Christmas the dope dealers made all of us proud. Made me very proud because they made sure that every kid in the building, in this building, they bought 'em all a gift, and they bought expensive gifts. . . . I think every little kid basically got what they needed. So they, I felt that they finally put the money in the community."

However, escalating gang tensions in the Homes meant increased intimidation and harassment, as rival gangs competed for control of buildings. Before the revitalization, two gangs—the Gangster Stones and the Conservative Vice Lords—controlled different sections of the Homes. As the revitalization began disrupting gang territories and the Gangster Disciples, who had controlled the Extension, became factionalized, competition for turf in the Homes increased. Wanda described the situation in her building in late 1995:

> It's like the boys they run everything. Nobody can come in.
> People don't even want to come visit you because they got to
> be stopped downstairs. . . . The security guards don't come out
> the booth . . . the boys doing all the searching of people. You
> know, "Who you going to see? Where you going?" You know,
> pulling guns out, putting them to people's heads, and all that
> type of stuff. . . . The kids can't come outside and play because
> everybody fighting and shooting and selling drugs everywhere.

Other residents, like LaKeisha, continued to say that the gang members and drug dealers generally left them alone unless they tried to interfere with their business. "They don't bother you. . . . It's like their only object is making money. Whoever they have to step on to do it, they'll do it. They're not just gonna come up and mess with you, or push you out of their way, or stuff like that. A tenant, no. . . . But if you fool with their money, then [they'll do something]."

Violent Crime Continues

As in Rockwell, the level of violent crime in Horner reflected the larger gang war that dominated CHA's high-rise developments. As figure 5.1 shows, residents' reports of major problems with violent crime—shootings, beatings, and sexual assaults both inside and outside their buildings—declined significantly from May 1995 to December 1996, as the revitalization initiative began affecting conditions in the development. In the Homes buildings, however, by December 1997, as the Gangster Disciples splintered and CHA's revitalization efforts disrupted long-held gang territories, residents' reports of serious problems with shootings increased again.[52]

There were striking differences between the Lake Street building and the two buildings in the Homes section. Because of the intense gang war afflicting the Extension in 1994, Lake Street residents initially reported much more serious problems with shootings and violence: In May 1994, more than 70 percent rated shootings both inside and outside as a "big problem," while 44 percent of residents from the Homes buildings said shootings were a big problem inside and 55 percent said they were a big problem outside.

The proportion of Lake Street residents reporting serious problems with shootings outside dropped dramatically to 37 percent, by May 1995. This reported reduction in gunfire in the Lake Street building was arguably the most positive change we documented at Horner, and the Horner Revitalization Initiative primarily precipitated that change. As she reflected on the relative peace in 1996, Barbara recalled the terror of the particularly intense gang war in 1994. "It was gang wars. . . . [Our building] was caught in the middle of that other gang. So we was surrounded on one side with the one gang and on the other side it was the same gang, so we was like caught in the middle. So, therefore, it was constant shootings." Our survey data suggested that this situation persisted for at least nine months, from May 1994 to January 1995. For reasons not fully known, the gangs in the Extension agreed on a "peace," or truce, and the gang war gradually died down in early spring of 1995. Some of this change may have been related to the announcement of the revitalization initiative (that is, the gangs realized that the turf they had been fighting over was about to disappear). However, a peace in Rockwell began in the summer of 1995 involved some of the same gangs, so the simultaneous truce in Horner may have reflected a higher-level decision by gang leaders. Whatever the reason, residents like Regina from Lake Street noted a marked drop in random violence: "They haven't been doing no shooting between our buildings. I mean—knock on wood—is about the same. But they haven't had a shooting, but that's good. . . . I don't know what changed." However, the price for this relative peace was that residents had accepted protection from the gangs and allowed them to control the building. Among the Lake Street residents we interviewed, only Clarice was unambiguous in her view of the gangs: "Because the gangbangers are getting out of hand. You know they always act like they own the building. Now they truly do." Despite her concerns, Clarice, like the other residents we interviewed, acknowledged that the gang presence improved general building safety: "Nothing gonna happen inside the building because the gangbangers got control of the building. They know not to do anything inside the building."

Ironically, although the gangs may have made residents feel safer overall, this situation probably contributed to the problems with the CHA police (described earlier). The police may have believed many Lake Street residents were allied with the gangs; tension between residents and police mounted. Conversely, in January 1995, residents from Lake Street, like Inez, began to report that much ongoing violence was attributable to the actions of the CHA police: "That's the problem. . . . That's everyone's main concern right now is CHA police."

Further, while conditions had improved somewhat, violent crime continued to be a serious problem. For example, in December 1995, Barbara said that her son had been threatened at gunpoint twice in the previous three months. Her account exemplified the complexity of crime in Horner. In both cases, the assailant was someone her son knew; in the second instance, it was someone who lived in their building:

> My son was, it hasn't been three months . . . had a gun pulled on him twice as a matter of fact. Once he was going to Western [Avenue] to take the bus, and he had a gun pulled on him by one of the gang members [who] told him he'd better not, asked him what gang he was in. So the guy made him open up his coat, so he could see that he didn't have any weapons or anything. He told me he said, "Well, you'd better hurry up and go get on the bus." And then he had a gun pulled on him another time, so I took care of that problem. [Interviewer: "What did you do?"] I talked to the guy that pulled a gun on him. . . . And I told him, you don't play that tough. Well, I was just upset with,

he didn't pull it on my son, but he pulled it on my son and a bunch of younger children. . . . It was only two older children, my son and a young lady, and the rest of them were like ten, eleven, twelve years old. "This is something you don't do, I don't care," [I told him], "How upset would you have been if that gun had went off and taken somebody's life?"

Although it did not eliminate the violence entirely, the revitalization effort clearly brought profound social changes to the Extension that truly improved the situation by late 1996. Obviously, the biggest benefit for Lake Street residents was the closing of the building that housed the rival gang. Tenants from the other buildings in the Extension—and many in the Lake Street building itself—left to take Section 8 vouchers or apartments in scattered-site developments. By late 1997, fewer than seven hundred households resided in Horner; most of them hoped to move into the new townhouses. The reduced population and the departure of many troublesome tenants meant that the level of violent crime dropped dramatically.

While conditions improved steadily for Lake Street residents, violence in the Homes section was more episodic. The Homes had a larger population at the outset—recall that most buildings in the Extension were already closed by 1994—and the effect of the revitalization initiative on this section of the development was much more gradual. According to residents, violence in the Homes varied considerably over time; the worst period was in May 1995, when 66 percent of the residents reported major problems with shootings in and around their buildings. However, even as the revitalization initiative moved forward and work began on some of the mid-rises in the Homes, residents' concerns about shootings and violence remained high, with about 40 percent of residents reporting major problems in both 1996 and 1997.

Wanda described one episode of gang violence in January 1995: "Just about a couple weeks ago. Yeah, they was at war for about a whole weekend—maybe a little longer than a weekend. . . . They were shooting back and forth at each other. Across the field and doing drive-bys and everything. And a little boy got killed, a lady got killed—innocent people that had nothing to do with what was going on, end up getting hurt." Later that year, in May, LaKeisha reported that there was another gang war in progress: "Well, there's one [a gang war] now . . . started yesterday afternoon, two o'clock in the afternoon. It's still continuing now. This happened like eleven o'clock this morning, they're out there shooting."[53]

In February 1996, several residents, including LaKeisha and Wanda, said that problems with gang conflicts had escalated after several powerful, local gang members were released from jail—the same situation that led to the outbreaks of extreme violence in Rockwell Gardens. LaKeisha described the ongoing conflict: "A lot of people were in jail that used to be over here, and they get out. . . . They want certain buildings, you know, they like they claim these buildings. . . . They just don't gonna give it up like that, so it cause conflict—shooting, arguments and fights and stuff." Wanda felt the violence was the worst she had ever seen: "The drug selling, the people that they letting move in, everything is worse . . . than it was two years ago. . . . The crime, the violence, kids getting killed. Little kids, innocent kids getting killed when they caught out in the gang wars. The people that don't even live around here, hanging and selling the drugs and everything, and nobody seems to care. Nobody."

Horner in Transition

The Henry Horner Homes changed dramatically between 1993 and 1996. In the early 1990s, Horner was truly a dismal place, with filthy grounds, miserable buildings, and a tenant population overwhelmed by drug trafficking and violent crime. By the end of the decade, Horner was a community in transition, in the midst of a massive revitalization that would eliminate the huge high-rise and some mid-rise buildings, change the look of the remaining mid-rises, and open many units to households with incomes between 50 to 80 percent of the local median.

It is safe to say that most of the CHA's Anti-Drug Initiative programs had no sustained impact on crime and gang activity in Horner. Residents reported that the sweeps had improved conditions in the short-run, but the improvements quickly disappeared without effective follow-up. The security guards were a particular source of complaints. Even in 1993, we found that residents viewed the security guards as ineffective; over time, their performance deteriorated even further. By late 1996, the gangs had pushed them out of the buildings almost entirely; if the guards did report for work, they generally sat in cars in front of the buildings. By the end of 1997, even the CHA gave up the effort; they stopped trying to station guards in the buildings and, instead, sent a reduced force to patrol the development.

Residents also perceived the CHA police as ineffective. Many residents, particularly those from the Lake Street building, reported problems with the CHA police harassing and sometimes abusing residents. Further, many residents said they were afraid to report crime to the police, for fear that the police would not protect their anonymity.

Because of the high levels of fear and relatively low levels of social cohesion, the CHA was unable to organize tenant patrols in Horner. The

CADRE center effectively organized prevention programs and worked with local schools, but it was less successful in getting residents into drug treatment. Finally, even as the revitalization initiative got underway, problems with graffiti and vandalism remained severe.

Despite the apparent lack of success of the Anti-Drug Initiative in Horner, residents did note some reductions in the rates of crime and vandalism over time, but it was clear that most of these reductions had little to do with the Anti-Drug Initiative programs. Most changes occurred after the revitalization initiative began; the biggest changes were limited to the Lake Street building, the first to be affected by the redevelopment. With the exception of the substantially reduced violence in the Lake Street building, most of these changes were modest; even after two years of revitalization efforts, problems with drug trafficking and gang dominance remained severe.

Barbara expressed sadness that any meaningful changes occurred only after threats of the impending destruction of the Horner community and outside legal intervention:

> The part that makes everybody sad is, why should we have somebody come in from the outside to step in and make changes for us? We should be able to do that for ourselves. Of course, we wouldn't have had that $50 million to do the much needed things that need to be done. But overall, we should have been able to straighten out a lot of the problems that we needed to straighten out. I think in order for any neighborhood to work, it take the people. You shouldn't wait for the police to come in or for HUD to come in. . . . You should be able to do those things on your own.

Westhaven

We returned to Horner in the spring of 1998 to assess the early phases of the Horner Revitalization Initiative. We conducted a survey of the entire Horner development, including the new townhomes, and of its surrounding community. We found a community still in the midst of dramatic transition. By 1998, 160 new townhomes had been constructed in and around Horner, and 98 of these new units were occupied, about half with former Horner residents. The physical appearance of the development and the surrounding neighborhood had been altered dramatically. Most remaining tenants of the Lake Street building had moved into the townhomes; the old building was scheduled to be closed, but not yet slated for demolition. A number of the other original buildings still remained, undermining the impact of the positive changes.

Photo 7. Redevelopment of Henry Horner Homes: New Townhomes at Corner of Leavitt and Lake Streets with View of Henry Horner Homes. *Photo by Jean Amendolia.*

With the physical improvements had come social changes as well. In May 1998, only 682 of the units in the original development were still occupied.[54] Fewer than 100 of the 409 original families affected by the first phase of the redevelopment chose to stay in Horner; most other families elected either scattered-site or Section 8 housing. Some original residents had been declared ineligible for replacement housing because either they had serious lease violations or someone in the household held a criminal record; no one knew how many tenants had been evicted or where they had gone when they left. In addition to the tenants who took relocation assistance and those who had been evicted, there were a few reports that some tenants left without waiting to be relocated, fearing that the Section 8 voucher would last only a year—a persistent rumor that the CHA was unable to dispel. Finally, new families had begun moving into the community, leasing the townhomes that were set aside for higher-income families.

In mid-1998, physical conditions in Horner had surely changed for the better, but it was less clear how much these changes had benefited the original Horner tenants. Relatively few had moved into the new townhomes, and little was known about the tenants who had left. Gentrification was moving closer to Horner, with expensive townhomes located only blocks away. Our 1998 survey indicated that residents feared that they might find themselves priced out of the development altogether. A majority of Horner residents (59 percent) said they believed the townhomes were only for higher-income people.

Further, about one-third (35 percent) believed that the neighborhood was becoming unaffordable for some residents, and only 39 percent expected to live in the neighborhood five years from now.

In addition to economic pressures, residents also feared that screening processes might exclude them from the new townhomes. In 1998, all residents of the new townhomes—both Horner and higher-income tenants—had to undergo criminal and credit checks, pass a housekeeping inspection, and undergo a needs assessment before being allowed to move into their new units. All residents were required to go through an orientation to introduce them to the nuances of townhome living (for example, utility payments, how to use and clean their new appliances, and other housekeeping tips). Concern about screening increased after May 1997, when a resident reportedly "trashed" her new unit, and another resident's housekeeping was alleged to be so bad it created a fire hazard.[55] Although there was little evidence for either of these claims, these incidents raised questions about whether Horner residents would be able to take proper care of their new units. Some community leaders involved in the redevelopment of the entire near west side argued that this orientation was not sufficient for Horner residents and that the residents and the redevelopment were being set up to fail.[56]

Because of concerns about Horner residents possibly damaging the new townhomes, the owner of the Chicago Bulls, the basketball team that plays in the nearby United Center, offered to donate $1 million to allow the CHA to provide mandatory housekeeping training for its new townhome residents. The money was given to a local community organization, which planned to develop the training. The Horner Resident Committee, which represented the tenants in matters related to the *Mothers Guild*, strongly opposed the training and considered it demeaning to Horner tenants. As late as 1999 the issue of how much support Horner tenants really need to make the transition to the new townhomes remained unresolved, and community residents continued to protest that Horner residents were "bringing their problems with them" (*Chicago Tribune*, February 28, 1999).

Inez was one of the original tenants lucky enough to move into a new townhome on the Horner site. While she was very happy with her new apartment, she was less sure about the changes in the community. She reported that there was little interaction between the original Horner residents and the new higher-income tenants: "So what it is divided right now. The people from Horner talk to each other and the market rate people still keep to themselves. They don't say anything to you. They don't even come to meetings."

Obstacles to Creating a Mixed-Income Community

Even after the revitalization effort had wrought substantial changes in Horner, problems with drug-related crime persisted— even outside the high-rises. In 1998,[57] we found that nearly three-fourths of Horner residents reported major problems with people selling drugs and people using drugs in their neighborhood; nearly 70 percent reported serious problems with gangs as well.[58] Finally, more than 50 percent said that shootings and violence were still a big problem in the development.

Providing adequate security for Horner remained an ongoing problem, which became more complex as the CHA's resources diminished. In 1998, because HUD required the CHA to spend its modernization funds on capital improvements, the amount of money the agency had available to spend on security services in its developments was significantly reduced; CHA was thereby forced to lay off security officers.

While Inez felt her new home was safe, she said that the gangs continued to dominate the development and feared that the changes brought about by the revitalization could actually increase the violence:

> Right now, everything is so peaceful. . . . It could be just getting out of the building. . . . But I do have some concerns because what they're doing is, from Damen to Western, if you notice, there are no vacant lots. The ones that are left, they're going to build something on, so there won't be any vacancies, which is real good. But what they're doing is bringing people from the other side of Damen and they're moving them down on Washington . . . just moving them and scattering them around. Well, it was different gangs. . . . So I'm just wondering, when is it that there's going to be a big blood bath? It's going to be one, because they're [the CHA] not considering it and of course, who would think they would have to, but when they're separating these people and even if the person took the person [with the criminal record] off their lease, boyfriend or brother, it's still a problem.

Gangs continued to control the remaining mid- and high-rise buildings in the Homes section of the development. By May 1998, the new townhomes had already experienced one likely gang-related shooting. In addition to the violence, the gang presence still brought vandalism and visible disorder: in 1998, two-thirds of Horner residents reported big problems with graffiti, and 46 percent said they had serious problems with trash and junk in the neighborhood. The persistence of these incivilities in the face of CHA's renewed management efforts underscores the power that the gangs and drug dealers maintained in the Horner community. Clearly, until these problems can be effectively addressed, crime will continue to present a serious threat to the long-term viability of the revitalization effort.

In addition to the problems with drugs and crime, the neighborhood continued to suffer from a lack of stores and other amenities that would entice higher-income residents. In 1998, more than 60 percent of Horner residents identified a lack of restaurants and grocery stores as a major problem. The desire for a "decent grocery store" was especially high on almost everyone's list. While liquor was available nearby, food was not, except for high-priced convenience stores. Residents also complained about lacking supportive neighborhood services, job training programs, and employment opportunities.

Relatively few original tenants—at least those from the Extension which had been redeveloped first—remained in Horner to experience the early effects of the revitalization initiative. Most residents who suffered through life in Horner during the early and mid-1990s chose to leave the development, and we know almost nothing about how they fared in scattered-site housing, Section 8, or other CHA developments. It is probably safe to assume that scattered-site or Section 8 units were higher quality than the apartments in Horner and at least somewhat safer. However, the neighborhoods were unfamiliar, and tenants certainly experienced more strenuous screening and lease enforcement than they had been accustomed to. One possible scenario is that many of these troubled tenants may not survive the Section 8 program in the private market and may ultimately end up in private-market slums that are as bad—or even worse—than where they lived before.[59]

Clarice moved out of Horner in late 1995 for a scattered-site unit in a poor Hispanic community a few miles away.[60] Her views about the move were mixed. She opted for relocation because she felt that it was too dangerous for her family to remain in Horner:

> I moved out of Horner because my daughters was starting to develop, and the guys around there wanted to talk to them. My daughters didn't want to talk to them. Then they started saying things, my daughter couldn't go this place and that place. I told my daughters they can go where they want. Then they say they couldn't go visit their cousins because it was in the next building, and the next building was a [different] gang. I told them

they could go. So they left them alone for a while, then they found a reason to jump on them. They jumped on them when it was real dark out, and there was no lights in the building. . . . I had to leave there because I was so angry because I knew these people and the head of the gang, I knew him ever since he was born! I was very upset. It got to the point that I was ready to kill him. I had told management if you don't move me, something's going to happen. And the day that I clicked and was about to do it, they called and said they had me a new apartment.

Clarice felt that her new neighborhood was much safer for her family; because they were not Hispanic, the local gangs left them alone. Although she missed Horner, she felt that she and her daughters had more opportunities to improve their lives when they did not constantly live in fear. She enrolled in a clerical training program, and both of her daughters went to college. Clarice said that without the constant fear of violence, she felt liberated:

Because I was so used to living there, it was a way of life. So when I moved, I felt like, oh God, I'm so free! . . . I didn't know I had these feelings until I moved. When I moved I felt like I was kind of free. Like I've been incarcerated so long it was a way of life and you didn't notice it. When I left, I felt I can go where I want to go, I had people over, I had more people coming. My old friends coming to visit me and whatnot. Go out when I want. Don't have to worry about coming in. . . . It was like I was free. Like somebody just took the key and said, okay, you're paroled.

While she was released from the oppressive fear of living in Horner, Clarice still had problems in her new community. She and her daughters were socially isolated. Although her new neighbors were not hostile, once they found out that she was not Puerto Rican, they ignored her. Although not as terrifying as Horner, her new neighborhood was also dangerous, dominated by the Latin Kings, another of Chicago's biggest gangs. Finally, her social world still revolved around Horner; most of her family still lived in the development, and she visited frequently. Thus, Clarice clearly was glad to have left Horner, but her situation was still far from ideal.

Epilogue: The High-Rises Close

By early 1999, it was still not clear whether the Horner Revitalization Initiative would succeed in its goal of creating a healthy mixed-income community. Security remained a major concern, and the redevelopment effort seemed stalled. In February 1999, the *Chicago Tribune* ran an article entitled, "Horner Homes Redevelopment Still a Rough Go," which documented delays in construction of the first 466 units, ongoing security problems, and concerns about the behavior of former Horner residents. In May 1999, the city of Chicago was poised to take control of the CHA. In late 1999 the implications of this take-over for the completion of the Horner Revitalization Initiative remained unclear.

While the revitalization effort continued, hundreds of Horner residents still lived in the original, unrehabilitated buildings. In January of 1999, Chicago was hit by a major snowstorm that dumped more than two feet of snow on the city. The snow was followed by fierce, sub-zero cold. The effect of the weather on CHA's failing high-rises was devastating. In Horner and the Robert Taylor Homes, the CHA had allowed vacancies to increase and had stopped repairing major building systems in anticipation of demolishing the buildings. When the cold wave hit, these buildings virtually collapsed: the heating systems failed and pipes burst, coating the buildings with sheets of ice. Hundreds of residents from Horner and the Robert Taylor Homes had to be relocated on an emergency basis, at a cost of nearly $7 million (*Chicago Tribune*, January 23, 1999). In the wake of this disaster, the high-rise buildings in the Homes section of the development were permanently closed, their remaining residents scattered in temporary shelters in suburban hotels or, gradually, relocated with Section 8 vouchers. How many of them will ever return to live in the new Westhaven development remains unclear.

6 | Harold Ickes Homes

The Residents of Ickes
Betty's Story

Betty was one of the first residents to move into the Harold Ickes Homes after the development opened in 1955.[1] A young single mother, she shared her first apartment with her mother and two of her siblings. Eventually she applied for her own unit and has stayed in the development since that time. Betty shares her initial impression: "When I first moved there, it was grass in front. . . . It was real clean outside. It wasn't any paper or anything around the building, the walls and everything was clean. . . . It was grass, little trees and everything all out in front. It was really beautiful around here. The building was clean."

Betty describes her upbringing as middle class because "we didn't never want for anything." Still, most of her clothes were thrift shop purchases, and she acknowledges that her mother "couldn't afford us too much though; she just bought us what she thought we needed." In spite of the fact that Betty has received public assistance for most of her adult life and has lived in public housing for more than forty years, she still says, "I'm not wanting for anything. I'm living decent, in my own apartment. I've got the things that I need, and I've got mostly just about everything I want as of now." When she moved into Ickes in 1955, Betty felt that Ickes was a good place to raise her children. Now Betty thinks of Ickes as a "dangerous" place for children: children playing in the hallways could fall out of broken windows or get electrocuted from "wires just hanging on the hall"; outside, gang members sell drugs, and the threat of violence erupting without warning looms.

Betty and her family have been fortunate in that none of the violence in Ickes has touched their lives directly; however, they have had other problems. Betty's daughter dropped out of high school and, like her mother, became pregnant at a young age. She now lives in Section 8 housing on the south side of the city. Betty's three sons finished high school and continue to live and work in Chicago, sometimes staying with their mother. None were involved with any gang activity while growing up in Ickes, although all three were arrested for various minor crimes.

Although Betty is "proud to live in Ickes" and believes she has lived a "blessed" life, she is concerned about the problems that plague the development. She has witnessed many changes during her forty years there. Where there used to be two-parent families, there are now teen mothers who have their own apartments. The buildings are no longer well-maintained, and crime and drug use have escalated. Today she says, "It's more gangbangers, they're dealing drugs more . . . and the lobbies be full of teenagers."

Nonetheless, she has not given up hope for Ickes. Instead, Betty has become active in the local resident council and has dedicated time to the tenant patrol in her building. She describes herself as an activist, and the work she does in Ickes makes her feel she has "a little power in what I'm doing." She explains that she got involved "because I wanted to see the building do better, and I wanted to see the tenants in the building do better." However, with the demolition of buildings in other CHA developments and gentrification rapidly changing the neighborhoods to the north and east, Betty believes that Ickes will soon be turned into condominiums and she will be offered a Section 8 voucher to use in another neighborhood.

Sondra's View

While Betty is still optimistic, Sondra, another long-term activist in the development, is angry about the changes in Ickes, particularly the devastation that drugs and gangs have brought to the community. Over the years, Sondra's passion to help residents who are unable or afraid to help themselves has driven her to stand up to gangbangers, feed neglected children, and counsel teenaged girls being abused by their boyfriends.

Sondra moved into Ickes more than twenty years ago, when she was a single mother in desperate need of shelter. After fighting with the sister with whom she was living, Sondra took her baby and walked out. As she aimlessly walked the neighborhood, it began to rain, so Sondra ducked into a phone booth to make a call. While she was on the phone explaining her predicament to a friend, a woman waiting to use the phone overheard her and offered to take her to Ickes: "I went into her office, she let me fill out an application for the Ickes development. . . . After I filled out the application, the rent was $26. I'll never forget that, the rent was $26. She said 'Do you have $26? 'Cause if you have $26, I want you to keep it. I'm gonna pay your rent.' She paid my rent, she gave me a ride to the building, and she took me inside that building, and she showed me my apartment, and she put the keys in my hand." This incident, clearly a watershed moment in Sondra's life, has shaped her willingness to help other young single mothers in trouble.

Sondra spent her childhood in Mississippi working in the fields and had a difficult time making the transition to the city. As she says, "When I look back on it, life in Mississippi was a breeze. You know, I didn't know nothing about locking doors. I didn't know nothing about locks, padlocks, violence, and gangs. I didn't know that until I got here to Chicago."

Sondra raised a son and a daughter in Ickes, and now she cares for her daughter's three children. Sondra speaks about her son with pride and affection. He graduated from high school and received a college football scholarship:

> I went to a banquet and they were showing tapes of him with the touchdowns and the passes and this, I had to laugh and I had to cry. Because it took me back to the time he was born, and then it took me back to the daily routines of how I had to really, really talk to this young man, let him know [about] drugs, guns, and violence, and he's a good boy. I'm not saying he's a good boy because he's mine. I'm saying he's a good kid because he is a good kid. I had to let him know clearly what I was gonna have and what I wouldn't tolerate. And he knew drugs and guns were something his mother wouldn't tolerate. It was almost overpowering because they got a tendency of coming at the young innocent ones. I had to go up against the gang, and I'm lucky to be alive, and I'm thankful to be alive. I had to go up against them several times and let them know, hey, he ain't going out like that. I couldn't stand for that.

Sondra's daughter did not fare as well, and, at one point, Sondra "wrote her off" as a disappointment because she dropped out of high school and became pregnant at a young age: "I wasn't as lucky with [my daughter] as I am with my son. I lost my daughter to Ida B. Wells [a housing development on the south side]. She met a boy in Ida B. Wells, and . . . he turned her whole head around. He just turned her world upside down. . . . And I wasn't informed that she wasn't [in school], and when it come down to the wire, she couldn't graduate 'cause she hadn't gone. Again, my heart was broken."

Sondra, active in her building for years, has served as an elected official as well as a tenant patrol member. She lives by the philosophy that "if I can do anything to make where I live better and safer, I'm for it." Often this means enforcing unpopular policies, like fining residents for not keeping the area outside their doorway clean, but more often it means being a shoulder to lean on and an advocate the residents can count on. She says she draws strength from the help she provides to other tenants: "that's the greatest feeling in the world, when you can go and get somebody off of crack rock. You just don't know how good that feel."

Until the mid-1990s, Sondra had no intention of ever leaving Ickes. But conditions in her building have deteriorated to the point that she's scared and "just tired of the city." She is thinking of moving: "Only change I see is everything has doubled, gotten worse. . . . You know, it's not a place you want to live anymore. . . . The gangbanging took over the neighborhood, or should I say take over the community."

To "calm her nerves," Sondra says she chain smokes two packs of cigarettes per day and takes high blood pressure medication and other prescription drugs. Although she says she has never been a social drinker or used illegal drugs, she confesses that she needs the cigarettes and medication to cope. "If you're not a drug addict, you're going to end up on something because you got to have something, and sometimes you just have to really, really not see, and to not see and not hear is very difficult. And you got to turn and walk the other way or you got to look the other way. . . . It's rough." Yet, despite her anxiety, Sondra does not want to leave Ickes while there are still residents that need her. She stays because she wants to see the violence and neglect end. "I want it to stop. I want to see it stop. Do you realize how sweet it would be to move on and know it would stop? How can you move on and be happy when you know it's still going on? Who gonna feed this little child if I'm gone so he can't knock behind my door? So will anybody else take the time out with this child and feed him?"

These women's stories offer two views of Ickes during a time of transition and uncertainty. In the early 1990s, Ickes had serious problems with drugs and crime, but it also had strong resident leaders like Sondra and Betty who were able to demand better services for their development. However, after HUD took over the CHA in 1995, budgetary pressures gradually forced the agency to shift its resources to more troubled developments; this shift left Ickes vulnerable to gangs and drug dealers. By the end of the decade, Ickes was a far more dangerous place than it had been in earlier years, and, although the development was not yet officially targeted for demolition, residents were uncertain about the future. Resident leaders like Betty and Sondra were overwhelmed. They were still committed to the community, but they now faced an uphill struggle.

Life in Ickes

The CHA invested millions of dollars in securing Ickes during the 1990s. Conditions in Ickes were not as bad as Rockwell and Horner, and the CHA's efforts there met with greater success. However, in early 1996, the CHA gradually began curtailing services in Ickes at the same time that demolitions in nearby developments were disrupting gang territories. This chapter tells the story of life in Ickes during the period of relative calm from 1994 to the middle of 1996 and during the period of chaos that followed, as the development was overtaken by vicious gang turf battles.[2]

In 1994, Ickes was one of the safest of CHA's high-rise developments; although more dangerous than other inner-city neighborhoods, it was not an urban war zone like Rockwell and Horner. Ickes's relatively small size also made the development seem less threatening. The entire development takes up only about four-square city blocks (by contrast, Horner runs nearly a mile). Opened in 1955, Ickes consists of approximately eight hundred units in twelve high-rise (nine- and seven-story) buildings. Many buildings appear to be extremely long, but in reality they are double buildings—physically connected on the exterior, but not the interior. Although smaller than the high-rises in Rockwell and Horner, the buildings are equally grim and forbidding.

The Ickes Homes are at the beginning of Chicago's infamous "State Street Corridor"—the four-mile strip of public housing that runs almost uninterrupted down State Street on Chicago's south side. Just north of the development are the Hilliard Homes, a small development consisting of three high-rise buildings. Just a few blocks away are two other relatively small developments, Prairie Courts and Dearborn Homes, followed by the enormous high-rises of Stateway Gardens and the Robert Taylor Homes.

Although it is part of the State Street Corridor, Ickes is not as isolated as Rockwell or Horner and is closer to businesses and services. To the north of the development lies Chicago's Chinatown, a neighborhood with many thriving restaurants and small businesses, and to the south lies the campus of the Illinois Institute of Technology. Across the street from the development are several food and liquor stores. Ickes is well-served by public transportation, with several bus lines running through the development, and less than two blocks away an elevated station for the transit line goes directly downtown.

As in CHA's other high-rise developments, Ickes's population is extremely poor. In 1997, the average income was about $6,000, and only about 10 percent of the residents were employed. Single females headed most households. However, Ickes had a larger proportion of older, long-term residents than either Horner or Rockwell.[3]

Barren Grounds

To an outsider viewing the development in 1993,[4] the development appeared much less menacing than either Horner or Rockwell; it was not unusual to see residents strolling around the development, standing and chatting, and walking through the development with their children. However, the grounds were just as barren as in the other developments. The grass had nearly disappeared, and there were no trees; nothing blocked the dirt and debris that blew across the sidewalks. The playgrounds consisted of cracked slabs of concrete with brightly painted cement tunnels; all the other equipment was long gone. The parking lots and walkways were pocked with holes, and when it rained Ickes became a sea of mud. As Sondra described, the mess was made worse by residents who occasionally dropped trash from apartment windows on unsuspecting passersby.

While the grounds were bleak, they were still cleaner than in either Horner or Rockwell. In May 1994, only about half of the Ickes residents thought that trash and junk (41 percent) and graffiti (55 percent) were big problems outside their building. One reason for this difference was that Ickes had more effective resident leadership than the other developments. Its Local Advisory Council, the CHA's official tenant organization, lobbied for more and better services. As a result, the buildings' exteriors were relatively well maintained; although physically unattractive, they were mostly free of graffiti, and few windows were boarded up.

The buildings' interiors were in worse shape than their exteriors. Although fewer than half (41 percent) of Ickes residents considered trash and junk inside the buildings to be a major problem in May 1994, nearly 60 percent reported big problems with broken light bulbs, and 72 percent reported big problems with graffiti. The janitorial staff routinely painted over graffiti on the interiors, but they could not compete with the resident gang members poised to "tag" the freshly coated walls. As in the Horner Homes, the enclosed hallways in Ickes consisted of a long

Photo 8. Harold Ickes Homes with View of Hilliard Homes. *Photo by Jean Amendolia.*

corridor with elevators at the midway point. The only windows were situated directly opposite the elevators, thus daylight did not reach many apartment entrances. When the lights were out, tenants were forced to navigate through darkened hallways and blindly grope for keys and doorways with little light. Sondra said that the dark stairways were particularly hazardous to elderly residents, a problem exacerbated by the fact that some stairways had partial or missing banisters: "We still need banisters. A lot of the time you don't have no lights, and you never know when you're gonna fall. You wanna reach for something, so what you gonna do? You reach for the banister, and then, maybe half of it is off and half of it is on."

While CHA's janitors tried to keep the Ickes buildings relatively clean, as in Rockwell and Horner, the buildings were rapidly decaying, and basic systems like elevators, plumbing, and heating, had begun to fail. The CHA maintenance crews were understaffed and poorly prepared for the magnitude of repairs. Many residents had serious problems with their plumbing, including rusted sinks, continuously running water in bathrooms or kitchens, and leaking ceilings. Several residents said they had problems with lead paint on exposed pipes and were worried about the long-term effects on themselves and their children. The roaches and rodents that infested the buildings forced residents to patch holes and set traps themselves. Major repairs often went undone, creating hazardous

Photo 9. Stairwell, Harold Ickes Homes. *Photo by Nina Taluc.*

conditions. Tondi, a woman in her early thirties, described how her child was scalded by an unprotected hot water pipe: "I'd complain, complain, complain. One day I'm in the kitchen cooking something . . . I hear my son, 'Ma!' When I went back . . . all his skin was wrapped around the pole. Third degree burn. . . . You see them pipes? They're supposed to be covered up. They're not covered up."

A "Bad Neighborhood"

In May 1994, Ickes was not contested gang turf and did not experience the "war" that terrorized residents in Horner and Rockwell. Ickes was a typical "bad neighborhood," with serious problems with drug trafficking and substance abuse, and relatively modest levels of violent crime. In 1994, only the Gangster Disciples were active in Ickes. Consequently, Ickes residents were spared the overwhelming gang violence that plagued the other developments. As one CHA staff person put it,

> I look at the development across the street, and I look at the development two blocks from here—no, they're not safe as here. One thing I've found that the developments that's surrounding here has a mixture of gang activity and two or three different kind of gangs. The gang that is in this development, they're all one. So they really don't have nobody to fight, nobody to do the things that they have to do. And then the other gangs don't even come down here.[5]

Because the Gangster Disciples dominated the development, Ickes residents were able to move freely through the development without having to fear they were violating another gang's turf. However, residents did think certain areas were worse than others: residents called the north end of the development the "terror zone," where drug dealing and violence were more likely to occur.

Even with only a single gang, many residents complained about high levels of gang activity. More than 40 percent said that "young people controlling their building"—that is, blocking entryways and halls—presented a serious problem; 56 percent reported big problems with groups of people "hanging out" inside; and 64 percent reported big problems with loitering outside.

Because Ickes was dominated by a single gang, drug trafficking and gang activity were not as closely linked to each other. "Neutrons," a term apparently only used in Ickes, were non-gang-affiliated dealers. Like the gang members, Neutrons were typically lifelong Ickes residents, who were allowed to sell drugs provided they paid money to the gang leaders for the privilege. This arrangement meant there were few skirmishes over "territory," and with fewer conflicts and less violence, drug sales proliferated.

The persistent drug market resulting from this arrangement was evident to the tenants, who were confronted daily with drug sellers, buyers, and users. In 1994, two-thirds of the residents considered drug use inside and outside their buildings to be serious problems. Likewise, 60 percent reported that drug sales inside their buildings were big problems, and even more, 68 percent, reported problems with drug sales outside. The consensus was that the situation had improved somewhat following the sweeps in 1993, although the problem had clearly not disappeared. Instead, as Sondra explained, in many cases the dealers had simply moved into individual apartments: "That's a hard one because they used to sell it down in the lobby, and that's stopped. They used to sell it all in the stairways, and that stopped. But they're still at the houses that was selling—the ones they was smoking in is still smoke houses."

Because gang violence was relatively rare, Ickes residents were more concerned about the effects of the pervasive drug trafficking and substance abuse on children growing up in the development. Sondra, for example, voiced concerns about children being neglected because their parents were using drugs. As a resident leader, she often intervened by feeding or tending to neglected children: "Their mama done got the money, but the dope man got it all. . . . They should be in my shoes where they can see it every day—a child running nasty and dirty, holding their pants up, playing with one hand and holding their pants with another because mama had time to get the drugs, but she didn't have time to wash him up and put some clothes on and make him look decent. She didn't have time to feed him."

Many residents complained that drug-addicted women failed to discipline their children adequately.[6] One mother said that bad mothers and poorly behaved children were the worst problems in the development. "Women are not raising kids. . . . They hold up children in the wrong way. If a child gets hit, the mother says, 'Come on, you gonna hit them back,' instead of disciplining the child." Parents, especially drug-using mothers, were known to put children out of the house when they did not want to be bothered with taking care of them. Outside and unsupervised, these children caused problems for other residents. An elderly resident complained that it was difficult to keep the area in front of her door clean because children were forced to eat food there instead of in their apartments. "Their mamas tell them to get out there and eat, . . . and they leave food and stains in my front door," she said.

Other residents worried about their children witnessing drug transactions and hostile exchanges between drug dealers and users. This problem was one of the greatest frustrations parents voiced about raising children in Ickes. Rakiah, who had three young children, said: "Yeah. It's a problem. I have to walk—I have to live here. . . . They [drug dealers] just don't care who's seeing them or nothing. No, it's just an exchange of hands. Then you have the little kids, and they're seeing them. . . . I'm getting tired of seeing it every day. It's a part of my life. My everyday life. It maybe shouldn't have to be that way." Many parents feared that their children would view the dealers as role models. Young children often idolized the drug dealers because of their perceived power and affluence. The problem was compounded by the fact that it was nearly impossible for parents to paint drug dealers as "dangerous" or "monsters"; instead, they were someone's brother or son, individuals familiar to the children, people who bought the children presents, and men who looked out for them. The facts that drug dealers were usually friends or family of the residents or residents themselves added to the complex problems that drugs introduced to the development.

Episodic Violence

In May 1994, while two-thirds of Horner and Rockwell residents reported serious problems with shootings and violence outside their buildings, just 35 percent of Ickes residents considered violence outside to be a big problem, and only 21 percent reported big problems inside. Although Rockwell and Horner residents described living in a war zone, Sondra could only remember one drive-by shooting in the previous year: "In the last twelve months, now I remember a drive-by shooting because it started, I'm right on the corner. Just when they get to that corner . . . somebody start shooting going out toward 22nd Street and that happen four times. But really the truth, that was the only drive-by shooting I had noticed since I been there. . . . Just as they'd get to the corner of my window they get to shooting going toward 22nd Street. . . . But they went on about four days—every day for four days."

Focusing on the contrast between Ickes and Horner and Rockwell creates a false sense of security. In spite of the relative "peace" and lack of gang conflict, during 1994 one out of ten residents reported a bullet was shot into their apartment; typically a bullet had inadvertently been shot through an apartment window while the tenant may or may not have been at home. When considering that event with the rates of other crimes, including the 11 percent of households who were burglarized and the 6 percent who reported assaults, the result is that more than one-quarter of Ickes residents said they had been victimized in the past year. Further, in 1994, one out of five Ickes residents ranked attacks or robberies, sexual assault, and burglaries as major problems in their development. These statistics are noteworthy, given Ickes's comparative "safety."

In addition to the gang and drug-related crime, domestic violence was a daily reality in Ickes. One resident said that she and her boyfriend often got into arguments that "got out of hand." She elicited the help of the security guards and the police on several occasions to have her boyfriend removed from her apartment. Another described an on going court battle between her daughter and an abusive former-boyfriend. Rakiah, a long-term resident, recounted an incident she had witnessed: "A neighbor of mine . . . her boyfriend jumped on her son, and [the boyfriend ran] through my house. I just went downstairs and called the police on them because I didn't feel it was right. No one has the right to hit another human being, nor abuse them. So I called. I called Chicago police and told them the situation. They took it from there."

Like many residents, Sondra acknowledged that problems with domestic abuse were widespread:

> Yeah, it's a pretty big problem. Because like I say, 99 percent of the women are single women, and 98 percent of them got men living with them. And 98 percent of them don't call no shots in their own house. A lot of time they got little gangbanging boyfriends that beats the crap out of them, and beat them all in the lobby. I don't know if they think this is the ways it's supposed to be, or I can't do nothing about it. I don't know what's going on with them. Because you look at them and you try to figure out if I gotta feed you and take care of you and pay the rent for you, why should I be abused? This is the way I would think, but a woman that's being abused don't think that way.

Living in Fear

As in Horner and Rockwell, Ickes residents were generally reluctant to report crime to the police. In May 1994, slightly more than one-quarter (26 percent) of the tenants said they had reported a problem in their building to either the police or guards in the past twelve months. Even in Ickes, where gang violence was comparatively rare, residents feared retaliation if they got involved and instead followed the credo of "minding their own business."

In one extreme incident, a resident told us that he and other tenants failed to report a dead body in the hallway for hours.[7] The man said that he was going to visit a friend who lived on the eighth floor, when he saw a man being dragged down a flight of stairs. He knew the man was dead because he was being pulled by his feet, and his face was bouncing off the steps. The man dragging the corpse looked up and said to him, "Man don't say nothing. . . . You ain't seen nothing." The resident stepped over the body, where he observed "white stuff" coming from its mouth, and went about his business. When he got home later, he told his girlfriend about the incident but did not call the police. At 5:00 a.m., he and his girlfriend were awakened by the screams of a neighbor who had found the body in the hallway. If his story is true, the body had remained in the hallway for more than six hours—where several residents must have seen it—without anyone calling the police. As Rakiah said, residents believed it was simply too dangerous to get involved: "I wouldn't feel safe reporting, because see, the way I figure, you never know who's listening. When you tell one person, that person tells another person. . . . So the things I see, I keep to myself."

Social Ties

Ickes had more of a sense of community than either
Rockwell or Horner. There was a core of long-term, older residents like
Betty and Sondra who were involved with tenant patrols and reached
out to tenants in need. Because the Local Advisory Council was effective, with connections to some Central Advisory Council members (the
CHA-wide tenant organization), it was able to demand better services
from the CHA. This clout meant that Ickes received a large share of CHA
services, including janitors and security programs, even though it was
far from the worst development.

Yet even with the advantages of effective resident leadership and
better services, Ickes was still a high-crime community, and residents
still struggled to cope. Although most residents believed the safest strategy
was to "mind their own business," they also wanted to find solutions
that would protect their children. Residents were generally conflicted
regarding how much they could—and should—do to help solve the problems in their development. Only about 20 percent of the residents thought
that "helping to solve problems of drugs and crime" was solely the tenants' responsibility, whereas the remaining residents were about evenly
split between those who considered it to be the responsibility of the CHA
management and those who thought the CHA management and tenants
should work together.

Carol, a woman in her thirties who had lived in public housing most
of her life, argued that every resident knew who the problem tenants
were: "I think the tenants could do the most because, see, they're here,
and you know, they know the neighborhood, they know the people. So
I think if anything, maybe they'd have a better chance of trying to get
whatever they want done." Others, including Sondra, noted that like the
residents, management was also aware of which tenants were responsible for the problems; moreover, it had the power to evict the troublemakers: "If management knows what's going on in this building, you
know where the drugs are, you know who's selling drugs, you know who
the troublemakers are, you know it, get rid of these people! . . . If you're
a troublemaker, then you should go. . . . You sign a lease and when you
break that lease you should be gone. And you got kids you can't control, you shouldn't be in here."

Rakiah felt that if management and tenants worked together, seemingly intractable problems could be resolved:

> You can go to one woman and knock on the wall, and you can
> hold a whole conversation and it go, it's just like a circle. What
> you hear in one apartment, you hear in another apartment. . . .

Everybody knows what's going on. . . . [CHA management] knows who's doing what. I feel by them knowing what's going on, they could have stopped it. . . . I feel parents should be held responsible for what their child is doing. If that child's out selling dope, gangbanging and is coming back in the building, I feel that parent should be evicted. . . . When [CHA management] stopped screening, everything just fell apart. . . . People in this development can make this development what it should really be.

However, as in Horner and Rockwell, while Ickes residents felt that tenants could probably solve some problems, they did not believe that many would try. Sondra pointed out that many residents were substance abusers and unlikely to care about improving conditions: "If tenants worked together [they could really do something], but you got so many drug addicts who are not going to turn in, they're not going to turn in their source of drugs. Drugs don't bother them. The ones in the hallways and stuff is not bothering them."

Ickes residents had a very real fear of retaliation if they tried to confront gang members or drug dealers. As in the other developments, the relationship between gang members and drug dealers and other residents was complex. Many troublemakers were either long-term residents themselves or were the friends or relatives of long-term residents. The complexity of these relationships made it much harder for residents to effectively take action against the crime in their development. In this environment, residents tended to keep to themselves rather than get involved in trying to make things better. In May 1994, the majority of residents (56 percent) thought that Ickes residents "went their own way," while only 35 percent thought residents generally "helped each other out."

Ickes residents had to cope daily with witnessing drug sales, stumbling upon substance abusers in the stairwell or hallways, real or attempted burglaries or muggings, abused and neglected children, and domestic violence. Other than the activist residents, tenants generally kept to themselves, relying only on a small, trusted inner-circle and asking neighbors for help only with small things like lending them groceries. Most residents focused on ensuring the physical and emotional survival of themselves and their children. They avoided becoming involved, ignored obvious criminal activity, and sometimes carried weapons such as mace or a knife. There were also personal ways to "avoid" the traumas that confronted residents in their daily lives; some, like Sondra, used legal means—that is, prescription medication and cigarettes—to manage their stress and anxiety, but many more turned to alcohol and illegal drugs.

As in Rockwell and Horner, many parents established rigid rules of conduct for their children to try to keep them from becoming involved in drug trafficking. Some, like Sondra, aggressively confronted gang members who tried to lure children into the drug market. To protect their children, some parents kept their children inside most of the time, allowing them to play outside only when they could supervise them closely.

Despite their fears, residents did not consider Ickes to be an unusually bad place to raise their children and assumed that gangs and crime would be equally bad in many other neighborhoods. But like Tenille, a lifelong Ickes resident raising four children in the development, they acknowledged that close parental involvement was crucial: "It's okay. It's not the development, it's just some of the people that live in it. As long as you raise your kids right, in the right way, your kids going to grow up in the right way. But if you just let them run wild, they're going to be wild. If you don't tell them and talk to them, they're going to be wild. There ain't nothing wrong with your kids growing up here because I grew up here. I don't think I'm a bad person."

In sum, in 1994, Ickes was a distressed community with some resources and promise. Although not subjected to the constant gang violence that terrorized residents in Rockwell and Horner, the development, indisputably a dangerous community, was dominated by a thriving drug market. Residents lived in fear of retaliation from the drug dealers—both gang members and Neutrons—and spoke of the stress of trying to prevent their children from being caught up in the destructive world of gangs and drugs. Still, there seemed to be more hope for Ickes; conditions had been stabilized by the CHA sweeps, and a core of activist residents were committed to reclaiming their community.

The CHA's Battle against Crime in Ickes

The CHA began its battle against crime in Ickes in the early 1990s, not in response to any particular incident, but rather as part of its policy of securing all high-rise developments. Pressure from the Ickes's Local Advisory Council to get Anti-Drug Initiative services for their development may have played a role in the CHA's decision to crack down on crime. In January 1992, the CHA opened a CADRE center in a first-floor apartment in a building in the middle of the development.[8] Even earlier, in 1991, CHA staff held meetings with residents to recruit those interested in starting tenant patrols in their buildings. Although it is difficult to pinpoint exactly when each tenant patrol started in Ickes, by 1994 a number of the buildings, including two of the three profiled in this case study, were sustaining functioning tenant patrols. The entire Ickes development was "swept" in May and June 1992. After the buildings were swept or "locked down," as the residents referred to the event, the CHA initially stationed private security guards in the lobbies. Eventually, likely through the clout of the Local Advisory Council, the CHA replaced these guards with officers from its CHA Security Force. Security Force officers were stationed in Ickes until the CHA began scaling back its services in mid-1996.

When we first visited Ickes as part of a preliminary assessment of the Anti-Drug Initiative programs, residents believed that the CHA's initial efforts had substantially improved conditions there (Popkin et al. 1993, 1995). In 1993, the majority (71 percent) of the Ickes residents said that they felt safer since the sweeps.

A year later, in May 1994, residents reported that these changes had been sustained. They attributed the improved conditions to the combined efforts of the Security Force officers, the tenant patrols, and the sweeps. First-floor residents, particularly vulnerable to the drug dealers' activities, noticed a difference in their hallways. Louella, an elderly resident, said, "Well, I think it's more safe. When they had it unlocked, because I live on the first floor, [drug dealers] stood at my door twenty-four hours a day. I couldn't even get out. . . . They just wouldn't move, so I'd just take the grocery cart and run over their feet." Carol agreed: "It's much safer. Before the building was locked down, with me on the first floor, it was hard for me and my kids to get to our apartment door because they [drug dealers] used to stand right there. . . . Sometimes now I have my door unlocked, and I don't have to worry about nobody coming in and taking nothing. It's much better. It's quieter."

In general, the CHA's antidrug programs were more successfully implemented in Ickes than in either Rockwell or Horner. For nearly four years, from 1992 to 1996, the development was relatively safe when compared to other high-rise developments or even to conditions in Ickes in earlier years. Strong resident leadership, proximity to services, lack of gang conflict, better security, and CADRE center staff who were willing to negotiate with gang leaders all contributed to the success of the Anti-Drug Initiative in Ickes. One CHA manager described the progress:[9]

> Ickes is a smaller development. That's one reason [the Anti-Drug Initiative's] been successful. It's got a strong resident leadership there which also helps. . . . It's surrounded by—although it's technically mostly surrounded by other CHA developments—the immediate community surrounding it does have some kind of business environment. There are some institutions there—you've got IIT [the Illinois Institute of Technology], you've got hospitals there.

All this, however, started to change following the HUD takeover of the CHA in 1995, when, as a result of policy reallocations, the agency's emphasis shifted from combating crime directly to large-scale revitalization of its worst properties. HUD ordered the new CHA administration to cut its spending on security, which by 1994 totaled nearly $80 million a year. Ickes, with its high levels of security and janitorial services and apparently relatively low need, seemed a natural place to cut dollars. In mid-1996 the CHA pulled its Security Force from Ickes, leaving only the tenant patrols and CADRE center on-site. CHA's battle against crime in Ickes from 1994 to 1997 featured several years of relative success, followed by a rapid deterioration of conditions.

Sweeps

Ickes residents believed the sweeps had profoundly reduced problems with violent crime. In contrast to Rockwell and Horner, where residents said that multiple sweeps brought only short-term improvements, Ickes residents believed the effects of the single sweep were long lasting. For example, in 1994, nearly two years after the June 1992 sweeps, Fran, a first-floor tenant, said the sweeps had reduced the number of people hanging around the development and had kept "violent people" out: "Well, like you say, you don't have that many violent people running in and out no more. People being more cautious and careful about who they let in they house. . . . It improved in many ways. Sometimes they would just be in the building all night. Just on every floor. They was keeping up a lot of noises all during the night. Since the sweep, we still get noises, but the noises is not as bad as it was before they done the sweep."

Ickes was only swept once before the sweeps were declared unconstitutional (see chapter 2) and never had the "emergency sweeps" or "swarms"—joint Chicago and CHA police building patrols—that were implemented in both Rockwell and Horner. As in the other developments, residents both welcomed the sweeps as an effective crime prevention strategy and simultaneously viewed them as an invasion of privacy where CHA "treated everyone like a criminal." Tenille expressed both views: "Because I think that really is an invasion of your privacy. I'm not against the sweeps, but they shouldn't just come and surprise. . . . It's an invasion of your privacy, but I see what they're trying to do, though. Because if they let people know about the sweep, then that gives people time enough to get rid of whatever weapons or drugs they've got in their apartments. So I understand about the surprise sweep, but it's really an invasion of our privacy." In May 1994, only 24 percent of the residents thought that the CHA should be allowed to enter people's apartments to search for weapons and drugs, yet 59 percent wanted their building swept again. As in Rockwell and Horner, residents expressed these consistently contradictory feelings for years.

By December 1996, as conditions in Ickes were growing worse, some residents began talking about wanting to bring the sweeps back. Olivia, a young mother in her early thirties who moved into Ickes in 1992, explained that the best thing that could be done to improve conditions was to reinstate the sweeps: "They need to do like they did before during the sweeps, when everybody who ain't on a lease don't be around here or either do like they do if they stop them and they ain't got no identification saying that they live around here or know people, visiting people. They can get rid of a lot of people like that."

Sondra was much more forceful in voicing her outrage and disappointment that the sweeps were no longer considered a viable option. She noted how "outsiders" from the ACLU "lobbied" the courts to consider the sweeps an infringement of civil liberties, to deny the CHA the option of "going into a house and looking for guns and getting the guns out." She believed that decision, coupled with the CHA's decision to scale down on security, contributed to creating an unsafe environment in Ickes. After a pregnant woman had been murdered by her boyfriend, Sondra's frustration was high:

> Had the security been there, well, the radar [metal detectors] would have went off when the gun come through. You see, they stopped a lot. You got people lobbying for us. We don't need nobody lobbying for us in the wrong way. Ain't nobody lobby for no damn lights, ain't nobody lobby to clean these damn hallways. But then when it come down to going into a house and looking for guns and getting the guns out, then you got people standing back there going to court and shit, all this stuff. Hell, they ain't helping me. You know, don't help me that way.

Security

Although Ickes was not one of the CHA's most dangerous developments, by May 1994, the CHA had stationed officers from its Security Force in most buildings. Given that resident pressure often influenced such decisions, Ickes's Local Advisory Council may have been responsible for the Security Force's presence. CHA's Security Force officers received considerably more training and were better paid and better screened than contract security guards. Consequently, both residents and staff viewed them as much more effective than the private security guards that patrolled developments like Rockwell and Horner, and they commanded more respect from the residents.

The first CHA Security Force officers were assigned to Ickes shortly after the 1992 sweeps; by 1994, all buildings had them twenty-four hours a day. Although residents were initially pleased with the officers' performance, over the next two years, they gradually became disillusioned.[10] However, residents recognized that having the officers stationed in their buildings provided them valuable, though minimal, protection by screening visitors and keeping problem people out of the lobbies and hallways. India, who had lived in Ickes since she was ten, noted: "Because [having the guards] do make the building safer, makes me feel much safer by me knowing that they're in here. Because at least after a certain time at night there is no running in and out. Like I say, they don't just let anybody walk in. They . . . pick who they let in, and I do feel safer with them there."

The Security Force officers at Ickes followed the protocols instituted after the sweeps: they screened anyone entering the building by asking tenants to show their resident identification cards and required residents to sign in all guests. This screening process, probably the most effective way of improving safety, was also ironically the biggest source of dissatisfaction for Ickes residents. In contrast to Horner and Rockwell, where residents complained about lax security, Ickes residents consistently complained that the rules were *too restrictive*, even with their sporadic enforcement. When the rules were enforced, they placed an undue burden on tenants; some had to travel up and down as many as nine stories to sign in their guests, and residents without phones had no way of knowing when they had a guest.[11] Shirelle, a young mother with four children, described what she had to do when she expected visitors: "Now, if I expect them to come over . . . I be looking out the window. But if I don't know they coming, you won't get in, because I don't know you're coming. . . . But I have family members that came up and knocked on the door. I'm like, 'Well, how'd you get up?' It's like sometimes you can, and sometimes you can't. You may get lucky today, you may not get lucky tomorrow."

Like Shirelle, many residents protested that the rules were only enforced occasionally: that is, sometimes guards checked people's identification, sometimes they did not, sometimes they let in drug dealers, and sometimes they demanded identification from "legitimate" tenants. However, several residents acknowledged that the guards might have been following the rules, even when letting in potential troublemakers. If drug dealers or gang members were residents or legitimate visitors (e.g., someone's brother or son), then the guards had no justification for keeping them from entering the building. Marsha, a woman in her forties who had lived in Ickes for sixteen years, explained: "The security can only do so much. You know, once a person signs a person in the building, they are on their own. But the security . . . they do they job to the best of they ability." Residents' expectations of the guards were often contradictory. On the one hand, they argued it was critical for guards to check everyone's identification consistently so no one would receive special treatment; on the other hand, residents insisted that the guards should recognize them and were frustrated by the inconvenience of having to show their identification card.

This security situation in Ickes changed radically on March 1, 1996, when the new CHA administration began shifting its resources from security to revitalization. With Ickes's comparatively low crime rate, it was difficult for the CHA to continue to justify the enormous expense of providing their Security Force officers twenty-four hours a day. The Security Force was one of the housing authority's most expensive Anti-Drug Initiative programs; only the CHA police force was more costly. The new administration, willing to risk resident protests, insisted on cutting services to the development. The CHA issued a new security plan that called for removing the guards during daytime hours. By March, residents, aware that security was no longer present around the clock, had heard rumors to the effect that they would be removed entirely. Betty explained, "As of today, [CHA guards] were here yesterday, but I don't think they're here today. They wasn't in my building. But as of the first, they all was supposed to been taken out. [Interviewer: "Did you have security twenty-four hours over the past three months . . . ?"] Most of the time. And then some they would have to take out to put over in the next building because it was worse in that building than it was in our building. So they wanted more security in that building because our building was pretty quiet. They just wanted the guards over there for up until the next shift came on."

By the fall of 1996, the CHA decided to remove the Security Force officers altogether. For a brief period, a small group of officers patrolled the development on foot, but the Security Force was eventually deployed to patrol other, more dangerous developments. In December 1996, only 33 percent of Ickes residents reported having security officers in their building (presumably representing one of the three buildings). By December 1997, all security officers had been removed.

The removal of security from Ickes, which began in March 1996, marked the beginning of alarming increases in levels of gang activity, drug-related crime, and violent crime. Gang territories in Robert Taylor and Stateway Gardens were being disrupted by demolition and building closings; these gangs were looking for new territory. At the same time, the dominant Gangster Disciples of Ickes was weakened by the arrest and conviction of its top warlords. Once the CHA Security Force was removed and the Gangster Disciples fragmented, Ickes was vulnerable to the gangs from other developments. Conditions degenerated rapidly. By December 1996, residents said that crime was as bad, or worse, than it had been before the sweeps. Betty gives her assessment: "Well it's worse because they have taken security out, and they have taken all the booths that the security was working, they've taken those out. Now the buildings are just open to whoever want to walk in. . . . When the security was there, they was stopping everyone that comes into the building and find out what apartments they were going to. So now they can just come in and catch the elevator or the stairs and just go right into the building."

In February 1998, approximately two years after the removal of the security officers, Geraldine, another resident activist who had lived in CHA housing for more than twenty-five years, reflected that removing the guards "made it a lot worse. All the security wasn't good, some of them was quite lazy. But even the lazy ones, it's a difference. Because whenever something comes up, they were there. Because they had to be alert on that, you know, so they were there to rescue you. It's a difference."

Tenant Patrols

CHA was much more successful in organizing tenant patrols in Ickes than in either Rockwell or Horner. In Ickes, residents had created active tenant patrols as early as 1991; some continued to be active into 1996 and beyond. By January 1995, nearly all the residents were aware of a tenant patrol in their building, yet few participated in it (about fifteen tenants, on average). Although the number of tenant patrol members was small, they had a visible presence. More than two-thirds of the residents (in buildings with tenant patrols) said there were members working in their building at least once a day.[12]

Unlike the patrols in Rockwell, the tenant patrols in Ickes reliably carried out the basic task of "walking down" their buildings each day. Walking down the building meant checking the hallways and stairwells for maintenance problems like broken light bulbs, broken elevators, trash, or graffiti and monitoring who was walking through the buildings. In addition to their basic duties, the tenant patrols in Ickes developed two initiatives specifically focused on children: Tenant patrol members escorted children to and from school and sponsored a student-run candy store to raise money for schoolbooks and supplies. The CHA resident programs' staff, who was responsible for organizing tenant patrols in each development, commended the Ickes tenant patrols for their exceptional work with children. One staffer remarked, "Ickes continues to have one of the strongest school patrols we have."[13] Residents also had positive views of the tenant patrols, consistently rating them as effective in reducing crime and fear.[14]

Ickes's strong resident leadership was likely responsible for the unusual success of the tenant patrols there. Some tenant patrol leaders were also building presidents, who served on the Local Advisory Council. They thus had an extra motivation to keep their buildings safe and clean for the families they represented. Further, the linkages between the tenant patrols and the Local Advisory Council allowed the tenant patrols to demand a level of support from the CHA that was unheard of in Rockwell and Horner. The CHA Security Force officers, deployed in the development in response to pressure from the Local Advisory Council, provided some protection for the patrols. As Local Advisory Council members, several tenant patrol leaders accompanied the development president and site manager to meetings with both the CHA and Chicago police departments. As a result, the tenant patrols in Ickes were able to rely on an unusually high level of support from the police.

As an example of the close relationship between the tenant patrols and police, in the spring of 1995, tenant patrol members across the development organized and temporarily began monitoring the entire development en masse instead of simply patrolling their individual buildings. Apparently, the CHA police noticed the group and joined the tenant patrol the first day. Geraldine, an early member of the Ickes tenant patrol, describes this event: "We done started walking the building down in groups. . . . Last Tuesday, as a group, about twenty tenant patrol walked about six buildings down. . . . Yes, everybody just got into one group and walked all the buildings. . . . We drew the attention of the police—they wanted to see what was going on, so they came out . . . and they joined the walk down for three buildings."

The tenant patrol members had two advantages over the security guards: first, because they lived in the buildings that they patrolled, they had a vested interest in making *their* homes safer; and, second, they were more familiar with residents, which made it easier for them to approach residents and spot intruders. In fact, residents described the tenant patrol as a "watchdog" over the security guards. Betty, active with the tenant patrol in her building for six years, served as the nucleus for their efforts. She described the relationship between security and patrollers: "The security guards—they know [the gangbangers] from the next building, and they lets them in. They get in that building when they get ready . . .

but in our building they're a little more particular because the tenant patrol is there, and we know most of the ones that live in the building and the ones that do not live in the building. . . . They come to the door, [but] when they see the tenant patrol they turn, go back out the door."

Yet the tenant patrols had three major limitations as a crime fighting force: first, they had neither weapons nor any official form of protection; second, they had less anonymity than the security officers; and third, at the end of their shift, the tenant patrol members went home to their apartments and risked retaliation from the drug dealers in their buildings. Sondra describes how the initial reaction to the tenant patrols involved mostly taunting and verbal threats:

> You get them talking about you and staring you down. . . . Oh you get the one who talkin', you know, you hear 'em talkin' about you, but if you do something to me you are definitely going to jail. No doubt about it, you are going to jail. . . . So they can talk, you know, and when I'm by myself and go upstairs to the office, I gotta think about they can catch me out here and hurt me, you know, nobody know they did it. Yeah, certain things run through your mind.

Verbal threats were not uncommon; tenant patrol members were often referred to as "snitch bitches." Occasionally though, the taunting went beyond verbal altercations, and tenant patrol members were threatened, intimidated, and suffered property damage.

In early 1996, with the shift of CHA resources from safety to renovation, the CHA began gradually removing its Security Force from Ickes, and leaving the tenant patrols responsible for security during the days. Sondra was skeptical of the plan from the beginning:

> See, we don't have no .38 [guns]. They not giving us a .45 [gun] on our side to protect ourselves. They putting us out there with a pen and pencil. I mean, Chicago Police Department got weapons. Because do you think by us being residents that it's gonna make a difference if this person want to get upstairs and buy some drugs? Drug addicts will kill you! When they want to come in that building to buy some drugs, you better move over and let them in.

Olivia participated in the patrols periodically, but like many others, left the group out of fear for her own safety when the security officers were removed. She explains: "I'm not here to protect the whole building. As far as being there, if I got security to help me, I don't mind. But as far as being tenant patrol and just working the building, no I can't do that because drug dealers, you know how they are, and I don't want to risk myself getting hurt and killed trying to run no building. . . . If security leave, I'm gonna leave."

In the months after the guards were removed, a few tenant patrol members continued actively patrolling their buildings, but their activities were becoming more dangerous. Geraldine, who had kept the tenant patrol in her building strong, was the victim of a number of property crimes and threats; once her smoke alarm woke her, and she found someone had burned a book at her door. "It was scary. Just think that someone would try to burn you up." Geraldine believed all the incidents were in retaliation for her reporting a boy defacing the hallways. She explained the situation, "They done did everything to my door—kicked in my door, urine on my door, put human feces on my door knob. They have did everything now. That's why I know exactly what's happening. One of them shot at my car with a BB rifle." Even though Geraldine was sure she knew who was committing the crimes and reported the incidents to the police, she was told that if she did not actually see the crimes committed, there was nothing the police could do. By 1998, many tenant patrol members had decided the risks were too great and quit; others, including Geraldine, planned to move out of the development altogether. Without the protection of the police and Security Force, Ickes residents, like those in Horner and Rockwell, decided that getting involved in trying to control crime in their development was simply too risky.

CADRE Center

The CADRE center in Ickes opened in January 1992, and, like the other Anti-Drug Initiative efforts, was successful, at least until conditions began to deteriorate in late 1996. From the outset, the center, centrally located in a first-floor apartment at 2330 South State Street, employed from four to six full-time staff members, many of whom were residents. The Ickes center offered a wide range of drug prevention and intervention services, as well as parenting and youth programs. At the nearby South Loop School, CADRE staff coordinated a Students' Assistance Program, which included in-school workshops on substance abuse, gang awareness, self-esteem, and decision making.[15]

The Ickes CADRE center also developed a unique relationship with local gang members that helped to create a safer environment for the residents. Staff at CADRE met occasionally with gang members to work out compromises regarding rules of conduct. For example, in May 1995, the gang leaders agreed that drug dealing would be "outlawed" during the hours when children would be going to and from school. Staff commented, "I think it's safer now. CADRE has also helped with gang activity in the development. They go in, and they establish a rapport with the gangs, and they get commitments from them. And with those commitments, so far we've not had any problems. We also just celebrated in August our 'Increase the Peace Week.' So we have not had any violent crimes here in Ickes for some time."[16]

However, this agreement was considered controversial because many resident leaders did not think there should be any negotiations with gang members who were responsible for the drug trafficking and violent crime in the development. As Sondra said, "I'm not going to sit down with no drug dealers and gangbangers, and they all work together. I'm not going to set down with them and try to solve nothing. Why should I? I know for a fact when they leave that meeting they go on and do their jobs and that's selling drugs and gangbanging. . . . And I myself refuse to sit down and negotiate anything with them."

In general, though, by the end of 1996, staff and residents alike perceived the CADRE center as an effective and helpful resource for residents. There was a high level of community awareness of the office, and, according to Resident Programs' staff, many residents who received drug-related help through CADRE were able to stay clean off drugs.[17] "I would say that [CADRE] is very successful in helping those tenants that are ready for help. They can't do anything for someone that comes in and they're not ready for help. But if they come in, and they have a sincere desire to kick the habit, then CADRE can assist."[18]

Impact on Conditions

It is useful to consider the history of Ickes in two parts: first, the period from 1994 to 1996 when the CHA poured resources into the Anti-Drug Initiative efforts in Ickes, and conditions continued to improve slowly but steadily. During those years, the CHA's strategy appeared to be working. Second, the period beginning in March 1996 when conditions deteriorated as the new CHA administration shifted resources from security to demolition and revitalization. The agency began layoffs of officers from its Security Force and could no longer justify the cost of providing twenty-four hour security for Ickes, which had one of the lowest crime rates of any high-rise development.

With the Security Force removed, Ickes was an inviting target for crime, and conditions deteriorated rapidly. In spite of the demonstrable success of the Anti-Drug Initiative in Ickes up until early 1996, the CHA began dismantling its programs, piece by piece, letting Ickes slide toward becoming an urban war zone to rival Rockwell and Horner.

By using scales to summarize the patterns of change over time in residents' perceptions of major problems in Ickes,[19] we describe the impact of the CHA's programs in that development. In addition, we discuss the reasons for these changes and the factors that allowed Ickes to become one of the CHA's most dangerous developments by 1997.

Physical Conditions

As figure 6.1 shows, the majority of Ickes residents consistently reported serious problems with vandalism inside their buildings—graffiti, trash and junk, and broken light bulbs—from May 1994 to December 1997. Reports of problems decreased somewhat from May 1994 to May 1995, but they increased again by December 1995 and remained high a year later.[20] A sharp increase in reports of problems with broken light bulbs (from 51 percent in December 1995 and 1996 to 72 percent in December 1997) corresponded to the increase in overall gang violence, a result of the Security Force removal and the movement of new gangs into Ickes.

Tenants' fears were palpable when they voiced their concerns. In Ickes, as in Horner, drug dealers and gang members were mostly responsible for removing or knocking out the bulbs. As Olivia explained, the gangs and drug dealers wanted the buildings dark so they could covertly sell and use drugs and to intimidate the other residents.

> Oh my God, it ain't been none over there in months. I even fell up the stairs. I went to housing and made a report, she put it in my file, but since then I done tripped up the stairs two more times. It's been like this for months. . . . They put lights in there, but they get broked out. I guess because it's not a cover on there, but that's why I say it's not Housing's fault as far as putting the lights in there. They will put the lights, but like I said, nine times out of ten, it's the people who don't want the lights in there that's knocking them out.

In addition to making it difficult to negotiate the hallways and stairwells, the constant darkness terrified residents. India said she was too frightened to open her door: "They bust out the lights. I mean they busts out the light bulbs so bad, you know, like somebody knock on your door, if it ain't no light, you be scared to answer your door. It be pitch black, the stairways, the hallways." Likewise, Sondra was afraid of being attacked in the dark:

> No I didn't have a flashlight, and it wouldn't do no good anyway because a flashlight wouldn't work. Because the only thing

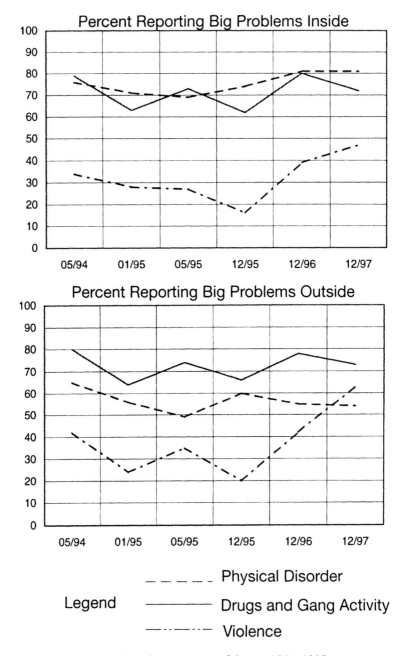

Figure 6.1. Ickes Residents' Perceptions of Crime, 1994–1997

they'd do is throw a coat or something over your head and they got you anyway. So now I've got to ride the elevator, and the elevator don't close when you want it to close, it close when it ready. And I want the elevator to hurry up and close, don't let nobody come in the elevator with me. . . . Now when the elevator door open, my heart is just pounding. . . . I got to go all the way down to the end of the hallway to get to my door. . . . I was scared, I was anxious, I was frustrated. You're damn near scared to death.

Yet elevators frequently broke down temporarily, forcing residents to climb the darkened stairwells, putting them in danger. Tenille summed up the situation: "Ok, for one thing, it's dark, and no lights. The elevators stay broke sometimes you know. Then all the lights, you know you can't see nothing ok. When the elevator's working you catch the elevator, then when the elevator's broke you got to walk down those dark stairs and you can't see nothing. And that's very dangerous."

The deteriorating situation inside the buildings, particularly the broken light bulbs, was particularly disheartening to residents. Many now believed that their development was slipping back into its condition prior to the sweeps in 1992. Further, they were pessimistic about what that meant for long-term prospects for the development. With nearby developments slated for demolition, rumors surfaced that the CHA was neglecting Ickes on purpose so that the vacancy rate would increase, the buildings razed, and new housing built for higher-income tenants. As Sondra said: "Five years from now? I think it'll probably be a beautiful place, because five years from now they're going to be done closed them down and brought the condominiums all the way down through here."

Drug Sales and Gang Activity
Modest Improvements

The CHA's Anti-Drug Initiative programs were intended to reduce drug-related crime. As discussed above, until late 1996, Ickes had a thriving drug market, but relatively low levels of violent crime. The CHA's efforts appeared to have had only a modest impact on drug sales and use over time, but they were more effective in reducing problems with gang activity. Residents provided numerous anecdotal accounts of how, prior to the sweeps, gangs and drug dealers had free reign of the development and boldly sold drugs both inside and outside the buildings. After the sweeps, residents said that conditions improved; while drug dealing still occurred, it was much less menacing or obvious.

Much drug trafficking moved from the lobbies and hallways to individual apartments, where it was less visible.

As figure 6.1 shows, between May 1994 and December 1995, residents' complaints about drug trafficking, substance abuse, and gang activity both inside and outside tended to vary seasonally: the proportion of residents reporting big problems was higher in May 1994 and May 1995 and lower in January and December 1995.[21] In the warmer months, about two-thirds of the residents reported big problems with drug sales and use; in the cooler months, the figure dropped to about 60 percent. Although concerns about gang activity—that is, young people controlling the building and people hanging out—also varied seasonally to some extent, there did appear to be a steady downward trend. For example, the proportion of residents reporting big problems with gangs controlling their building fell from 42 percent in May 1994 to 19 percent in December 1995. Likewise, the proportion of residents reporting big problems with groups of people hanging out outside their buildings fell from 64 percent in May 1994 to 50 percent in December 1995. Thus, the Anti-Drug Initiative programs seem to have been somewhat effective in reducing the more obvious signs of the thriving drug business: they reduced the number of dealers and their customers in lobbies and entryways.

Still, even with these modest improvements, residents remained concerned about the pervasive drug trafficking, particularly the potential impact on children. As Rakiah said, "[Drug dealers] just don't care. They have no respect. They sell in front of the kids. They come in, smoke their stuff—sometimes the kids be playing in the hallways, and there they are, just right there. It's just like they don't even see them. They see them, they just don't care."

Violent Crime: Dramatic Improvements
While the Anti-Drug Initiative programs appeared to have only a modest impact on drug trafficking, violent crime dropped dramatically between May 1994 and December 1995. As figure 6.1 shows, the proportion of Ickes residents reporting serious problems with shootings and violence, assault, and rape inside their buildings was more than halved, from 34 percent in May 1994 to just 16 percent in December 1995; reports of problems outside fell from 42 percent to 20 percent.[22] This marked improvement clearly had an impact on the overall quality of life in Ickes; residents felt safer, and they were increasingly willing to participate in community crime-prevention efforts.

During 1995, residents typically reported hearing gunshots once or twice every few months. They seemed to have little concern that the violence would escalate or that they themselves were in danger. In early

1996, when asked to reflect on the effects of the Anti-Drug Initiative over the past two years, each resident we interviewed noted the drop in violent crime. Sondra said with almost pleasant surprise: "Well, you know what. I'm just about 100 percent sure it is [less]. . . . Because if they're shooting, you hear it. You don't hear it now. Every now and then, and it's so spaced out that you don't pay that much attention to it like it used to be. Used to hear so much gunfire 'til you wonder who done got killed now."

Residents attributed the decline in violence to a variety of factors: one tenant felt that the community was better organized and worked more closely together to fight crime than in the past; several mentioned the sweeps; and several others, including Geraldine, thought the local gang leaders were instrumental in keeping the level of violence down. "I think the gang members is more concerned about the community, and they controlling it themselves better. . . . I guess they just changed. They know that if all of them keep up with the shooting, it would bring in more police force on them, and I think there would be a police problem there. If they [are] shooting, [there] would be more police in the neighborhood, so they don't do any shooting. They mostly sell drugs."

Rakiah agreed, "It's not hardly no shooting and violence here, unless somebody that don't live down here come down here and start something with the gangbangers that live down here. But there don't be too much violence down here because, I don't know how it go. The gangbangers down here, whoever their leader is, they got their little meetings . . . they tell them try not be have too much violence down here."

The War Zone: Mid-1996 to Early 1998

In March 1996, the CHA began to remove its Security Force from Ickes; by the end of 1996, the guards were all but gone. With the lack of security, problems with gangs and drugs rapidly worsened. Residents' complaints about drug trafficking and gang activity rose sharply: the proportion reporting big problems, both inside and outside, increased from just over 60 percent in December 1995 to about 80 percent in December 1996. In essence, the proportion reporting problems in the winters of 1996 and 1997 was about the same as the proportion reporting problems during the warmer weather, when drug trafficking tended to be more visible (see figure 6.1).[23] Clearly, residents believed the situation had deteriorated. For example, complaints about big problems with drug sales inside the buildings increased from 46 percent in December 1995 to 69 percent a year later; reports of problems with gangs controlling the buildings nearly doubled, rising from just 19 percent in 1995 to 36 percent a year later. Most striking, the proportion of Ickes residents reporting problems with drug trafficking, substance abuse, and gang activity now *exceeded* the figures for both Rockwell and Horner, the more notoriously dangerous developments. It may be that residents in Ickes were less accustomed to extreme problems with drugs and violent crime and so perceived their problems as worse. Nevertheless, Ickes residents were hardly naive about drug-related crime, and it was clear that conditions were uncharacteristically severe.

When we visited Ickes for the last time in February 1998, we tried to understand why conditions had deteriorated so drastically; residents resoundingly complained about the number of drug dealers selling from inside their buildings. Without any form of security, Ickes had become extremely attractive to outside drug dealers. Geraldine explained:

> A lot of teenagers, and they're selling drugs on the stairs, in the lobbies, in the front. . . . Most of them don't live in the neighborhood. They just come up here and work. That's what they call working, selling drugs. [Interviewer: And the people who buy drugs, do they come from all over?] It's this postman, it's a mailman. . . . You'd be surprised at the people that come and buy drugs. It's so many people they come over here, and they . . . work there, and they pulls up in cars and on the street and buy.

With no security, gang members were easily able to gain control of the building lobbies and use that space to market their drugs. Olivia denounced the situation: "It's just ridiculous. They're just, like I said the CHA don't even come around here. It's just wide open with the drugs. They just do what they want to do. . . . It don't matter if you're a man or lady, old or young, they do what they want to do to you. They don't have no respect for one another."

Not only did residents have little recourse or protection, but they suffered the indignity of being locked out of their own buildings and intimidated by the large groups of young men routinely congregating in the lobby. Geraldine described how gang members had literally taken over: "They lock the back door with an iron pipe and residents have to knock on the door to get in. And then they escort them out the back door. . . . They close it back up with the pipes. And they end up they have to open the door for them to come in so they sell drugs in the lobby then."

The drug trafficking was not confined to the lobbies or the first floor; drug dealers moved upstairs. With stepped up evictions, the vacancy rate in the three buildings in Ickes doubled in 1997 to more than 20 percent from a steady rate of less than 10 percent from 1991 to 1996. By 1997, the CHA was enforcing stricter eviction policies, and more residents were being forced out. According to Sondra, in 1998, there were more than two hundred vacant apartments in Ickes, many of which were used by drug dealers. Betty said the vacancies were creating more problems for residents: "They are a problem because they [the drug dealers] have been getting into vacancies. Some of them, they have been breaking into, and then they've been hiding the drugs in the vacant apartments. A few children have been in the vacant apartments also, and some is living in the vacant apartments."

Most seriously, after the CHA removed the security officers, problems with violent crime skyrocketed. In 1998 Tenille said:

> For one thing, the little gangs around here, ok, they used to have respect. Now they walk around now with pistols, shooting up and down the lane. They used to didn't do that. Now it seem like they just don't care no more. . . . They just shoot while kids outside and stuff now. There used to didn't be no shooting around here that much, but now they do. It seem like it's more now. . . . Just about three times a week now. . . . When the change start happening, when they took away the security. It started getting worser then. Now it getting even worse.

Without security, Ickes was particularly vulnerable to outside gangs. By 1996, the CHA was vacating and demolishing buildings in other developments along the State Street Corridor, displacing their gangs members from their usual turf. The dominant Gangster Disciples had been weakened by the conviction of more than thirty of its top warlords on federal conspiracy charges related to drug sales; as a result, Ickes did not even have an effective gang to fight off intruders.[24] Without guards or gangmembers to protect the development from outsiders, Ickes quickly became a battleground.

As figure 6.1 dramatically illustrates, residents reported enormous increases in problems with violent crime. The proportion of residents reporting serious problems with violent crime (shootings, assaults, and rapes) inside their buildings rose from just 16 percent in December 1995 to 39 percent in December 1996 and 47 percent in December 1997. Likewise, the proportion of residents reporting major problems outside doubled from 20 percent in December 1995 to 40 percent in December 1996 and rose again to 63 percent in December 1997.[25] Shockingly, the rates of violent crime reported in Ickes in 1997 were *more than double those reported in Rockwell Gardens* and about 20 percentage points higher than those reported in Horner. From being just a "bad neighborhood," Ickes had become an urban war zone to rival CHA's worst high-rise developments.

Sondra described a development caught up in a brutal gang war in 1998: "I don't know if [the gang war] ended or if it's still going on. We had drive-by shootings and somebody right by my window got hit. And several other people got shot. And the kids are feuding with the Dearborn Homes. The school is in the Dearborn . . . backyard. I don't know if the war's over because since then we don't have no peace. I mean you constantly hear the shooting so I don't know if it's over or not." Ickes residents used to note when shooting occurred; now they noted when it stopped. Olivia said she had heard gunfire so often in the past year that "I can't even count." Sondra concurred: "It becomes like a daily thing. Usually when I don't hear no shots, I can hardly go to sleep. I'm laying there waiting on them. And a mother like me, and I say a mother like me because I got a teenage son, you don't rest until that kid is in the house. Smaller kids might get on your nerves, but the older kids be on your heart." She described the intense anxiety Ickes residents lived with day to day: "You don't have to see them. When I get up in the morning time and I go downstairs, and I see fresh blood all the way down the stairs, you see what I'm saying. And then you wonder, whoever did it, did they kill him? Is that person still living? Wonder who it was. I wonder how bad they was hurt. You don't wonder what it was about because you know what it was about."

An Uncertain Future

The residents of the Ickes Homes were the unintended victims of the CHA's changing priorities. From 1992 to the beginning of 1996, when the CHA was focusing its management efforts on combating crime, Ickes residents benefited greatly from the agency's efforts. Staff implementing the CHA's Anti-Drug Initiative programs in Ickes were able to capitalize on the relatively high level of social cohesion and effective resident leadership to produce a real and lasting impact on conditions in the development. With CHA's security officers guarding the lobbies, residents reported fewer problems with vandalism, drug trafficking, and especially gang violence. However, by 1996, national public housing policy had shifted away from promoting community crime prevention to demolishing and revitalizing "distressed" developments. After HUD took control of the CHA in mid-1995, it mandated that the new administration reduce spending on security and begin using its funds for a more long-term solution: CHA needed to redevelop its worst sites. This change in policy left the CHA with less money for its Anti-Drug Initiative; with reduced resources, the agency could no longer justify large expenditures for securing Ickes because, when compared to other CHA developments, Ickes was relatively safe.

The decision to abandon the Anti-Drug Initiative efforts in Ickes seems particularly disheartening, given that, of the three developments profiled in this book, only in Ickes were virtually all the programs at least somewhat successful in reducing crime and disorder. The entire development was swept, the CADRE center functioned effectively, tenant patrols actively patrolled in a number of buildings, and CHA security officers kept drug dealers out of lobbies and halls. CHA's programs were able to succeed because of both the higher level of social cohesion in Ickes—the core of older, long-term activist residents who struggled to maintain order—and the development's domination by a single gang. Without gang conflict, residents were able to use the CADRE center, and tenant patrols were able to form and monitor their buildings, with much less fear of retaliation than in Horner and Rockwell.

As documented above, when the CHA pulled its Security Force from Ickes, gangs losing turf in other developments moved into Ickes and violence increased rapidly. With escalating gang warfare, tenant patrollers no longer felt safe monitoring crime in their buildings, and many long-term residents who had sustained the social life of the development fled.

Ickes residents reported a bewildering array of problems: gangs had taken over the development; residents were being locked out of their buildings; residents who had been hired as janitors were being intimidated, threatened, and beaten; the vacancy rate had more than doubled; and residents were generally terrified. If not for the consistency of the stories, the description of this change might seem unbelievable. Ickes had been the "success story": the Anti-Drug Initiative had worked there, and conditions had stabilized. Although the development was by no means a paradise—drug use among residents posed a never ending challenge, and gangs still sold drugs in the neighborhood—it had not been a hellish war zone like Rockwell or Horner. But by the end of 1997, Ickes was as bad, or even worse, than the other developments.

By 1998, Ickes residents were uncertain about the future of their long-time home. More and more buildings in other CHA developments were vacated and torn down, and the vacancy rate in Ickes increased; residents came to believe that their development would not remain intact much longer. Even as conditions in Ickes deteriorated, gentrification began just a few blocks north and east of the development, and the city began developing plans to revitalize the entire area.[26]

In early 1998—perhaps to help it blend into the higher-income neighborhood growing up around it—the CHA invested in physical improvements in Ickes. The agency planted trees, installed a wrought iron fence around the development, and constructed two new playgrounds. All this effort improved the developments' appearance, but it was uncertain, and

Photo 10. Landscaping at the Harold Ickes Homes, 1998. *Photo by Jean Amendolia.*

unlikely, that simply beautifying the grounds would help control crime. Further, despite this cosmetic investment, the agency's plans for the development were unclear. Although Ickes had not officially undergone a viability assessment as of this writing, the CHA had begun talking to residents about rehabilitating some buildings in Ickes, while tearing down others to reduce the density of the development.[27]

Ickes residents were convinced that their development was going to be demolished and that they would be displaced. Betty said that Ickes would be "great big beautiful condominiums" but that all the current residents would have to leave. Geraldine, who was in the process of moving out of the development, commented: "It probably be condemned. . . . They'll be empty. . . . If they condemn the building, I think really, truly, since HUD been here, they not doing any work inside the building, trying to fix it up or anything. I think really since this is prime property here, they really just want the buildings just to close up. Just so they can just demolish it so they can use it for something else."

The CHA administration has ambitious plans to "transform the State Street Corridor" by demolishing buildings in the Robert Taylor Homes, Stateway Gardens, and Dearborn Homes. By late 1999 some of these efforts are already underway.[28] Although Ickes has not yet been specifically slated for demolition, its future seems tenuous. In the meantime, other than the landscape work, the CHA appears to be making little effort to secure the development. Sondra has given up hope for Ickes and blames the CHA for abandoning her and her fellow residents so it can meet its larger goals:

You know, you can't get no light. You can't get housing to, the electrician told me when I told him one building, one complete building was black, he said "these people don't want light." What the hell do you mean about "these people"? I live in here too, and I want some lights. . . . So now you tell me, why is it we can't get nothing done, we can't get hallways cleaned, can't get the lights on, everybody living in fear. No, do you think they're going to put these condos all the way down through here and let us live here? Absolutely no. You're on your own, you know. That's the purpose of letting us suffer. Well if we let them suffer long enough, we won't have to make them move. They all will move on their own. And you know what? They're just about right.

7 | No Simple Solutions

Communities trapped in dire poverty, Rockwell, Horner, and Ickes are public housing developments so troubled that millions of dollars of crime prevention and other services had almost no sustained impact on the quality of life for individual residents. With the exception of the revitalized sections of the Horner Homes, physical conditions remain dismal, the result of poorly designed buildings, vandalism, and years of mismanagement and maintenance neglect. The remaining residents struggle with a host of challenges from high rates of unemployment and welfare dependency to substance abuse and mental illness. City services are poor, stores are few, and the local schools and parks are nearly as distressed as the developments they serve. Gangs and the drug trade dominate the social world; there is no underlying social structure strong enough to oppose them and enforce community standards and norms.

Massive revitalization efforts like the one now underway in Horner hold the promise of reducing the urban blight. Since 1995, the high-rises in Horner have all been closed, and five buildings have been demolished. A new, attractive mixed-income community of townhomes has emerged, providing superior housing for a few former residents. However, the benefits for the other remaining tenants—those neither evicted nor motivated to leave on their own—remain unclear. Having lived for years with the terrifying violence around them, these Horner residents and the residents of the other CHA developments undergoing revitalization now fear losing the only home they have known. The CHA has served as the housing of last resort for vulnerable families; many may lack the resources to make a successful transition to Section 8 or mixed-income housing.

Thus, the stories of Rockwell, Horner, and Ickes offer insights into both the failure of so many well-intended efforts and the risks that these residents face as the CHA begins to transform its public housing developments into mixed-income communities. Understanding the depth of the problems in these communities suggests that an intensive, targeted, and long-term commitment is necessary to bring about fundamental change for many of these vulnerable families.

The Failure of the CHA's War on Crime

By the 1990s, Rockwell, Horner, and Ickes, like CHA's other high-rise developments, had become urban war zones. Long-time residents remembered that when they first moved into the developments in the late 1950s and 1960s, they offered a hopeful alternative to the slums where many of them had lived before. The grounds were landscaped with grass and trees, there were playgrounds for children, the apartments were clean and big enough to comfortably house large families. Residents watched out for each other's children, and, while there were problems, there was also a real sense of community. But after thirty years, the grass and trees had been replaced by dirt and garbage, the playground equipment was broken, the plumbing and heating systems had failed, the buildings were infested with vermin, and the walls were covered with graffiti. Crime, drug trafficking, and substance abuse were epidemic. Only a few older, determined residents still tried to enforce some social order; most focused on getting through the days and protecting their children from the many constant dangers.

When social reformers finally gained control of the CHA in the late 1980s, they believed that they would not be able to bring about any positive changes unless they were also able to reclaim the developments from the gangs and drug dealers. Under Chairman Lane's direction, the CHA and HUD poured hundreds of millions of dollars into an expensive war on crime. From 1994 to 1996, the CHA spent nearly $250 million on its massive Anti-Drug Initiative. After HUD took control of the CHA in mid-1995, the programs were gradually scaled back, but security costs remained extremely high—approximately $40 million per year for the CHA police and Security Force.

As the individual stories of Rockwell, Horner, and Ickes show, all this effort had little sustained impact on the crime and violence in CHA's high-rise developments. Despite some short-lived improvements, all three developments were still gang dominated, still extremely dangerous, and still overwhelmed by the drug trade. Indeed, Ickes was arguably worse off than it had been before the CHA's war on crime began. As the case studies illustrate, three major factors undermined the CHA's programs: (1) the crime problems were so severe that short-term, intensive law enforcement actions were nearly useless; (2) the social world was so dominated by gangs and the drug economy that residents were unable to organize effectively to combat their common problems; and (3) the housing authority was so dysfunctional that bad management undermined even its best-designed initiatives.

Ineffective Law Enforcement

The CHA's Anti-Drug Initiative was modeled on successful community crime-prevention efforts in other, less distressed, settings. The agency, incorporating the elements that law-enforcement experts and researchers thought were key, created what was, at least initially, a comprehensive and collaborative program that involved law enforcement, housing authority management, tenants, and social service providers. The program included police and security guards, tenant patrols, on-site drug prevention centers, and the installation of security measures like guard booths and metal detectors. According to Chairman Lane, who created the Anti-Drug Initiative, in theory if the CHA could secure the buildings with its police and security forces and enforce its own management rules, then residents could reclaim their developments.

But the three case studies demonstrate that in communities as distressed as CHA developments, traditional assumptions about community crime-prevention programs do not apply. For residents to participate freely in an organized anticrime effort, police protection must be sufficient for them to feel reasonably safe from retaliation. But, as these case studies illustrate, for the most part, the law-enforcement efforts intended to secure CHA developments did not have much impact on the level of drug sales and gang violence. In Horner and Rockwell, the sweeps and police patrols had a temporary impact at best: gangs and drug dealers left for a few days, and initially the guards kept them out of the lobbies and stairwells. However, without a strong, continuing police presence and with only poorly paid, untrained contract security guards to protect the entryways, the gangs quickly regained control of the buildings.

In contrast, the sweeps and other law-enforcement efforts had a much more sustained impact in Ickes, where trained security officers from CHA's own Security Force worked for several years. While the Security Force guarded the entryways, the level of violence was very low, the drug dealers mostly stayed out of the lobbies and stairwells, and other residents felt confident enough to participate in tenant patrols and other activities. But when budget cuts forced the CHA to remove its security officers from Ickes, conditions quickly deteriorated, and the violence escalated dramatically. The resident-managed Monroe Street building in Rockwell followed a similar trajectory: When the CHA Security Force protected residents and screened out problem tenants, drug trafficking and violence almost disappeared. But when the CHA withdrew this protection and began to fill up vacant units with displaced unscreened tenants from other buildings, the crime quickly returned.

Without a strong twenty-four-hour presence, the police and CHA staff trying to control the crime faced a nearly impossible task, particularly in Rockwell and Horner. The CHA's poorly designed buildings offered innumerable places for criminals to hide. The well-armed gangs had considerable economic resources and power. A seemingly endless supply of vulnerable young boys was available to replace members who were arrested or killed. The CHA's short-term, intensive law-enforcement interventions and untrained contract security guards were simply not enough to secure extremely dangerous developments like Rockwell and Horner. Although the sweeps and Security Force were enough to secure Ickes and the Monroe Street building, the rest of Rockwell and Horner was contested gang turf and consequently much more violent—at least until the gang war overwhelmed Ickes in 1996, and it, too, joined the ranks of insurmountable difficulties. It is not clear that anything short of an oppressive police presence—an option both constitutionally and financially unfeasible—would have made a significant difference in these two developments. However, Rockwell and Horner residents were so desperate that they often advocated such heavy-handed measures as the only realistic solution to their plight.

To the difficulty of challenging the powerful gangs add the element of danger; most residents—even in Ickes—were afraid to cooperate with the police. After watching one highly visible police action after another fail, many tenants gave up hope for improvement and believed that neither the police nor CHA officials could protect them effectively. With the gangs and drug dealers dominating their developments, residents desperately feared retaliation by the perpetrators. Given these harsh realities, it is not surprising that residents often chose to cooperate with the gangs that controlled their buildings instead of the police because "their boys" provided them with at least some measure of protection from rival gangs.

The Importance of Social Cohesion

Police and security efforts were also ineffective, particularly in Horner and Rockwell, because the community itself was so disorganized. Crime-prevention efforts like the Anti-Drug Initiative assume a level of social cohesion that simply does not exist in these extreme environments. These programs require that residents unite against a common outside enemy; further, residents should have the confidence and the social and psychological resources to successfully cooperate and confront their community's problems.

But with the gangs and drug dealers wielding most power and controlling nearly all economic resources, these assumptions were unrealistic. Like other similar programs, the CHA's Anti-Drug Initiative focused on excluding outsiders: removing illegal tenants during sweeps, putting guards and metal detectors at front entrances, and blocking off other building exits. But this strategy ignored the fact that many people causing problems—selling drugs, using drugs, vandalizing buildings, and committing violent crimes—were not outsiders, but neighbors, relatives, partners, and friends of the crime witnesses or victims.

As a result, even law-abiding tenants in CHA developments were enmeshed in the social world created by the gangs and the drug economy. The resident population as a whole was itself extremely troubled. Unemployment and welfare recipiency were high, substance abuse and depression were rampant, and teen pregnancy was an accepted fact of life. Residents—especially the children who lived in these developments—were traumatized by the constant stress of coping with the violence and disorder. With rare exception, no strong social structure opposed the gangs and drug dealers. To survive in this complex environment, residents had developed intricate and interdependent relationships with the criminals. Residents did not view the gang members who dominated the developments as strangers; rather, they saw them as "the boys" or "the gangbangers," often young men they had known all their lives. The relationship between the criminals and other residents recalled the old *Pogo* adage "We have met the enemy, and they is us." Standing up to the drug dealers and gangbangers entailed both the risk of possible retaliation and the potential loss of relationships. Therefore, a crime-prevention strategy based on excluding outsiders missed the point; that plan necessarily had little chance of success.

The fact that, despite the odds, the CHA's Anti-Drug Initiative programs seemed relatively successful in two sites—Ickes and the Monroe Street Building in Rockwell—highlights the critical importance of social cohesion for successful community crime prevention. These two communities had less extreme initial problems. Until 1996, they were not contested gang turf and had a somewhat higher proportion of employed residents. Even more significant, both Ickes and the Monroe Street Building had older, stable tenant populations with strong resident leadership. These tenant leaders lobbied the CHA for more services, particularly protection from the Security Force, and more and better janitors. It is telling that Ickes and Monroe Street were the only sites where the CHA's tenant patrol program was successful. Feeling relatively safe, leaders in Ickes felt empowered to work with the CADRE center to negotiate with the gangs to protect children from drug dealing and gang activity. Likewise, the resident managers in the Monroe Street building demanded the right to screen new tenants, fought with the CHA over the pace of rehabilitating their building, and negotiated with the drug dealers to take their business elsewhere. In both Ickes and Monroe Street, residents' complaints about violent crime dropped dramatically; it then seemed possible to begin both addressing the deeper problems of substance abuse and poor parenting and meeting residents' needs for education and job training.

But even in Ickes and Monroe Street, the social structure was fragile. Gangs and drug dealers still held sway over their communities, and order required substantial support from the housing authority and police. When the CHA could no longer sustain the higher level of service, violence and disorder skyrocketed, particularly in Ickes. As the violence increased, threats against the tenant patrol members escalated. Residents stopped participating in the patrols, and some leaders, fearing retaliation, fled the development. Those who remained were overwhelmed and dismayed by the chaos that seemed to be engulfing their community.

The Monroe Street community began to fray when the CHA began closing other buildings in Rockwell and housing the remaining tenants in empty units in the Monroe Street building. The Resident Management Corporation was not allowed to screen these new tenants, and problems with crime and disorder immediately began to increase. Some new tenants, affiliated with rival gangs, brought their conflicts to the long-peaceful building. With the Security Force removed, drug dealers once again hung out in front of the building and in the lobby and stairwells. But the biggest blow came when Wardell Yotaghan, the Resident Management Corporation president who had struggled to hold the community together for nearly a decade, died suddenly of a heart attack in June 1999.[1] In late 1999, it is not clear whether the remaining resident leaders will have the power to unite to overcome the escalating challenges.

The Role of Bad Management

Finally, bad management and poor implementation clearly undermined many CHA efforts. For almost two decades the housing authority was in a nearly constant state of management turmoil. The social reformers who took control of the CHA in the late 1980s were frustrated by the dysfunctional culture of the agency, which still bore the vestiges of the Swibel administration and thus the old Democratic political machine. Even into the 1990s, resources were frequently distributed by clout or cronyism; investigators were still uncovering evidence of fraud in contracting; and the resident councils functioned as quasi-political organizations. The HUD-imposed administration that took control of the CHA in 1995 complained that they could not identify all the people on the payroll, that staff would not cooperate in implementing new programs, that imposing order over CHA's financial management was nearly impossible, and that the resident councils fought every effort that might undermine their clout. When the Chicago city government gained control of the CHA in 1999, the new administrators identified many unresolved management problems and claimed to have uncovered a $50-million deficit.

In this environment, it was nearly impossible for CHA staff to function effectively. The agency failed at even basic tasks like collecting rents and tracking the number of occupied units in its developments. Thus, on paper, between 1994 and 1996 the CHA operated what appeared to be a model community crime-prevention program, but in reality, poor management undermined most attempts to run these programs effectively. Even when dedicated staff succeeded in overcoming the many obstacles to start new initiatives, ineffective follow-up and rapid strategic changes undermined their efforts. For example, the original strategy for sweeps involved collaboration with CHA management, security, law enforcement, and social service providers. This promising approach was abandoned relatively quickly, however, because of legal remedies and financial constraints; it cost the CHA nearly two hundred thousand dollars to sweep a single building. The sweeps subsequently became strictly a law-enforcement strategy. The security measures installed after the sweeps— security doors, guard booths, turnstiles—were not maintained; sometimes they ultimately benefited the gangs and drug dealers rather than the security guards. Finally, although the agency spent tens of millions of dollars hiring private security guards, the untrained, poorly supervised personnel had little impact on crime in CHA's developments.

The CHA's strategy often seemed to consist of trying one poorly thought-out measure after another; even the better ideas had no time to take hold, let alone determine effectiveness. The history of Rockwell provides numerous examples of this inconsistency. The sweeps there were not followed up with effective law enforcement. The Nation of Islam guards, in theory, were supposed to both provide security and organize the community, but with poor implementation, they failed to do either. The private managers substantially reduced vandalism and disorder, but they complained that they lacked sufficient funding to make substantial repairs. Empty apartments, never rehabilitated, remained vacant for years. The Monroe Street Resident Management Corporation brought about major improvements in their building, but they lost ground when the CHA lost enthusiasm for resident management and began to shift resources elsewhere.

Thus, shifting priorities, poor planning, and ineffective program implementation undermined virtually all CHA efforts to contain the crime in its developments. Each new administration brought a new set of senior staff and a new set of initiatives. Without strong champions or continuity, existing programs were misunderstood or neglected. Constant administrative turnover ensured that no staff had any institutional memory or thorough knowledge of the circumstances in individual developments. Given this level of turmoil, it is not surprising that even the best designed and most expensive of CHA's interventions had little long-term impact on the crime in its developments.

The Future of Public Housing in Chicago

As the case studies illustrate, by the end of the 1990s, all efforts to substantially improve life in CHA's high-rise developments had failed. Indeed, the situation was so extreme that the only alternative seemed to be demolition and replacement housing. Because the problems in these communities are so layered and deep and because the CHA remains a troubled institution, even this redevelopment brings tremendous risks for the current residents. These tenants now face searching for and securing housing in the private market, where their lack of experience and their complex personal problems will make it difficult for many to make a successful transition to either Section 8 or mixed-income housing. Given the history and limited resources of the CHA, there are no guarantees that they will receive the kinds of intensive services they are likely to need to overcome these challenges.

Transforming Public Housing

CHA housing is now undergoing an incredible transformation. As in Horner, the high-rise buildings are coming down; the new townhomes will serve a broader range of tenants. This transformation of CHA housing is possible because of several changes in federal housing policy intended to address the problems of distressed public housing on a national level.

These changes include the HOPE VI program, created in 1993 to provide funding for the revitalization and reconstruction of more than sixty thousand units of "distressed" public housing throughout the United

States. The repeal of the "one-for-one replacement rule" in 1995 made it easier for housing authorities to take advantage of this new funding by substantially reducing the cost of tearing down public housing. Housing authorities no longer have to construct a new unit for every unit they demolish; instead, they need only replace occupied units. Moreover, CHA can replace the demolished units with either new housing or a Section 8 certificate or voucher. The demolition of public housing has accelerated since 1997, when the federal government began mandating housing authorities to conduct "viability" assessments of all their properties with more than three hundred units and vacancy rates of more than 10 percent.[2] "Nonviable" developments, where the costs of rehabilitation exceed the costs of providing residents with Section 8 vouchers, are supposed to be demolished within a five-year period.

Finally, federal policy now emphasizes the creation of mixed-income developments. Much public housing being demolished under the HOPE VI program will be replaced with smaller developments designed to serve a more varied tenant population. The Quality Housing and Work Responsibility Act of 1998 allows housing authorities to take a number of measures to attract higher-income residents, particularly reinstituting "ceiling rents," which keep rents at a set level even as tenants' income increases.[3] These new residents will include working families, still low-income, but much less poor than the population in public housing today.

At the same time that HUD has made it easier for housing authorities to revitalize or replace some of their worst public housing properties, federal policy has shifted away from constructing new public housing and is focusing instead on providing Section 8 assistance for the poorest tenants. Section 8 participants receive certificates or vouchers that allow them to search for housing in the private-rental market.[4] Since 1998, the majority of all new Section 8 assistance has been set aside for the poorest households; this change will shift many of the poorest tenants from public housing into the private market. HUD hopes that this strategy will help to keep the poorest tenants from being concentrated in a few inner-city neighborhoods and has even allowed some housing authorities, including the CHA, funding to provide counseling to help Section 8 tenants find housing in higher-income, low-poverty neighborhoods.[5]

Will These Changes Benefit CHA Tenants?

These policy changes have had a dramatic impact on Chicago. Nearly all CHA high-rise developments failed the viability test. As discussed in the case studies, Rockwell and Horner were among the developments that failed; Ickes, not yet assessed, will likely fail on the next round. The agency scrambled to come up with a plan that would preserve some of this housing, which constitutes a substantial portion of the low-income housing available in the city of Chicago. The 1998 CHA plan calls for the demolition of more than eleven thousand units— 38 percent of the current family housing stock—during the next ten years. This number may increase as developments like Ickes are assessed throughout 1999.

Most developments that failed the viability assessment will be re-developed by creating a mix of new townhomes and rehabilitated mid- and high-rise buildings, which are much smaller and of lower-density than the current developments.[6] The housing authority then plans to turn much of this new and revitalized housing into mixed-income de-velopments for market-rate tenants and the working poor, who make up only a small proportion of the current resident population of agency hous-ing (see Chicago Housing Authority 1998). Many current residents will receive Section 8 subsidies and assistance in finding a new unit or be moved into apartments in smaller, scattered-site developments.

Planners intend these changes to bring about a better quality of life for CHA residents; however, local policymakers are concerned about the potential for current tenants to become reconcentrated in poor neigh-borhoods, where it is relatively easy to find landlords who will accept Section 8. Some Chicago neighborhoods are already complaining about the influx of CHA residents to their communities, fearing an increase in crime and disorder (McRoberts and Pallasch 1998). To try to avoid creating new pockets of extreme poverty, the CHA plans to provide resi-dents who receive Section 8 with mobility counseling—assistance to encourage them to move to low-poverty areas.[7] There is much debate about defining these areas; one plan calls for defining them as neigh-borhoods where less than 24 percent of the households have incomes below the poverty line and less than 30 percent of the households are nonwhite.

Policymakers in Chicago hope that this strategy of creating mixed-income communities and assisting tenants in moving to higher-income areas will help solve the problems of both the residents and the CHA. The theory is good: residents will benefit by gaining access to safer neigh-borhoods with better educational and employment opportunities, and employed residents in higher-income communities or mixed-income developments will serve as role models for children and unemployed residents. On the housing authority side, mixed-income developments are presumed easier to manage; the communities should be more stable, with fewer turnovers of residents than traditional public housing. The pressure of attracting and keeping higher-income tenants will force the property managers to be more responsive; the city should also be more willing to provide services to keep higher-income residents. Businesses and institutions may be more willing to invest in a mixed-income community; thus, problems with isolation and lack of access to services will be reduced. Further, because the developments are being revitalized, the housing authority may be able to budget for on-site resident services and programs.[8]

Like the Anti-Drug Initiative, this transformation of CHA housing is grounded in current social science theory. Much of the impetus for the changes in federal housing policy is based on the consensus among policy makers and researchers that high concentrations of very low-income families in public housing create an "underclass culture" (Wilson 1987; Schwartz and Tajbakhsh 1997). This underclass culture is characterized by high rates of unemployment, welfare recipiency, teen pregnancy, female-headed households, drug use, and crime. Certainly, CHA's high-rise developments all experience this kind of dire poverty, with problems so complex that they seem to defy solution.

It is not at all certain that the new mixed-income and dispersal strategies can either reverse these effects or prove any more beneficial to current CHA residents than all the anticrime efforts that preceded them throughout the 1990s. No one is sure how bad neighborhoods cause bad outcomes for residents or how these problems are best addressed (Turner and Ellen 1998). Although social structure and organization seem crucial, it does not necessarily follow logically that constructing a better designed mixed-income development will lead to the creation of the kind of community where different kinds of people interact and provide each other with help and support (Smith 1999). Nor is there strong evidence that exposing low-income public housing tenants to higher-income residents will help them either to become self-sufficient law-abiding citizens or overcome their other complicated personal problems.[9]

The experience of the *Gautreaux* program is one main reason that policy makers in Chicago and elsewhere are hopeful that providing CHA residents with Section 8 certificates or vouchers or creating mixed-income developments will help to resolve their problems. The settlement of the *Gautreaux* case initiated a court-ordered desegregation program that provided Section 8 certificates to current and former CHA residents who were willing to move to areas that were less than 30 percent black or city neighborhoods that were undergoing "substantial revitalization." Surveys of *Gautreaux* participants indicated that those who moved to white suburban communities were somewhat more likely to be employed after they moved and that their children were more likely to stay in school, to be employed after graduation, and to attend four-year colleges or universities.[10]

Although the *Gautreaux* results appear to support the CHA's current strategy, in reality, they may have little relevance for today's much more troubled resident population. First, *Gautreaux* participants were volunteers: these motivated residents were willing to act as pioneers and move to unfamiliar communities. Second, the program heavily screened the participants. Finally, the majority of families who came through the program never moved; those who succeeded—and were therefore represented in the research—were the most determined and motivated.[11]

Today's CHA residents are likely to have tremendous difficulty making the transition to mixed-income or private-market housing. Thus far, CHA's housing has served as the housing of last resort for very vulnerable families. Many of these tenants, with their multiple, complex problems, are desirable tenants for neither public nor private landlords. Even the least troubled are extremely poor and have little formal work experience. The resident population consists mostly of single-parent, female-headed households, many with several small children or teenagers.[12] Even leaving aside other problems, there may simply not be enough large units available to house all these families.

Further, because of their very low incomes and personal problems, many CHA residents may not qualify for housing in mixed-income developments or for Section 8 assistance. Our assessment of the early phases of the revitalization of Henry Horner Homes (Popkin et al. 1998b) suggests that the ultimate outcome of that effort may be a much-improved development with few original tenants living there. Many Horner tenants have had trouble passing the screening process for the new mixed-income units. Even those tenants who do qualify for the new units may not be able to sustain the level of housekeeping and personal behavior required to avoid eviction.

CHA residents who receive Section 8 subsidies may fare no better, particularly as the number of residents searching for low-income housing increases. Recent research on Section 8 participants in Chicago who could not find apartments to lease indicated that a substantial proportion was from CHA developments (Popkin and Cunningham 1999). Searchers had difficulty locating apartments that would accept large families, particularly those with teenagers. Residents reported that they encountered discrimination on many levels: racial discrimination; unwillingness to take children; bias against Section 8 participants and the Section 8 program in general; and bias against CHA residents (for example, assuming that any CHA resident would be gang-connected).

By federal law, residents who are "vouchered out" (that is, who receive Section 8 vouchers) of their developments must receive relocation assistance. However, this assistance can be minimal: no more than locating an apartment and paying the security deposit, and far less than actual counseling to prepare physically and mentally for this big move. Many CHA residents have already been relocated—often to housing in other inner-city neighborhoods where it was easy to find landlords who would accept Section 8. The CHA hopes to avoid concentrating its families in vulnerable neighborhoods by providing residents with extensive assistance to encourage them to move to middle-class suburban areas like the ones where *Gautreaux* participants moved. This counseling may help residents find an apartment—possibly even one in a good neighborhood—but unless the agency is willing to invest in intensive, long-term follow-up, there is considerable doubt whether many CHA residents will be successfully integrated in the private market. As in mixed-income developments, troubled residents may be evicted, and they may end up either living with relatives or homeless.

Even if they succeed in keeping their new apartments, new housing for these troubled families may not necessarily lead to new jobs or better outcomes for their children. Most of these families are also coping with the implications of the changes in the welfare system that will force them into the labor market (Newman and Harkness 1999). Undoubtedly, some will benefit from the new housing opportunities, but without intensive support, the magnitude of these changes may overwhelm many former residents and undermine any potential benefits of a better environment.

Revitalizing Neighborhoods Requires Improved CHA Management

In late 1999 the CHA remains an agency plagued by poor management. The 1995 HUD takeover eventually brought some administrative improvements, but the agency still ranked low on overall management. The CHA was turned back over to the city government in May 1999. Mayor Richard M. Daley agreed to take back responsibility for the troubled agency only if he was given substantial latitude to make drastic changes in administration, a tactic he used successfully to improve Chicago's public schools.[13]

The newest CHA administration will have to guarantee that conditions in the new mixed-income public housing developments are much better than those in current CHA developments if they hope to attract and retain higher-income residents. The fact that the city now has control of the agency offers the hope that the mayor will now be able to integrate CHA needs with other city agencies and programs. But, given the agency's reputation, the CHA faces a dual test: it will have to work hard to meet the challenge of attracting new tenants, and it must undertake a substantial public relations effort to erase the stigma associated with its projects for nearly forty years. The costs of building housing nice enough to attract market-rate tenants—and of providing high-quality maintenance—may make such a large-scale approach impractical. The CHA recently opened a small mixed-income development near Cabrini-Green, with units selling for nearly $200,000 in the open market. Not surprisingly, this new development provides housing for only sixteen former CHA residents (McRoberts 1998).

After rehabilitation and replacement of its worst properties, as of mid-1999 the CHA planned to have about eleven thousand units in these developments. However, approximately half of these new and rehabilitated units will be set aside for market-rate and working households; because so few of CHA's residents are employed, only a small proportion of these households can come from CHA's current population. The remaining residents will receive Section 8 subsidies, which they may be unable to use in the private market for reasons described above. As of late 1999, the new CHA administration has introduced another, even more ambitious, plan. Regardless of whether any version of these plans succeeds in creating much better housing or, with the city's involvement, revitalizing neighborhoods, the conclusion is inescapable: a much smaller supply of public housing will be available for the neediest tenants. With a limited supply of housing, it may not be possible for the CHA to effectively serve both higher-income tenants and its current, extremely needy population. Without careful management, these residents may indeed become the "tenants that nobody wants" (Quercia and Galster 1997).

No Simple Solutions

It might be tempting to dismiss the CHA's tenants as undeserving. As the stories of Rockwell, Horner, and Ickes document, many residents are gang members, drug dealers, and substance abusers. Many more, complicit in these crimes, pretend not to notice both to avoid the risk of retaliation and to preserve relationships with friends and relatives. CHA residents have had the advantage of free—or nearly free—housing for many years, and some have abused it. However, many good people have lived in CHA housing; activists like Wardell in Rockwell Gardens, Barbara in Horner, and Sondra in Ickes have fought hard to try to strengthen their communities, and other residents have simply focused on doing their best to raise their children in a risk-filled environment.

The CHA families—physically, socially, and psychologically isolated—

need to be brought back into the mainstream of community life. Physically, they have been isolated in huge apartment complexes, cut off by expressways and other barriers from neighborhoods with services, shopping, and employment opportunities. Their social contacts, the few friends and family members they feel they can trust, have generally all lived in public housing; many know no other way of life. For many, welfare and the underground economy have provided their only financial support. Psychologically, to deal with their constant struggle with violent crime, they have emotionally shut down—"minded their own business" and tried not to see too clearly the drug dealing, shootings, assaults, and vandalism that they encounter daily. Although it may be impossible to help everyone, CHA families—especially the children growing up in its terrible developments—need access to the kind of comprehensive services that may help them overcome their problems.

As things now stand, there are some indications that residents are right to view the current transformation of the CHA as another round of "urban renewal." Even though the redevelopment of its housing is just beginning, the CHA has already removed a number of its more difficult tenants. In the late 1990s, the agency began enforcing the "one-strike" provision that calls for the eviction of families where any household member has a felony or drug conviction. The agency also began enforcing its rent collection provisions for the first time in many years. As in Rockwell Gardens, these changes in policy led to a huge increase in vacancies in many CHA developments. Some residents have simply left CHA housing; others were relocated very quickly in response to emergency situations like the lack of heat in the Horner buildings in the winter of 1999.[14] The whereabouts of many of these former tenants is unknown. Some may have landed in better housing in better neighborhoods, but it is equally likely that many have ended up in worse housing in even worse neighborhoods.

Whether the remaining residents will benefit from the transformation of the CHA is uncertain. It is likely that some will do well, but others will not—and it is not known how large this second group will be. CHA's new mixed-income developments have the potential to serve low- to moderate-income families—and the potential to create nicer, better managed developments than currently exist—but they may offer more opportunities for higher-income tenants than for CHA current residents. The Section 8 program was originally intended to serve low- to moderate-income families already in the private market. Even if the CHA's troubled residents succeed in finding housing, it is not clear that they will succeed in keeping it. And even if they keep the housing, it is not clear that the anticipated benefits will likewise follow.

After decades of financial malfeasance, weak administration, short-sighted management decisions, inadequate services, and misguided policies, the agencies that oversaw the growing tragedy in CHA housing—the CHA, HUD, and the city government—have an obligation to the residents. They owe CHA residents, especially the thousands of children who still live in the terrible high-rises, a serious effort to try to help them improve their lives. There are no simple solutions, and none are inexpensive. But withholding this intensive assistance risks another public housing disaster: a significant number of residents could end up as badly off as the patients who were "deinstitutionalized" from mental institutions during the 1970s and 1980s, many of whom comprise today's homeless population.

Models can help avert further humanitarian disaster. Efforts to house and stabilize homeless families and refugee resettlement programs both offer lessons that can be applied to the CHA residents. The major lesson is that bringing about even modest positive outcomes for the most troubled families will require long-term—up to two years—intensive support (Blank 1997). If HUD and the new city-sponsored CHA administration truly want to try a Gautreaux-like approach of counseling to help tenants move to better neighborhoods, the federal government will have to provide funds for more assistance than merely finding housing. Any such program, including comprehensive social services and multiyear follow-up, should be linked to the transitional case management services the state of Illinois is providing for welfare recipients. The city will also have to work to ensure that there is enough affordable private-market housing to serve these tenants. Policymakers should also consider options such as providing families who are not yet ready to make the move to mixed-income or Section 8 housing with supportive housing that would offer a range of on-site social services. This approach has been used to help the homeless. Finally, policymakers may also have to face the fact that some residents are so damaged that they will never make a successful transition; there should be some way of ensuring that these most vulnerable families—and their children—live in housing that is decent and safe.

Without this kind of intensive assistance, the future for CHA's current residents is in doubt. Many residents suffer problems that are owing, at least in part, to years of exposure to traumatic stress. Their current situation is intolerable, but it is not yet clear that what awaits them outside CHA housing is better. It would be a terrible irony if former CHA residents end up concentrated in overcrowded private-market slums, much like the housing that CHA's high-rise developments replaced. Residents like Dawn from Rockwell Gardens, LaKeisha from Henry Horner, and Sondra from Ickes all fear that they will be displaced and left without even what little they now have. Wardell Yotaghan devoted his final years to trying to ensure that CHA residents would have a decent and safe place to live; it would a terrible tragedy if his efforts came to nothing and residents' fears proved prophetic.

Research Methods

STUDY SITES

The evaluation focused on the impact of the CHA's Anti-Drug Initiative in three of the agency's high-rise developments: Henry Horner Homes (1,777 units), Harold Ickes Homes (803 units), and Rockwell Gardens (1,313 units). Included in a preliminary evaluation, Horner and Ickes (Popkin et al. 1993, 1995) were selected because of their diversity in crime rate, level of social organization, and implementation of Anti-Drug Initiative program components. Horner was a very high crime development with a long history of management problems and a low level of social cohesion. Ickes had a moderately high crime rate, better site management than at Horner, and relatively strong resident organizations. Rockwell Gardens was selected because it offered an interesting comparison: like Horner, it was plagued with very high crime rates, but, like Ickes, it had a higher level of resident organization. In addition, the CHA had implemented two intriguing new programs in Rockwell: (1) private management and security services provided by a partnership of Moorehead and Associates, an experienced management company, and New Life Self-Development Company, an affiliate of the Nation of Islam; and (2) resident management in one building.

DATA COLLECTION

The Anti-Drug Initiative comprises a complex set of programs that the CHA began implementing in 1988. This research on the CHA's battle against crime in its high-rise developments spanned the period from 1994 through late 1997. During the study period, the CHA frequently changed its crime-prevention strategies, and life in its developments was affected by other events (that is, redevelopment initiatives, HUD takeovers, and so on). Therefore, to paint a full picture of the CHA's struggle against crime in Rockwell, Horner, and Ickes, we collected various types of data that allow us to tell the story of how these events affected residents' lives from multiple perspectives:[1]

Resident Surveys

We conducted six waves of resident surveys: the first four were approximately six months apart—May 1994, January 1995,[2] May 1995, and December 1995—and the last two followed at twelve-month intervals in December 1996 and December 1997.[3] In each round of data collection, we attempted to interview one adult in every household in each selected building. After the first round of surveys we attempted to reinterview the same respondent in each subsequent wave, using birth date and gender as identifying information. If that person was not available, we interviewed any adult who lived in that household.[4] Our interviewing staff consisted of current and former CHA residents who were trained to work as interviewers. We conducted most of the interviews between 9:00 a.m. and 3:00 p.m., Monday through Friday; because of safety concerns, interviews were only occasionally conducted in the evenings or on weekends.[5]

We completed a total of 396 interviews in May 1994, for an overall response rate of 66 percent. In January 1995 we increased our number of completed surveys to 547, a 77 percent response rate, and maintained that level of cooperation in May 1995 and December 1995. Because the number of vacancies increased (particularly in Horner) as the CHA's redevelopment efforts got underway, the number of completed interviews dropped down to 396 with a 71 percent response rate in December 1996 and 360 completed interviews with an 80 percent response rate in December 1997.[6]

The survey respondents were representative of the CHA's resident population; this, like the populations of most distressed properties, consists largely of female-headed households with children (National Commission on Severely Distressed Public Housing 1992a).[7] Not surprisingly, then, the majority of respondents in our sample (about 80 percent) were female; about half were thirty-four or younger; the majority (again about 80 percent) had three or fewer children; more than 70 percent had lived in CHA housing for five years or more; and less than half had graduated from high school. We found few differences between the residents in the three developments or between survey waves.

The survey included a series of outcome measures designed to capture the impact of various components of the Anti-Drug Initiative. The key variables included: the perceived severity of violence and other crime problems; the perceived severity of specific physical disorder (vandalism, trash) and social disorder (drug trafficking, visible loitering, gang activity) problems; levels of fear of crime; victimization experience; and residents' sense of empowerment. Residents were also asked about various components of the Anti-Drug Initiative (guards, tenant patrols, sweeps, maintenance, and social services); special attention was given to their awareness of, participation in, and evaluation of these programs and activities.

We constructed indices from the items measuring residents' perceptions of the severity of problems with physical disorder, social disorder, and violent crime both inside and outside the buildings; these indices allowed us to test for changes over time. To construct the scales, we subjected individual items in the first four waves of the survey to principal-components factor analysis to determine scale composition and unidimensionality. We also conducted reliability analyses to measure each scale's internal consistency. (For complete information on scale properties, see Popkin et al. 1996, 1999.)

All six indices are binary variables equal to one if the respondent reports any of the scale items are a "big problem" and zero if the respondent reports all items in a scale are "no problem" or "some problem." It should be noted that we constructed the scales for the analyses in this book somewhat differently than in our previous work (for example, Popkin et al. 1996, 1999), which included only the first four waves of data. The binary variables provide a more intuitive measure than the means we used previously and allow us to more easily discuss changes over time. The differences in scale construction did not affect the overall results.[8] Detailed information about scale properties is provided in Table A.1.

SCALE COMPONENTS

For the scales measuring perceptions of conditions inside the building, respondents were instructed as follows.

Please think about the inside of your building—the stairwell, hallways, elevators, and lobby of your building—and inside your apartment. Tell me if the following items are a big problem, some problem, or no problem in those areas *inside* your building.

The following items were included in the "inside the building" scales.

Table A.1 Scale Characteristics

SCALE NAME	MEAN	STANDARD DEVIATION	MINIMUM	MAXIMUM	N	CHRONBACH'S ALPHA
Physical disorder inside	0.81	0.40	0.0	1.0	2786	0.72
Physical disorder outside	0.65	0.48	0.0	1.0	2775	0.63
Social disorder inside	0.75	0.43	0.0	1.0	2774	0.85
Social disorder outside	0.74	0.44	0.0	1.0	2772	0.86
Violence inside	0.45	0.50	0.0	1.0	2779	0.72
Violence outside	0.49	0.50	0.0	1.0	2774	0.77

Physical Disorder Inside (1) Graffiti, that is, writing or painting on the walls? (2) Broken light bulbs that are not replaced for at least twenty-four hours? and (3) Trash and junk in the halls and stairwells?

Social Disorder Inside (1) People selling drugs? (2) People using drugs? (3) Young people controlling the building? and (4) Groups of people just hanging out?

Violence Inside (1) People being attacked or robbed in the stairwells, hallways, elevators, and lobby of your building or inside your apartment? (2) Shootings and violence? and (3) Rape or other sexual attacks?

For their perceptions of conditions outside their building, respondents were instructed:

(Now let's go over these activities again, but this time) Please think about the area right *outside* your building—the parking lots, the lawns, the street, the sidewalks right *outside* your building. Tell me if the following items are a big problem, some problem, or no problem in those areas *outside* your building.

The following items were included in the "outside the building" scales.

Physical Disorder Outside (1) Graffiti, that is, writing or painting on the walls? and (2) Trash and junk in the parking lots and lawns?

Social Disorder Outside (1) People selling drugs? (2) People using drugs? (3) Groups of people just hanging out?

Violence Outside (1) People being attacked or robbed outside your building? (2) Shootings and violence? and (3) Rape or other sexual attacks?

In addition to the longitudinal survey discussed above, we conducted a survey of a representative sample of Henry Horner and neighborhood residents in May 1998 for the *Gauging the Effects of Public Housing Redesign* study (see Popkin et al. 1998b). The survey contained some of the same questions on perceptions of disorder and violence as in the longitudinal survey and also included questions on their perceptions of the comprehensive neighborhood revitalization effort.

In-depth Resident Interviews

To supplement the findings from the resident surveys, we conducted in-depth interviews with a small sample of well-informed residents from all three sites. Each respondent was asked general questions about some or all of the following topics: crime and maintenance problems in the selected buildings; awareness of and opinions on various Anti-Drug Initiative components including tenant patrols, CADRE centers, sweeps, and security guards; resident empowerment, including residents' ability to work together to control crime; victimization experiences; and experiences in reporting crime to police or guards.

The first round of in-depth resident interviews was completed in June 1994, immediately after the first survey wave. We asked the resident staff of the CADRE centers to help us identify residents whom they considered well informed about conditions in the developments and who represented a range of views. In the first round, we completed seventy-seven interviews divided almost evenly between the three sites. For the subsequent rounds of interviews (conducted in January 1995, May 1995, September 1995, December 1995, and February 1996) we selected thirty-two of these respondents, who were particularly articulate and well informed, to serve as our "key informants."[9] The purpose of the follow-up interviews was to inquire about changes in CHA's Anti-Drug Initiative procedures or policies, such as the security guards, tenant patrols, social services, and crime. We also asked about any major problems or events that might have occurred in the development, including gang wars or other incidents that might have affected residents' perceptions of crime and safety in their neighborhood.

In addition to the rounds of interviews conducted as part of the main data collection, we conducted life history interviews with seven key informants (two from Rockwell, three from Horner, and two from Ickes) in May 1996. We reinterviewed two key informants from Horner as part of the follow-up study there in 1998 (Popkin et al. 1998b). Finally, we conducted a set of interviews with seven key informants from Ickes in February 1998 to help us understand why conditions there had deteriorated so dramatically since 1996.[10]

Staff Interviews

In addition to the resident interviews, we conducted periodic interviews with site staff members and interviewed all key Anti-Drug Initiative program staff members at least once. We conducted formal interviews with both Vincent Lane, the chairman of the CHA Board from 1988 to mid-1995, and Joseph Shuldiner, the CHA executive director from mid-1995 to mid-1999. We also interviewed other key actors outside the CHA, including the chief of the Chicago Police CHA unit and attorneys representing tenants in the lawsuits over the constitutionality of the Anti-Drug Initiative. In addition to general questions about crime and conditions in the CHA, staff interviews included more specific questions about the respondent's role or the role of his or her office in implementing the Anti-Drug Initiative. These interviews were taped when possible; in the few cases where the respondent refused to be tape-recorded, staff members took extensive notes. These transcripts were hand-coded and then analyzed.

Ethnographic Observations

The project ethnographer observed the study sites over a fifteen-month period. His goal was to speak with a broader range of residents than we reached through the surveys and key-informant interviews; he particularly sought the young men who lived in the developments. He observed drug trafficking and gang activity and talked to residents to learn how they coped with the pervasive dangers. Beginning with Horner in May 1995, the ethnographer conducted observations over a period of several months in each development and generally made about thirty visits to each site.[11] He kept field notes on his observations and interviews, analyzed these notes for salient issues and themes, and prepared an ethnographic report on each development.

ANALYSIS STRATEGY

Survey Data

Analyzing change between survey waves was quite complex because of the change in the composition of the survey sample over time. Researchers typically assess change by comparing independent samples (that is, respondents at wave 1 are completely different from respondents at wave 2) or by testing for change within correlated samples (that is, the same respondents are surveyed at both waves). The present study combines these two types of samples; therefore it cannot be analyzed easily with conventional statistical techniques.[12]

The solution to this problem was to use a generalized estimating equations (GEE) analysis strategy for longitudinal data (Liang and Zeger 1986); this took into account the nonindependence of data for some respondents while retaining the statistical power associated with the full sample. In our previous work (Popkin et al. 1996, 1999) on the first four waves of data, we used MIXOR (see Hedeker 1993; Hedeker and Gibbons 1994; Hedeker, Gibbons, and Davis 1991), another program that can address the same analytic issues. We opted to change to GEE for these analyses for computational convenience; however, we ran analyses to confirm that the results did not change as a result of the change in analysis strategy.

We separately analyzed the data in all three developments in a logistic regression model using the GEE approach with robust standard errors. The assumed "working correlation" structured for the within-person correlation was "exchangeable." The model was estimated both with and without controls for demographic characteristics,[13] and it tested whether there were statistically significant differences in the indices relative to the first wave (for example, wave 6 compared to wave 1) and relative to the prior wave (for example, wave 5 compared to wave 4). The results are shown in Table A.2.

Qualitative Data

The resident interviews were tape-recorded and transcribed. On the basis of reviews of the interview transcripts, we developed a codebook that identified key themes and issues discussed in the interviews; we then coded each interview. To ensure consistency and reliability, the same pair of analysts coded all the interview transcripts. Any questions about the way to code certain segments were discussed and resolved. A third member of the team reviewed the coding as she entered the material into the database.

The coded interviews were entered into The Ethnograph (Qualis Research Associates 1998), a qualitative database program, for analysis. The Ethnograph allows researchers to sort a large database of qualitative interviews by the codes they have developed. For example, we used The Ethnograph to bring up all the occasions when our key informants discussed instances of drug trafficking in their buildings. We then read through the output, and it allowed us to assess whether respondents generally felt that the problem was better, worse, or about the same. We also used The Ethnograph to compare responses about how the drug trade affected life in the development. Finally, we compared responses on the same topics across interview waves to help track trends over time. Because some staff interviews were not recorded, we analyzed them by hand rather than entering them into The Ethnograph database.

Table A.2 Residents Reporting "Big Problem" with Any Scale Items (in percentages)

SCALE NAME	MAY 1994	JAN. 1995	MAY 1995	DEC. 1995	DEC. 1996	DEC. 1997
			Henry Horner			
Physical disorder inside	93.8	95.7	91.6	87.6†	89.2	83.3†
Physical disorder outside	86.8	85.5	79.7	67.3†*	56.3†*	58.5†
Social disorder inside	89.5	90.2	85.2	74.6†*	71.3†	68.1†
Social disorder outside	85.7	87.6	79.7*	73.6†*	70.1†	68.9†
Violence inside	63.7	61.2	63.7	46.3†*	31.2†*	43.7†*
Violence outside	65.4	61.3	65.4	55.0†*	42.3†*	47.5†
			Ickes Homes			
Physical disorder inside	76.1	70.5	68.6	73.6	80.7	81.1
Physical disorder outside	65.2	56.1	49.0†	60.4	55.1	54.3
Social disorder inside	79.3	62.9†*	72.5	62.0†*	79.7*	71.7
Social disorder outside	80.4	64.0†*	73.9	66.5†	78.2*	72.6
Violence inside	33.7	27.9	27.5	15.7†*	38.7*	47.1†
Violence outside	42.4	24.5†*	34.6*	20.4†*	41.5*	62.9†*
			Rockwell Gardens			
Physical disorder inside	91.9	87.2	74.9†*	55.2†*	56.8†	68.7†*
Physical disorder outside	86.4	68.0†*	61.1†	43.3†*	41.5†	44.8†
Social disorder inside	86.8	77.9†*	80.6	62.2†*	53.8†	59.0†
Social disorder outside	87.1	73.1†*	76.0†	56.4†*	61.2†	61.1†
Violence inside	70.8	47.7†*	65.7*	33.9†*	32.2†	21.6†*
Violence outside	73.6	42.1†*	67.4*	39.0†*	47.9†	29.9†*

NOTE: Binary scale indices were multiplied by 100 to put them in percentage point units. Model results reported here were estimated separately for each development and control for the correlation in wave means due to reinterviewing the same respondent. A model that included demographic characteristics showed almost the exact same statistically significant changes.

† Indicates mean is significantly different than mean in wave 1.

* Indicates that the mean is significantly different from immediately prior wave at 5 percent significance level.

Finally, we performed a content analysis of the two major Chicago newspapers, the *Tribune* and the *Sun-Times*, to track major events that had affected the CHA over time. We conducted a LEXUS/NEXUS search to track coverage before 1994 and then tracked both papers throughout the course of the study. We maintained a database highlighting key events that affected the CHA and created a timeline on which we could compare our survey and interview data. The in-depth interview data, staff interview data, ethnographies, and information from the content analysis were integrated with the survey data to allow for comparisons and to enrich our understanding of change over time.

Notes

CHAPTER 1   INTRODUCTION

1. The approximate dates for these interviews were June 1994, February 1995, June 1995, August 1995, December 1995, and February 1996.

CHAPTER 2   THE CHICAGO HOUSING AUTHORITY

1. One of the archetypal stories about Swibel is that he used funds from the Flat Janitors Union, whose members were janitors in CHA housing, to fund the development of Marina City, two large downtown luxury high-rises. When the project ran into financial trouble in 1967, he obtained funds from Continental Bank. A few weeks later, the CHA shifted its multimillion-dollar development funds into low-interest accounts at Continental (Gittelson, 1982).
2. Gautreaux v. Chicago Housing Authority, 304 F. Supp. 736 (N.D. Ill 1969) *enforcing* 296 F. Supp. 907 (N.D. Ill 1969) and Gautreaux v. Landrieu, 523 F. Supp. 665, 674 (N.D. Ill 1981).
3. The receiver, the Habitat Corporation, eventually constructed more than one thousand units in non-impacted areas, that is, areas that were less than 30 percent black; however, nearly all of this housing was located in Hispanic neighborhoods, which were not considered "minority communities" under the 1969 decree.
4. The federal Section 8 program provides subsidies to low-income families to use in the private market. Participants must find units that meet HUD's housing quality standards and fall within what are called "fair-market rents." Once a family has found an acceptable unit, they pay approximately 30 percent of their income for rent (40 percent under the Section 8 voucher program) and the housing authority pays the rest.
5. Ultimately, this approach of using Section 8 certificates to disperse public housing residents throughout the metropolitan area became a central part of HUD's strategy for dealing with the problems of distressed public housing.

6. The Brooke Amendments to the Housing Act of 1937 were enacted in 1969 and 1970. The Omnibus Budget Reconciliation Act (OBRA) of 1981 changed rent requirements from a maximum of 25 percent to a minimum of 30 percent of adjusted income, 10 percent of gross income, or the welfare shelter rent, whichever of the three is greater. This policy also increased housing authorities' dependence on the federal government for operating subsidies.

7. Federal preferences were added in Section 206 of the Housing and Community Development Amendments of 1979 and then expanded in the Housing and Urban-Rural Recovery Act of 1983. Likewise, the 1981 OBRA reduced the eligibility rate for public housing from 80 percent to 50 percent of the area median income. Several laws in the 1990s gave housing authorities more flexibility to use local preferences.

8. Ceiling rents were eliminated in the 1981 Omnibus Budget Reconciliation Act (OBRA). Under a 1987 law, PHAs could apply for a waiver from HUD, while 1992 and 1994 laws allowed ceiling rents based on fair market rents or the 95th percentile of pre-ceiling rents. In the 1998 Quality Housing and Work Responsibility Act, ceiling rents were finally reestablished and could be calculated based on market conditions for public housing units.

9. Washington defeated Mayor Jane Byrne and Richard M. Daley, who became mayor in 1991.

10. The Metropolitan Planning Council's original plan called for Lane to become executive director, while Richard Ogilvie, the well-respected former governor, became the chairman of the board. However, Ogilvie died suddenly before the appointments were final, and it was then decided that Lane should hold both positions. Lanes dual appointment was approved by the city council in the spring of 1988.

11. Interview with Vincent Lane, former CHA executive director and chairman, December 13, 1994.

12. Ibid.

13. *Summeries v. Chicago Housing Authority* (1988). This suit was settled by consent decree in 1989, in a decision that allowed the continuation of the sweeps (but restricted the CHA's actions during apartment searches) and mandated that the CHA create a more liberal visitation policy.

14. Interview with Vincent Lane, former CHA executive director and chairman, December 13, 1994.

15. In 1988, HUD created a new national antidrug program, the Public Housing Drug Elimination Program, known as PHDEP; the CHA received its first grant in 1989. PHDEP was funded under the Anti-Drug Abuse Act of 1988 (P.L. 100–690), which authorized HUD to fund drug-control programs in local housing authorities.

16. The CHA also used this incident as additional justification for seeking the demolition and redevelopment of the Cabrini-Green site. This redevelopment plan itself led to greater controversy, as the agency encountered resistance from both residents and city government. This controversy bolstered the image of an agency in turmoil and may have hastened the HUD takeover.

17. The CHA had been in the process of replacing all the windows in its high-rise developments, but it had not yet gotten to the Taylor Homes.

18. Interview with Vincent Lane, former CHA executive director and chairman, December 13, 1994.

19. *Pratt v. the Chicago Housing Authority* (1993).
20. In June 1994, the CHA revealed that its own investigations showed that all six of the private security firms it contracted with to provide security in its high-rises had billed for services not rendered (*Chicago Tribune*, June 24, 1994). In October, the housing authority canceled a contract with one firm because of ongoing problems with overbilling during the investigation period (*Chicago Tribune*, October 21, 1994). Also during 1994, the Securities and Exchange Commission uncovered a major pension fraud scheme at the CHA, and HUD denied a CHA request for a $25-million expansion of its Section 8 program, citing chronic mismanagement and understaffing (*Chicago Tribune*, October 28, 1994).
21. New Life was owned by Leonard Farrakhan Muhammad, Nation of Islam leader Louis Farrakhan's son-in-law and financial manager. For a number of years the Nation of Islam had been involved in providing security for other public housing authorities around the nation through its Nation of Islam Security Agency. But in 1994, several members of Congress objected to the group's receiving federal funds for its security services because of Farrakhan's statements about Jews and whites in general. Because of these congressional objections, then-HUD Secretary Cisneros announced an investigation of New Life in January 1995 (*Washington Post*, January 21, 1995).
22. Since 1993, HUD has provided funds for revitalization and reconstruction of more than sixty thousand distressed public housing units through the HOPE VI program.
23. Section 202 of the Omnibus Consolidated Reconciliation Act (OCRA), 1996.
24. *Henry Horner Mothers Guild v. the Chicago Housing Authority and the Department of Housing and Urban Development* (1995).
25. Much of the financing for the Horner Revitalization comes from funds obtained through the *Gautreaux* settlement. See Popkin et al. (1998b) for details on the Horner settlement.
26. Section 202 of the Omnibus Budget Reconciliation Act (OBRA), 1996.

CHAPTER 3 FIGHTING CRIME IN PUBLIC HOUSING

1. Much of the material in this chapter appeared in S. J. Popkin et al., "Combating Crime in Public Housing: A Qualitative and Quantitative Longitudinal Analysis of the Chicago Housing Authority's Anti-Drug Initiative," *Justice Quarterly* 16 (3) 1999: 519–557.
2. The Public Housing Drug Elimination Program was funded under the Anti-Drug Abuse Act of 1988 (P.L. 100–690), which authorized HUD to fund drug control programs in local housing authorities.
3. As cochair of the Commission, Lane testified before Congress and was considered a leading candidate for secretary of Housing and Urban Development in 1992.
4. Less than ten years after its construction, the city closed the development. Pruitt-Igoe was ultimately demolished in 1973, after vandals had rendered it uninhabitable (Pate 1984).
5. For a review of the literature on crime prevention through environmental design, see D. P. Rosenbaum, A. J. Lurgio, and R. C. Davis, *The Prevention of Crime: Social and Situational Strategies* (Belmont, CA: Wadsworth, 1998).
6. For summaries of the research on situational crime prevention strategies,

see Rosenbaum et al. (1998) or R. V. Clarke, "Situational Crime Prevention," *Building A Safer Society: Strategic Approaches to Crime Prevention*, ed. M. Tonry and D. P. Farrington, Crime and Justice Series, vol. 19 (Chicago: University of Chicago Press, 1995).

7. More research is needed on the important topic of the relationship between situational crime prevention measures and crime displacement.

8. Specifically, adding police, conducting random patrols, aggressively arresting people in response to specific complaints, or community policing efforts without a clear focus on crime risk factors did not prevent serious crime (Sherman et al. 1997).

9. In one controlled experiment, raids of crack houses produced a drop in crime rates (Sherman and Rogan 1995), but the effects lasted no longer than one week.

10. These neighborhoods did not include public housing developments.

11. For a discussion of disorder reduction interventions and the limitations of their effectiveness, see R. B. Taylor, "Crime and Place: What We Know, What We Can Prevent, and What Else We Need to Know" (paper presented at the National Institute of Justice Annual Research and Evaluation Conference, Washington, D.C., July 1997).

12. For reviews, see Hope 1995; Lurigio and Davis 1992; Rosenbaum 1988; Rosenbaum, Lurigio, and Davis 1998.

13. An evaluation of a comprehensive public housing crime-prevention program in Spokane showed promising preliminary results, but it is not clear whether this approach could be transferred to a more troubled setting (Giacomazzi, McGarrell, and Thurman 1995).

14. In recent years, many housing authorities have begun to enforce rules and regulations more strictly, including the federal "one-strike-and-you're-out" provisions that ban households with criminal records.

15. The Housing Opportunities for People Everywhere or HOPE programs were a series of HUD programs initiated by then HUD Secretary Jack Kemp.

16. One of the greatest challenges of this project was tracking the rapid changes in the CHA's efforts. Each change in CHA leadership during the study period brought with it a corresponding set of changes in crime-prevention strategies. Because of the complexity of these programs and the amount of management turmoil at the CHA, it is likely that the following overview may yet contain some errors or omissions.

17. *Summeries v. the Chicago Housing Authority* (1988) and *Pratt v. the Chicago Housing Authority* (1993). See chapter 2 for a discussion of these cases.

18. Interview with Chicago Police Department administrator, April 25, 1995.

19. Interview with CHA security staff, February 21, 1996.

20. Ibid.

21. Because of these tensions, it is likely that the Chicago police department will absorb the CHA police in 1999.

22. Interview with senior CHA security staff, October 14, 1994.

23. Interview with senior CHA security staff, October 4, 1994.

24. Ibid.

25. Interview with CHA administrative staff, August 19, 1994.

26. Interview with the CHA Resident Programs staff, April 4, 1996.

27. Interview with CHA Resident Programs staff, September 23, 1994.

28. Interview with CHA Resident Programs staff, May 1, 1996.
29. Over the next three years, the CHA demolished buildings and began revitalization initiatives in Cabrini-Green, the ABLA Homes, Robert Taylor, Ida B. Wells, Washington Park, and the Lakefront Properties.
30. A management assessment of the CHA conducted in 1992 suggested that the sweeps had led to major improvements in CHA's maintenance of its high-rise properties (National Commission on Severely Distressed Public Housing 1992b). Likewise, our own preliminary assessment of residents' perceptions of the Anti-Drug Initiative in two CHA developments indicated that the program had a significant effect on reducing crime and drugs in one development and a more limited impact on the other (Popkin et al. 1993a, 1995). This assessment, focusing on Anti-Drug Initiative activities from 1991 to 1992, was only an exploratory analysis that did not permit an examination of the causes of these differences or assess whether the impact of the Anti-Drug Initiative was sustained over time.

CHAPTER 4 ROCKWELL GARDENS

1. With one exception, all resident names are pseudonyms.
2. Several CHA staff, including former Executive Director and Chairman Vincent Lane, voiced this belief in interviews. Our project ethnographer found that the outreach workers who worked with him, who were used to walking into shooting galleries, refused to go into Rockwell because of its reputation. This reputation was also reflected in media coverage; for example, an essay by Alex Kotlowitz describes Rockwell as the worst of CHA's developments ("The Quiet Riot Next Door," *Chicago Tribune*, August 27, 1996).
3. Mr. Yotaghan, who became a public figure in Chicago during the mid-1990s, agreed to allow us to use his real name for this book. In addition to being president of the Monroe Street Resident Management Corporation, he was also the leader of the Coalition to Protect Public Housing, a group opposed to the rapid demolition of CHA's developments.
4. As discussed in chapter 1, under Section 202 of the Omnibus Consolidated Reconciliation Act (OCRA) of 1996, all PHAs are required to conduct a "viability" assessment of any of their properties with more than three hundred units and a vacancy rate exceeding 10 percent. Nonviable developments are those where the costs of rehabilitation exceed the costs of demolishing them and providing residents with Section 8 vouchers.
5. Interview with Vincent Lane, former CHA executive director and chairman, December 13, 1994.
6. Interview with CHA administrative staff, August 19, 1994.
7. The assessment was conducted by On-Site Insight, a private consulting firm (On-Site Insight, "Physical Needs Assessment and Modernization Cost Estimates: Rockwell Gardens," Final Report to the Chicago Housing Authority, 1991).
8. One building in Rockwell (2450 West Monroe Street) under renovation is 70 percent vacant; four other buildings, with no major renovation or construction work, had vacancy rates exceeding 50 percent in July 1995.
9. CHA Resident Profile 1991 and 1997.
10. In 1987, Congress amended the U.S. Housing Act of 1937 to encourage increased resident management of public housing developments, formalizing

a movement that began in the mid-1970s through tenant initiatives in St. Louis, Washington, D.C., and Chicago. Resident management corporations undergo a multiyear training process before taking over management of their developments, after which time they are held to the same standards as private management companies (U.S. Department of Housing and Urban Development, 1992).

11. Because the surveys were conducted door-to-door, with the interviews frequently taking place in the hallways, we tried not to ask any items that might place respondents at risk if they were overheard. For safety reasons, we did not want to ask respondents directly about gang activity; therefore, we used the phrase "young people controlling the building" as a proxy. Respondents appeared to have no difficulty interpreting this question.

12. We conducted a subanalysis, comparing the percentages for 2450 West Monroe Street to the other two buildings. In 1994, the sample N for 2450 West Monroe Street was 32; the total for the other two buildings was 79. Because of the small numbers involved, we must use caution in interpreting these results. However, the trend was for residents of 2450 West Monroe to be more positive about conditions in their building.

13. Crack did not become a major street drug in Chicago until 1990, some years after it hit other major cities (Oullett et al. 1991).

14. As described in chapter 3, CADRE stands for Combating Alcohol and Drugs through Rehabilitation and Education.

15. Interview with CHA resident programs staff, May 1, 1996.

16. Interview with Vincent Lane, former CHA executive director and chairman, December 13, 1994.

17. Interview with Rockwell site staff, February 21, 1996.

18. Ibid.

19. Interview with the site management staff, February 21, 1996.

20. Interview with Vincent Lane, December 13, 1994.

21. We combined two measures of guards' performance (effectiveness in preventing crime and reducing fear) to create an index. The results reported here reflect changes in the index by survey wave. Our trend analyses show that overall there were no significant changes from the first round of the survey in May 1994, when residents were evaluating the contract security guards, to the fourth round in December 1995, eighteen months after the arrival of the New Life guards. Residents' ratings were not affected by their gender, age, or length of residency. See Popkin et al. 1996 for details.

22. Failure to provide adequate training for its security guards is allegedly one of the most common problems with the Nation of Islam's security companies (*Washington Post*, September 2, 1996).

23. Interview with senior CHA security staff, October 14, 1994.

24. *Chicago Tribune*, October 13, 1995.

25. The guards were not completely removed until the fall of 1996. Interview with CHA administrative staff, September 26, 1996.

26. Neither of these attitudes about the sweeps changed linearly over time, although female residents were significantly more likely than male residents to favor both allowing searches and having their building swept again.

27. Interview with senior CHA security staff, February 21, 1996.

28. Interview with senior CHA security staff, October 14, 1994.

29. We recognize that changes in reporting behavior are hard to interpret, and many possible explanations are available. Also, in the first wave of the survey (May 1994), we asked respondents if they had reported a problem in their building to the police or guards in the previous twelve months; as we were able to expand the study to include two additional survey waves, we changed the reference period to the past six months. Because of this change, drawing conclusions about change over time is problematic; however, we are able to make observations about general trends. Our analyses show that there were no linear trends in reporting behavior over the four survey waves from May 1994 to December 1995. This question was not asked in subsequent waves.

30. Interview with CHA resident programs staff, May 1, 1996.

31. Interview with CHA resident programs staff, September 23, 1994.

32. As with the guards, we created a composite index of the tenant patrol ratings and analyzed the trends in residents' evaluations across the four waves of surveys. While the level of tenant patrol activity varied, there were no significant trends over time in residents' assessment of the tenant patrols.

33. Interview with Rockwell site staff, April 4, 1996.

34. We created six scales to track changes over time: physical disorder inside and outside (problems with trash and junk, graffiti, and broken light bulbs); social disorder inside and outside (problems with drug use, drug sales, young people controlling the building, groups of people hanging out); and violence inside and outside (problems with assaults, shootings and violence, and rape). For a full description of the scales and scale characteristics, see the Appendix.

35. As discussed in the Appendix, we performed a trend analysis to examine the significance of changes over time. Our results show that these changes in residents' perceptions of physical disorder inside and outside were statistically significant. Residents' perceptions of problems with physical disorder inside their buildings decreased significantly ($p < .05$) in January 1995, May 1995, and January 1995; perceptions of physical disorder outside decreased from May 1994 to January 1995 and again from May 1995 to December 1995.

36. Our trend analysis indicated that residents' reports of serious problems with physical disorder increased significantly ($p < .05$) between December 1996 and December 1997, although they remained lower than in May 1994.

37. Reports of problems with physical disorder outside were significantly lower ($p < .05$) than in May 1994 from December 1995 through December 1997.

38. Our trend analysis indicates that residents' reports of problems with social disorder both inside and outside decreased significantly ($p < .05$) from May 1994 to January 1995 and dropped again between May 1995 to December 1995.

39. This story was reported in the *Chicago Tribune*, June 24, 1994.

40. Our trend analyses indicate that residents' perceptions of problems with violent crime dropped significantly ($p < .05$) from May 1994 to January 1995, rose significantly ($p < .05$) in May 1995, and fell again in December 1995.

41. Our ethnographer confirmed that violence had escalated in most CHA developments.

42. Our project ethnographer's observations during the spring and summer of 1996 suggested that the situation in Rockwell remained very tense and that

the gangs retained their control of the development. He described the faces of the young gang members in Rockwell as "serious-looking masks," appearing hardened much beyond their years. In the other developments in this study, he observed the young gang members joking around with each other; in Rockwell, the young men always appeared tense, as if waiting for trouble. Even making eye contact with the gang members was uncomfortable; they appeared ready to challenge anyone at the slightest provocation.

43. Our analyses indicated no significant ($p < .05$) changes in residents' perceptions of problems with drug trafficking and gang activity between December 1995 and December 1997.

44. Interview with Rockwell site staff, February 21, 1996.

45. Our analyses show a significant ($p < .05$) decrease in residents' perceptions of violent crime from December 1996 to December 1997, mostly because of the lack of violence in the Monroe Street building. In both years, reports of problems with violence were significantly ($p < .05$) lower than in May 1994, again primarily because Monroe Street residents skewed the overall results.

46. As a comparison with residents' reports, we examined residents' calls for police service over an eight-year period from 1988 to 1995. These data came from the Chicago Police Department, but they include information from the CHA Police Department, which reports to the same system, called RAMIS. Using interrupted time-series analysis, we tested the impact of five different interventions in Rockwell: the sweeps in February 1989, August 1989, and November 1992; the CHA's response to the gangs' attempt to drive out the New Life guards in July 1994 (pulling the guards out, bringing in CHA police and CHA Security Force officers); and the HUD takeover in May 1995. The results indicated that, once we controlled for other variables, only the incidents in the summer of 1994 led to a statistically significant decrease in residents' monthly calls for police service. See Popkin et al. 1996 for a full discussion.

47. Interview with Joseph Shuldiner, CHA executive director, June 14, 1998.

48. Interview with Wardell Yotaghan, Resident Management Corporation president, August 19, 1998.

49. The Bromley-Heath Resident Management Corporation was accused of allowing residents to engage in massive drug dealing and failing to enforce the federal "one-strike-and-you're-out" policy ("Bromley Director Could Face Eviction Under 1–Strike Rule," *Boston Globe*, Judy Rakowsky, Metro/Region, A1, November 3, 1998). LeClaire Courts, the first resident-managed development in Illinois, was taken over by the CHA on July 16, 1996, after reports of mismanagement of funds by staff ("Housing Complex Wary of Changes," *Chicago Tribune*, Janita Poe, Metro Chicago, July 17, 1996).

50. Interview with Joseph Shuldiner, CHA executive director, June 14, 1998.

51. See Chicago Housing Authority. 1998. *Chicago Housing Authority Draft Viability Analysis Summary and Proposed Revitalization Schedule: Briefing Packet*. April 9.

CHAPTER 5 HENRY HORNER HOMES

1. All resident names are pseudonyms.

2. The Local Advisory Council (LAC) is the CHA's resident council. Residents from each building elect a building president and vice president who serve

on the LAC. In addition, residents from each development elect a development president who sits on the CHA's Central Advisory Council.

3. The Brooke Amendments to the Housing Act of 1937 were enacted in 1969 and 1970. These amendments limited tenant payments for rents to 25 percent of income to make public housing affordable to very low-income families. The Omnibus Consolidated Reconciliation Act (OCRA) of 1981 changed rent requirements from a maximum of 25 percent to a minimum of 30 percent of adjusted income, 10 percent of gross income, or the welfare shelter rent, whichever of the three is greater. As discussed in chapter 2, these regulations reserving public housing for the poorest tenants were changed under the Quality Housing and Work Responsibility Act of 1998 (Section 513.d.2).

4. The sample sizes in Horner gradually declined as the population fell. See Appendix.

5. The Chicago Bulls pressed for the Annex to be demolished as part of the revitalization of Henry Horner so that they could construct a parking lot on the site. However, Annex residents ultimately voted to have their buildings rehabilitated. *Chicago Tribune*, December 18, 1995.

6. CHA Residential Statistical Summary for Year-End 1991 and 1997.

7. Order Approving Consent Decree, *Henry Horner Mothers Guild v. Chicago Housing Authority*, March 10, 1995.

8. Interview with CHA administrative staff, August 19, 1994.

9. *Henry Horner Mothers Guild v. the Chicago Housing Authority and the Department of Housing and Urban Development*, 1991.

10. The "one-for-one" replacement law was intended to prevent the loss of low-income housing units, but in cities like Chicago with large aging developments it made the cost of redeveloping prohibitive. The law was repealed by Congress in late 1995, and housing authorities are now required to replace only occupied units. These units may be replaced by either new development or Section 8 assistance.

11. Order Approving Consent Decree, *Henry Horner Mothers Guild v. Chicago Housing Authority*, March 10, 1995.

12. For a full discussion of the history of the Horner Revitalization Initiative, see Popkin et al. 1998b.

13. Our first visit to Horner was part of a preliminary evaluation of CHA's anti-crime programs. See Popkin et al. 1995.

14. The Gangster Disciples also controlled a number of buildings in Rockwell. Indeed, according to the 1995 Chicago Crime Commission report, the gang had a significant presence in more than two-thirds of the CHA's developments. As discussed in chapter 4, the splintering of the Gangster Disciples in 1996 led to a rapid increase in violence across the CHA.

15. As described in chapter 3, CADRE stands for Combating Alcohol and Drugs through Rehabilitation and Education.

16. Interview with CHA administrative staff, August 19, 1994.

17. Ibid.

18. Interview with Vincent Lane, December 13, 1994.

19. The *Mothers Guild* case was settled when the one-for-one replacement rule was still in effect, and housing authorities had to build a new unit for every unit they demolished. Congress repealed the one-for-one replacement

rule in 1995. Henceforth housing authorities need only replace occupied units, and they can replace them with either "hard" units (public or scattered-site units) or "soft" units (a Section 8 certificate or voucher). This change in the law, paving the way for demolition of numerous distressed developments, meant that the CHA was not required to replace as many units in its other developments.

20. See chapter 2 for a full discussion of the controversy over the sweeps and the consequences for the CHA.

21. Interview with senior CHA security staff, October 14, 1994.

22. Linear trend analysis showed that the proportion of residents who opposed unauthorized searches increased over time, but the proportion of residents who favored having their buildings swept again did not. Female residents were significantly more likely to favor sweeps.

23. Residents' views about the security guards remained extremely negative throughout the study period. Our wave-by-wave analysis showed that residents' evaluations of the guards grew more negative between May 1994 and January 1995 and remained at this level in May 1995. We were unable to assess residents' views in December 1995 because the guards were so rarely present that the vast majority of residents simply answered that no guards were present in their building. See Popkin et al. 1996.

24. *Memorandum in Support of Plaintiff's Motion to Hold Defendants in Civil Contempt, to Award Sanctions Against Them and to Extend the Move-out Date, Henry Horner Mothers Guild v. the Chicago Housing Authority,* September 1995.

25. Interview with CHA administrative staff, August 19, 1994.

26. According to the *Chicago Tribune* (July 24, 1997) and *Chicago Sun-Times,* (July 24, 1997), Federal Security Inc. was charged with fraudulently collecting $19 million in federal funds and inflating its employee roster to cheat the CHA. Company paperwork showed that some guards manned several stations simultaneously; at one point, Federal Security Inc. apparently claimed to be providing four hundred to five hundred guards, while actually employing only half that number.

27. By 1994, the CHA was spending about $77 million per year on security and antidrug programs, most of which were funded through its modernization funds; the CHA's 1998 security budget was reduced to be $39 million (*Chicago Tribune,* May 27, 1998).

28. Interview with senior CHA security staff, October 14, 1994.

29. Part of the CAPS program involved "beat officers" holding regular community meetings to discuss problems and concerns. See Skogan and Hartnett 1997.

30. Interview with senior CHA security staff, October 14, 1994.

31. In the first wave of the survey, we asked residents if they had reported a problem in their building to the police or guards in the past twelve months; as we were able to expand the study to include two additional survey waves, we changed the reference period to the past six months. Because of this change, drawing conclusions about change over time is problematic; however, we were able to make observations about general trends. The linear trend analysis showed that the proportion of residents indicating that they had reported a problem to the police or guards declined significantly over

time. Residents' demographic characteristics did not significantly affect their reporting behavior. See Popkin et al. 1996.

32. Interview with CHA resident programs staff, September 23, 1994.

33. Ibid.

34. Because Horner never had active tenant patrols, we did not ask the survey respondents about this Anti-Drug Initiative component.

35. Some tenant patrol participants in Rockwell Gardens had to be relocated for their own protection. See discussion of tenant patrols in chapter 4. Residents in Ickes also experienced retaliation, particularly after CHA security was removed from the development in 1996 (see chapter 5).

36. Interview with CHA resident programs staff, April 4, 1996.

37. Interview with CADRE center staff, September 16, 1994.

38. Ibid.

39. Interview with CADRE center staff, April 1996.

40. The discussion in this section is based primarily on a follow-up study of the Horner Revitalization Initiative. See Popkin et al., *Gauging the Effect of Public Housing Redesign: An Assessment of the Early Phases of the Henry Horner Revitalization Initiative* (A Report to the Department of Housing and Urban Development and the John D. and Catherine T. MacArthur Foundation, Abt Associates Inc., 1998).

41. As will be discussed in more detail in chapter 7, the CHA was mandated to either demolish or rehabilitate virtually all of its high-rise properties under Section 202 of the Omnibus Budget Reconciliation Act of 1996. Because of the consent decree, Horner is the only site where the CHA is required to replace all the demolished units with new construction.

42. Half of the tenants are to be "very low-income," (that is, with incomes less than 50 percent of the area median) and half are to be "low-income" (with incomes 50 to 80 percent of the area median).

43. Residents may be disqualified from receiving housing assistance if, after the signing of the consent decree, they do not remain a tenant in good standing (i.e., if they violate terms of the lease, such as not paying rent, or if they are evicted for-cause), and/or they are convicted of a felony. Similarly, no one convicted of a felony may reside in a leaseholder's unit.

44. The public housing units built near, but not on, the Horner site are considered in-fill or off-site units; these units, built as part of the Horner redevelopment, are not associated with the CHA's similar, but separate, scattered-site housing program.

45. Interview with CHA Project Manager of Henry Horner Redevelopment, May 15, 1998; interview with East Lake/Grenadier Horner site manager and the Horner redevelopment leader on June 19, 1998.

46. Order Approving Amended Consent Decree, *Henry Horner Mothers Guild v. Chicago Housing Authority*, August 9, 1995.

47. We created six scales to track changes over time: physical disorder inside and outside (problems with trash and junk, graffiti, and broken light bulbs); social disorder inside and outside (problems with drug use, drug sales, young people controlling the building, groups of people hanging out); and violence inside and outside (problems with assaults, shootings and violence, and rape). For a full description of the scales and scale characteristics, see Appendix.

48. See Popkin et al. (1998b).

49. Our longitudinal analysis of the survey data on physical disorder problems inside the Horner buildings in our study confirms that there was relatively little change over time (Appendix). Residents' complaints about physical disorder increased slightly between May 1994 and January 1995 and did not decrease significantly ($p < .05$) until December 1995 when the revitalization was underway. Residents' complaints about problems in their buildings increased somewhat in December 1996 and decreased again in December 1997, a decrease reflecting the marked improvement in problems with broken light bulbs.

50. Our longitudinal analyses (see Appendix) show that residents' perceptions of problems with physical disorder outside their buildings decreased significantly ($p < .05$) between May 1995 and December 1995 and again from December 1995 to December 1996.

51. Our longitudinal analyses indicate statistically significant ($p < .05$) decreases in residents' reports of problems with social disorder inside from May 1995 to December 1995; residents' perceptions of social disorder inside remained significantly lower than in May 1994, December 1996, and December 1997. Residents' perceptions of problems with social disorder outside decreased significantly ($p < .05$) from January to May 1995 and continued to decrease slightly for the remainder of the study.

52. Our longitudinal analyses showed that residents' perceptions of problems with violent crime inside their buildings decreased significantly ($p < .05$) from May 1995 to December 1995 and again from December 1995 to December 1996. However, residents' reports of problems with violent crime inside increased significantly from December 1996 to December 1997. Residents' perceptions of violent crime *outside* their buildings decreased between May 1994 and January 1995, fell significantly between May 1995 and December 1995, and fell again between December 1995 and December 1996. There appeared to be an upward trend between December 1996 and December 1997, but this change was not statistically significant.

53. Indeed, our interviewers heard gunfire while they were conducting the interviews.

54. Interview with CHA administrative staff, May 15, 1998.

55. Ibid.

56. Interview with representatives of the Central West Community Organization, May 14, 1998.

57. This study involved surveying a random sample of residents from all buildings in the development rather than from the three sample buildings we tracked from 1994 through 1997.

58. See Popkin et al. 1998b.

59. Changes in federal housing policy have pushed many very low-income tenants into the private market. Without adequate tracking, it is unclear how these changes will affect these residents. See chapter 7 for a discussion of this issue. Also see Popkin, Buron, and Levy 1999.

60. In the 1990s, the vast majority of CHA's scattered-site housing was constructed in low-income Hispanic neighborhoods. The provisions of the *Gautreaux* case prohibited the agency from building any new housing in neighborhoods that were more than 30 percent black; resistance in white neighborhoods and higher land prices made locating new housing in these communities

nearly impossible. See Rubinowitz et al. *Crossing the Class and Color Lines*, forthcoming.

CHAPTER 6   HAROLD ICKES HOMES

1. All resident names are pseudonyms.
2. As in Rockwell Gardens and the Horner Homes, we conducted six rounds of surveys in three buildings between May 1994 and December 1997, six rounds of in-depth interviews with twelve residents from these buildings, and ethnographic observations. In addition, because of the dramatic changes in Ickes, we conducted an additional round of in-depth interviews there in early 1998. (For a complete description of our research methods, see Appendix.)
3. Chicago Housing Authority, *Resident Statistical Profile*, 1991 and 1997.
4. Our first visit to Ickes was part of a preliminary evaluation of CHA's anticrime programs. See Popkin et al. 1995.
5. Interview with Ickes site staff, September 26, 1994.
6. These comments were made to the project ethnographer while he was visiting Ickes.
7. One of our project ethnographer's regular informants told him this story to illustrate how he did not feel safe reporting crime in Ickes.
8. Combating Drugs and Alcohol Through Rehabilitation and Education Center.
9. Interview with CHA administrative staff, August 19, 1994.
10. Our analysis of the four waves of survey data showed a significant increase in residents' dissatisfaction with the security officers' performance over time. The wave-by-wave analysis showed that residents' ratings of the guards were stable from May 1994 to January 1995 but that dissatisfaction increased significantly by May 1995. The ratings remained low in December 1995. See Popkin et al. 1996.
11. One of the three Ickes buildings had a working intercom system in 1994, and guards would call residents to let them know they had a visitor. However, in the other two buildings (and when the intercom was not working), residents either had to be prepared to meet visitors, or the guests had to stand outside and "holler up" to residents' windows to get them to come down.
12. We asked survey respondents, "How often does the tenant patrol work in your building?" In May 1994, 76 percent of respondents (in buildings with tenant patrols) said they saw tenant patrol members working at least once a day. A linear trend analysis found no significant change in perceptions of the amount of patrolling over time. See Popkin et al. 1996, for a complete discussion of these trends.
13. Interview with CHA resident programs staff, May 1, 1996.
14. As with the guards, we asked Ickes residents to evaluate the performance of the tenant patrols in terms of reporting crime and reducing residents' fears. We created a composite index and conducted a linear trend analysis to test for changes in evaluations over time. The results showed no significant change (or trend) over time. See Popkin et al. 1996, for a complete discussion.
15. Interview with Ickes site staff, April 4, 1996.
16. Interview with Ickes site staff, September 26, 1994.
17. Interview with Ickes site staff, April 4, 1996.
18. Interview with Ickes site staff, September 26, 1994.

19. We created six scales to track changes over time: physical disorder inside and outside (problems with trash and junk, graffiti, and broken light bulbs); social disorder inside and outside (problems with drug use, drug sales, young people controlling the building, groups of people hanging out); and violence inside and outside (problems with assaults, shootings and violence, and rape). For a full description of the scales and scale characteristics, see Appendix.

20. Although there was some variation in residents' reports of problems with physical disorder inside their buildings, our longitudinal analyses indicate that none of these was statistically significant.

21. Our longitudinal analyses showed clear evidence of seasonal variation. Ickes residents' complaints about big problems with social disorder inside their buildings dropped significantly ($p < .05$) from May 1994 to January 1995, rose again to May 1994 levels in May 1995, and fell significantly ($p < .05$) again in December 1995. Social disorder outside followed a nearly identical pattern: at higher levels in May 1994 and May 1995 and significantly lower levels in January 1995 and December 1995.

22. Our longitudinal analyses showed a downward trend in residents' reports of problems with violent crime inside, with the biggest decrease ($p < .05$) occurring between May 1995 and December 1995. Reports of problems outside showed more seasonal variation, dropping significantly ($p < .05$) between May 1994 and January 1995, rising again somewhat in May 1995, and falling again in December 1995.

23. Our longitudinal analyses showed significant increases ($p < .05$) in residents' reports of problems with social disorder both inside and outside between December 1995 and December 1996. Residents' concerns remained high in December 1997. However, our analyses also indicated that these higher levels were not significantly different than the levels reported at wave 1 in May 1994.

24. See, for example, *Chicago Tribune*, July 3, 1997. The weakening of the Gangster Disciples was partially responsible for the deterioration of conditions in Rockwell Gardens in 1996. See chapter 4.

25. All of these changes were statistically significant ($p < .05$). Moreover, the levels of violence reported in December 1996 and December 1997 were significantly higher than in May 1994.

26. Interview with Joseph Shuldiner, CHA executive director, June 14, 1998.

27. Ibid.

28. "CHA Sets Sights on its State Street High-Rises," *Chicago Tribune*, September 11, 1996.

CHAPTER 7 NO SIMPLE SOLUTIONS

1. Mr. Yotaghan died of a heart attack on June 15, 1999. He was eulogized in the *Chicago Tribune* (June 18, 1999) as a man who "worked tirelessly to help relieve the misery" of public housing.

2. Section 202 of the Omnibus Consolidated Reconciliation Act (OCRA), 1996.

3. The Quality Housing and Work Responsibility Act of 1998 (Section 513.d.2) requires that at least 40 percent of a housing authority's units made available in a year must be occupied by families with incomes at or below 30 percent of the area median income. If more than 75 percent of the new or turnover Section 8 vouchers are used by families with incomes below 30

percent of the median income, then this 40 percent requirement can be reduced to as low as a 30 percent share.

4. All units must meet HUD's housing quality standards and fall within what HUD has determined to be fair-market rents; under recent regulations, participants must also pay a full security deposit for their unit. The CHA pays the security deposit for residents who are relocated because of demolition or renovation; other participants may apply to the security deposit loan fund if they are willing to move to low-poverty areas. Otherwise, Section 8 applicants must come up with these funds independently.

5. HUD has provided some housing authorities with funds to provide mobility counseling—search assistance to encourage families to move to low-poverty areas that the department hopes will offer greater job opportunities. HUD is funding mobility counseling through a variety of programs including: the Moving to Opportunity research demonstration, the Regional Opportunity Counseling Initiative, programs funded as part of desegregation litigation settlements, and as counseling for public housing relocatees under the Vacancy Consolidation Program. For an overview of different types of existing mobility programs, see Turner and Williams 1998.

6. The CHA has HOPE VI funding to revitalize four of its largest developments—ABLA, Cabrini-Green, Henry Horner, and Robert Taylor—and is using its own modernization funds for redevelopment of several others.

7. There are a number of planned and existing mobility programs in the Chicago area. These include a small program in the Cook County suburbs run by Housing Choice Partners, CHAC's new program (which includes special counseling services for the disabled and for Latino families), and the two contractors that run CHA's relocation services. The Gautreaux program ended in 1997. Finally, CHAC was a site for the Moving to Opportunity research demonstration; the last families in this study moved in mid-1998. Since 1998, the Metropolitan Planning Council has been coordinating a group of agencies that provide mobility counseling services to help Section 8 holders locate housing in low-poverty, nonminority areas. CHAC Inc., which manages the CHA's Section 8 program, has developed a mobility program for existing Section 8 holders; the agencies providing relocation services for CHA residents also will be providing similar mobility counseling.

8. For discussions of the presumed benefits of mixed-income and dispersal strategies, see Epp 1996; Brophy and Smith 1997; Stegman 1992; Nelson and Khadduri 1992.

9. For a full discussion of the research on mixed-income and dispersal strategies for public and assisted housing, see Popkin, Buron, and Levy 1999.

10. For discussions of the research on the Gautreaux program, see Rosenbaum et al. 1991; Kaufman and Rosenbaum 1992; Popkin, Rosenbaum, and Meaden 1993.

11. HUD's ten-year Moving to Opportunity Demonstration (MTO) is intended to address some shortcomings of the Gautreaux research. MTO was implemented in five cities (Baltimore, Boston, Chicago, Los Angeles, and New York). In each city, samples of public housing residents were randomly assigned to one of three groups: families to receive a special MTO certificate, which could be used only in census tracts where less than 10 percent of the households were below the poverty level; families to receive a regular

Section 8 certificate; or families to remain in public housing. While MTO should answer many of the questions about the effects of dispersal strategies, it will be some years before results are available on outcomes for participants (U.S. Department of Housing and Urban Development 1996).

12. The CHA's Residential Statistical Summary for family units in 1997 shows that almost one-fifth of the households have five or more people living in the same apartment, more than half the residents are children, and only 6 percent of the households are headed by a married couple.

13. G. Washburn and M. Garza, "As City Regains CHA, New Managers Are Named," *Chicago Tribune*, Metro Chicago, P 1, May 28, 1999.

14. *Chicago Tribune*, January 13 and January 23, 1999.

APPENDIX

1. The original study also included an analysis of crime statistics from 1988 through 1995. For a complete description of the study methodology, see Popkin et al. 1996, 1999.

2. The second round of data collection was conducted in January rather than December because of a funding delay.

3. The last two waves of the survey were conducted as part of a broader project to gauge resident satisfaction and management needs in CHA housing. This study was conducted at the request of HUD in order to assess the effects of the 1995 HUD takeover of the CHA. In addition to the sample for the Anti-Drug Initiative study, this study included residents from other high-rise developments, senior buildings, and low-rise developments. See Popkin et al. 1998a for a report on this study.

4. The unit of selection was the building with its corresponding apartment numbers, not individuals. Typically, only one adult lives legally in the apartment; by choosing a respondent in this manner, we might have obtained viewpoints of illegal residents. Such residents represent a substantial proportion of the CHA population.

5. For more detail on our survey methods and interviewer training, see Gwiasda, Taluc, and Popkin 1997.

6. The sample sizes for waves 1 through 6 are: 193, 235, 237, 201, 158, and 120 for Henry Horner; 92, 140, 153, 159, 119, and 106 for Ickes; and 111, 172, 175, 165, 119, and 134 for Rockwell Gardens.

7. Although adult males live in the developments, few are primary leaseholders; most are not legal tenants but the boyfriends or relatives of leaseholders.

8. We did calculate the scales as means for this analysis as well to ensure that there were no substantial differences in the results.

9. At the end of the first round of interviews, the interviewer was asked to answer a few questions about the quality of the information obtained from the respondent. That information was used as the basis for selecting our key informants. We attempted to reinterview four residents per building, but, because of difficulties in locating some respondents, the actual number of key informants from each building ranged from three to five.

10. These interviews were part of the *CHA Resident Satisfaction and Management Needs Survey* conducted for HUD (Popkin et al. 1998a).

11. The observations in Horner were conducted from May to September 1995, with a return visit in September 1996 to update our information about the

development. The observations in Rockwell and Ickes were conducted between December 1995 and July 1996.

12. Treating the four waves of data as independent (when in fact this was only partially true) would have resulted in an underestimation of standard errors. This bias would have increased the chances of making a Type I error: falsely concluding that statistically significant changes occurred between waves. Alternatively, if only the panel (repeat) sample had been used to conduct a repeated measures analysis, then considerable statistical power would have been lost because the sample sizes would have declined by approximately 60 percent.

13. The demographic characteristics included in the model were binary covariates representing educational level (high school graduate), gender (female), number of children (three or more), and length of residency in CHA housing (greater than five years).

Bibliography

Annan, S. O., and W. G. Skogan. 1992. *Drugs and Public Housing: Toward an Effective Police Response*. Washington, DC: Police Foundation.

Baron, H. M. 1969. Building Babylon: A Case of Racial Controls in Public Housing. In *Revolt of the Powerless: The Negro in the North*, edited by H. Hill. New York: Random House.

Blank, R. M. 1997. *It Takes a Nation: A New Agenda for Fighting Poverty*. Princeton: Princeton University Press.

Bourgois, P. 1995. *In Search of Respect: Selling Crack in El Barrio*. Cambridge, UK: Cambridge University Press.

Bowly, D. 1978. *The Poorhouse: Subsidized Housing in Chicago, 1895–1976*. Carbondale: Southern Illinois University Press.

Boydstun, J. 1975. *The San Diego Field Interrogation Experiment*. Washington, DC: Police Foundation.

Brophy, P. C., and R. N. Smith. 1997. Mixed-Income Housing: Factors for Success. *Cityscape: A Journal of Policy Development and Research* 3 (2): 3–31.

Buerger, M. E. 1994. A Tale of Two Targets: Limitations of Community Anticrime Actions. *Crime and Delinquency* 40: 411–436.

Bursik, R. J., and H. G. Grasmick. 1993. *Neighborhoods and Crime: The Dimensions of Effective Community Control*. New York: Lexington Books.

Chicago Housing Authority. 1998. *Chicago Housing Authority Draft Viability Analysis Summary and Proposed Revitalization Schedule: Briefing Packet*, April 9. Chicago: Chicago Housing Authority.

———.1997. Office of Management Analysis and Monitoring. *Residential Statistical Summary: Year-End 1997*. Chicago: Chicago Housing Authority.

———. 1994. *Crime Incidence in Chicago Housing Authority Developments, 1988–1993*. Chicago: Chicago Housing Authority.

———. 1991a. *Office of Management Analysis and Monitoring. Residential Statistical Summary: Year-End 1991*. Chicago: Chicago Housing Authority.

————. 1991b. *The Public Housing Drug Elimination Program. A Request to the U.S. Department of Housing and Urban Development.* Internal document. Chicago: Chicago Housing Authority.

Clarke, R. V. 1980. Situational Crime Prevention: Theory and Practice. *British Journal of Criminology* 20: 136–147.

————, ed. 1992. *Situational Crime Prevention: Successful Case Studies.* New York: Harrow and Heston.

————. 1995. Situational Crime Prevention. In *Building a Safer Society: Strategic Approaches to Crime Prevention,* edited by M. Tonry and D. P. Farrington. Chicago: University of Chicago Press. 91–150.

Clarke, R. V., and P. H. Mayhew. 1980. *Designing Out Crime.* London: Her Majesty's Stationery Office.

Conklin, J. F. 1975. *The Impact of Crime.* New York: Macmillan.

Coulibaly, M., R. L. Green, and D. M. James. 1998. *Segregation in Federally Subsidized Low-Income Housing in the United States.* Westport, CT: Praeger.

Cuyahoga (Ohio) Metropolitan Housing Authority. 1993. Police Division Overview. Paper presented at the Council of Large Public Housing Authority Conference on Public Housing Security, Washington, DC.

DuBow, F., and D. Emmons. 1981. The Community Hypothesis. In *Reactions to Crime,* edited by D. A. Lewis. Beverly Hills: Sage. 167–182.

Dunworth, T., and A. Saiger. 1993. *Drugs and Crime in Public Housing: A Three-City Analysis.* Santa Monica: RAND.

Epp, G. 1996. Emerging Strategies for Revitalizing Public Housing Communities. *Housing Policy Debate* 7 (3): 563–588.

Feins, J., J. C. Epstein, and R. Widom. 1997. *Solving Crime Problems in Residential Neighborhoods: Comprehensive Changes in Design, Management, and Use.* Issues and Practices Series. Washington, DC: National Institute of Justice.

Fosburg, L. B., S. J. Popkin, and G. P. Locke. 1996. *Historical and Baseline Assessment of HOPE VI Program: Volume 1: Cross-Site Report.* Washington, DC: U.S. Department of Housing and Urban Development.

Furstenberg, F. F., Jr. 1993. How Families Manage Risk and Opportunity in Dangerous Neighborhoods. In *Sociology and the Public Agenda,* edited by W. J. Wilson. Newbury Park, CA: Sage. 231–257.

Garbarino, J., K. Kostelny, and N. Dubrow. 1991. *No Place to be a Child: Growing Up in a War Zone.* Lexington, MA: Lexington Books.

Gautreaux v. Chicago Housing Authority, 304 F. Supp. 736 (N.D. Ill 1969) *enforcing* 296 F. Supp. 907 (N.D. Ill 1969) and *Gautreaux v. Landrieu,* 523 F. Supp. 665, 674 (N.D. Ill 1981).

Giacomazzi, A. L., E. F. McGarrell, and Q. C. Thurman. 1995. Community Crime Prevention and Public Housing: A Preliminary Assessment of a Multi-Level, Collaborative Drug-Crime Elimination Strategy. Paper presented at the 47th annual meeting of the American Society of Criminology, November, Boston, MA.

Gittelson, S. 1982. The Secret Battle over Charles Swibel. *Chicago,* July, 101–132.

Goering, J., A. Kamely, and T. Richardson. 1997. Recent Research on Racial Segregation and Poverty Concentration in Public Housing in the U.S. *Urban Affairs Review* 31 (5): 723–745.

Greenberg, S., W. Rohe, and J. R. Williams. 1982. *Safe and Secure Neighborhoods:*

Physical Characteristics and Informal Territorial Control in High and Low Crime Neighborhoods. Washington, DC: National Institute of Justice.

Greensboro Housing Authority. 1993. "Police Neighborhood Resource Centers: Making a Difference." Paper presented at the Council of Large Public Housing Authority Conference on Public Housing Security, Washington, DC.

Gwiasda, V., N. Taluc, and S. J. Popkin. 1997. Data Collection in Dangerous Neighborhoods: Lessons from a Survey of Public Housing Residents in Chicago. *Evaluation Review* 21 (1): 77–93.

Hagedorn, J. M. 1998. *People and Folks: Gangs, Crime, and the Underclass in a Rustbelt City.* Chicago: University of Chicago Press.

Halpern, R. 1995. *Rebuilding the Inner City: A History of Initiatives to Address Poverty in the United States.* New York: Columbia University Press.

Hammett, T. M., J. D. Feins, T. Mason, and I. Ellen. 1994. *Public Housing Drug Elimination Program Evaluation.* Vol. 1, *Findings.* Washington, D.C.: U.S. Department of Housing and Urban Development.

Hedeker, D. 1993. *MIXOR: A Fortran Program for Mixed-Effects Ordinal Probit and Logistic Regression.* Technical Report. Chicago: University of Illinois at Chicago.

Hedeker, D. and R. D. Gibbons. 1994. A Random-effects Original Regression Model for Multilevel Analysis. *Biometrics* 50: 933–944.

Hedeker, D., R. D. Gibbons, and J. M. Davis. 1991. Random Regression Models for Multicenter Clinical Trials Data. *Psychopharmacology Bulletin* 27: 73–77.

Heinzelmann, F. 1981. Crime Prevention and the Physical Environment. In *Reactions to Crime*, edited by D. A. Lewis. Beverly Hills: Sage. 87–102.

Henry Horner Mothers Guild v. Chicago Housing Authority. 91 C 3316 (N.D. Ill 1996).

Hirsch, A. R. 1998. *Making the Second Ghetto.* Chicago: University of Chicago Press.

Holzman, H. R., C. R. Kudrick, and K. P. Voytek. 1996. Revisiting the Relationship between Crime and Architectural Design: An Analysis of Data from HUD's 1994 Survey of Public Housing Residents. *Cityscape* 2 (1): 107–126.

Hope, T. 1995. Community Crime Prevention. In *Building a Safer Society: Strategic Approaches to Crime Prevention*, edited by M. Tonry and D. P. Farrington. Chicago: University of Chicago Press. 21–89.

Jacobs, J. 1961. *Death and Life of Great American Cities.* New York: Random House.

Jones, L., L. Newman, and D. Isay. 1997. *Our America: Life and Death on the South Side of Chicago.* New York: Scribner.

Kaufman, J. E., and J. E. Rosenbaum. 1992. The Education and Employment of Low-Income Black Youth in White Suburbs. *Educational Evaluation and Policy Analysis* 14 (3): 229–240.

Kelling, G. L., and C. M. Coles. 1996. *Fixing Broken Windows: Restoring Order and Reducing Crime in Our Communities.* New York: Free Press.

Keyes, L. C. 1992. *Strategies and Saints: Fighting Drugs in Subsidized Housing.* Washington, DC: Urban Institute Press.

Khadduri, J., and M. Martin. 1997. Mixed-Income Housing in the HUD Multifamily Stock. *Cityscape: A Journal of Policy Development and Research* 3 (2): 33–69.

Kleiman, M.A.R. 1988. Crackdowns: The Effects of Intensive Enforcement on Retail

Heroin Dealing. In *Street-Level Drug Enforcement: Examining the Issues*. Washington, DC: National Institute of Justice.

Kleiman, M.A.R., A. Barnett, A. V. Bouza, and K. M. Burke. 1988. *Street-Level Drug Enforcement: Examining the Issues*. Washington, DC: National Institute of Justice.

Kotlowitz, A. 1991. *There are No Children Here: The Story of Two Boys Growing Up in the Other America*. New York: Doubleday.

Lavrakas, P. J. 1985. Citizen Self-Help and Crime Prevention Policy. In *American Violence and Public Policy*, edited by L. A. Curtis. New Haven: Yale University Press. 47–63.

Liang, K. Y., and S. L. Zeger. 1986. Longitudinal Data Analysis Using Generalized Linear Models. *Biometrika* 73: 13–22.

Lurigio, A. J., and R. C. Davis. 1992. Taking the War on Drugs to the Streets: The Impact of Four Neighborhood Drug Programs. *Crime and Delinquency* 38: 522–538.

McRoberts, F. 1998. "A New World—Down the Block." *Chicago Tribune*, October 8.

McRoberts, F, and A. M. Pallasch. 1998. "Neighbors Wary of New Arrivals." *Chicago Tribune*, December 28.

Massey, D. S., and N. Denton. 1993. *American Apartheid*. Cambridge, MA: Harvard University Press.

Meehan, E. J. 1985. The Evolution of Public Policy. In *Federal Housing Policy and Programs: Past and Present*, edited by J. P. Mitchell. New Brunswick, NJ: Rutgers University Press. 287–318.

Merry, S. E. 1981. Defensible Space Undefended: Social Factors in Crime Control through Environmental Design. *Urban Affairs Quarterly* 16: 397–422.

Metropolitan Planning Council. 1990. *Partners in Hope: A Case Study of a Project to Recommend Improvement Strategies for the Chicago Housing Authority*. Chicago: Metropolitan Planning Council.

Meyerson, M., and Banfield, E. C. 1955. *Politics, Planning, and the Public Interest: The Case of Public Housing in Chicago*. New York: Free Press.

National Commission on Severely Distressed Public Housing. 1992a. *The Final Report of the National Commission on Severely Distressed Public Housing*. Washington, DC: U.S. Government Printing Office.

———. 1992b. *Case Study and Site Examination Reports of the National Commission on Severely Distressed Public Housing*. Washington, DC: U.S. Government Printing Office.

Nelson, K. P., and J. Khadduri. 1992. To Whom Should Limited Housing Resources be Directed? *Housing Policy Debate* 3 (1): 1–55.

New York City Housing Authority. 1993. Description of Security-Related Activities. Paper presented at the Council of Large Public Housing Authorities Conference on Public Housing Security, January, Washington, DC.

Newman, O. 1972. *Defensible Space*. New York: Macmillan.

———. 1996. *Creating Defensible Space*. Washington, DC: U.S. Department of Housing and Urban Development.

Newman, S. J., and J. Harkness. 1999. The Effects of Welfare Reform on Housing: A National Analysis. In *The Home Front*, edited by S. Newman. Washington, DC: The Urban Institute Press. 29–80.

Olson, L. M., and T. Herr. 1989. *Building Opportunity for Disadvantaged Young*

Families: the Project Match Experience. Center for Urban Affairs and Policy Research Report. Evanston, IL: Center for Urban Affairs and Policy Research.

On-Site Insight. 1991. *Physical Needs Assessment and Modernization Cost Estimates: Rockwell Gardens.* Final Report to the Chicago Housing Authority.

Ouellet, L. J., A. D. Jimenez, W. A. Johnson, and W. W. Wiebel. 1991. Shooting Galleries and HIV Disease: Variations in Places for Injecting Illegal Drugs. *Crime and Delinquency* 37 (1): 48–64.

Pate, A. 1984. *An Evaluation of the Urban Initiatives Anti-Crime Program: Final Report.* Washington, DC: U.S. Department of Housing and Urban Development.

Patillo, M. E. 1998. Sweet Mothers and Gangbangers: Managing Crime in a Black Middle-Class Neighborhood. *Social Forces* 76 (3): 747–774.

Popkin, S. J., L. Buron, and D. Levy. 1999. Mixed-Income and Dispersal Strategies: Excluding the Most Troubled Public Housing Residents? Paper presented at the Fannie Mae Foundation Research Seminar, January, Washington, DC.

Popkin, S. J., and M. Cunningham. 1999. *CHAC Inc. Section 8 Program: Barriers to Successful Leasing Up.* Report prepared by the Urban Institute for CHAC, Inc. Washington, DC: The Urban Institute.

Popkin, S. J., V. E. Gwiasda, D. P. Rosenbaum, J. Amendolia, W. Johnson, and L. M. Olson. 1999. Combating Crime in Public Housing: A Qualitative and Quantitative Longitudinal Analysis of the Chicago Housing Authority's Anti-Drug Initative. *Justice Quarterly* 16 (3): 519–557.

Popkin, S. J., V. E. Gwiasda, L. Buron, and J. M. Amendolia. 1998a. *Chicago Housing Authority Resident Satisfaction and Management Needs Survey: Final Briefing Report.* Report to the U.S. Department of Housing and Urban Development, Bethesda, MD: Abt Associates Inc.

Popkin, S. J., V. E. Gwiasda, J. M. Amendolia, L. Buron, and L. Olson. 1998b. *Gauging the Effects of Public Housing Redesign: Final Report on the Early Stages of the Horner Revitalization Initiative.* Report prepared by Abt Associates Inc. for the U.S. Department of Housing and Urban Development and the John D. and Catherine T. MacArthur Foundation.

Popkin, S. J., V. E. Gwiasda, J. M. Amendolia, A. A. Anderson, G. Hanson, W. A. Johnson, E. Martel, L. M. Olson, and D. P. Rosenbaum. 1996. *The Hidden War: The Battle to Control Crime in Chicago's Public Housing.* Report to the National Institute of Justice, Bethesda, MD: Abt Associates Inc.

Popkin, S. J., L. M. Olson, A. J. Lurigio, V. E. Gwiasda, and R. C. Carter. 1995. Sweeping Out Drugs and Crime in Public Housing. *Crime and Delinquency* 41 (1): 73–99.

Popkin, S. J., L. M. Olson, V. E. Gwiasda, A. J. Lurigio, and R. C. Carter. 1993a. *An Evaluation of the Chicago Housing Authority's Public Housing Drug Elimination Program.* Chicago: Department of Criminal Justice, Loyola University of Chicago.

Popkin, S. J., J. E. Rosenbaum, and P. M. Meaden. 1993. Labor Market Experiences of Low-Income Black Women in Middle-Class Suburbs: Evidence from a Survey of Gautreaux Program Participants. *Journal of Policy Analysis and Management* 12 (3): 556–573.

Pratt et al. v. Chicago Housing Authority. 93 C 6985, F. Supp. 792 (N.D. Ill 1994).

Qualis Research Associates. 1998. The Ethnograph. Thousand Oaks, CA: Scolaril Sage Publications Software.

Quercia, R. G., and G. C. Galster. 1997. The Challenges Facing Public Housing Authorities in a Brave New World. *Housing Policy Debate* 8 (3): 535–569.

Rainwater, L. 1966. Fear and the House-As-Haven in the Lower Class. *Journal of the American Institute of Planners* 32: 23–37.

———. 1970. *Behind Ghetto Walls: Black Families in a Federal Slum*. Chicago: Aldine.

Reiss, A. J., Jr. 1985. *Policing a City's Central District: The Oakland Story*. Washington, DC: National Institute of Justice.

Rosenbaum, D. P. 1988. Community Crime Prevention: A Review and Synthesis of the Literature. *Justice Quarterly* 5: 323–395.

———. 1993. Civil Liberties and Aggressive Enforcement: Balancing the Rights of Individuals and Society in the Drug War. In *Drugs and the Community: Involving Community Residents in Combating the Sale of Illegal Drugs*, edited by R. C. Davis, A. J. Lurigio, and D. P. Rosenbaum. Springfield, IL: Thomas. 55–82.

Rosenbaum, D. P., A. J. Lurigio, and R. C. Davis. 1998. *The Prevention of Crime: Social and Situational Strategies*. Belmont, CA: Wadsworth.

Rosenbaum, J. E., S. J. Popkin, J. E. Kaufman, and J. Rusin. 1991. Social Integration of Low-Income Black Adults in Middle-Class White Suburbs. *Social Problems* 38 (4): 448–461.

Rouse, W. V., and H. Rubenstein. 1978. *Crime in Public Housing: A Review of Major Issues and Selected Crime Reduction Strategies*. Vol. 1. Washington, DC: U.S. Department of Housing and Urban Development.

Rubinowitz, L. S. 1992. Metropolitan Public Housing Desegregation Remedies: Chicago's Privatization Program. *Northern Illinois University Law Review* 12 (3): 589–669.

Rubinowtiz, L. S., J. E. Rosenbaum, S. Dvorin, M. Kulieke, A. McCareins, and S. J. Popkin. Forthcoming. *Crossing the Color and Class Lines: Low-Income Black Families in White Middle-Class Suburbs*. Chicago: University of Chicago Press.

Sampson, R. J., and W. B. Groves. 1989. Community Structure and Crime: Testing Social-Disorganization Theory. *American Journal of Sociology* 94 (4): 774–802.

Sampson, R. J., and J. H. Laub. 1993. *Crime in the Making: Pathways and Turning Points through Life*. Cambridge, MA: Harvard University Press.

Sampson, R. J., S. W. Raudenbush, and F. Earls. 1997. Neighborhoods and Violent Crime: A Multilevel Study of Collective Efficacy. *Science* 277: 918–924.

Schwartz, A., and K. Tajbakhsh. 1997. Mixed-Income Housing: Unanswered Questions. *Cityscape: A Journal of Policy Development and Research* 3 (2): 71–92.

Shaw, C. R., and H. D. McKay. 1942. *Juvenile Delinquency and Urban Areas*. Chicago: University of Chicago Press.

Sherman, L., D. Gottfredson, D. MacKenzie, J. Eck, P. Reuter, and S. Bushway. 1997. *Preventing Crime: What Works, What Doesn't, What's Promising*. Washington, DC: National Institute of Justice.

Sherman, L., and D. P. Rogan. 1995. Deterrent Effects of Police Raids on Crack Houses: A Randomized, Controlled Experiment. *Justice Quarterly* 12: 755–781.

Skogan, W. G. 1990. *Disorder and Decline: Crime and the Spiral of Decay in American Neighborhoods*. Los Angeles: Macmillan.

Skogan, W. G., and S. Annan. 1994. Drugs and Public Housing: Toward an Effective Police Response. in *Drugs and the Criminal Justice System*, edited by D. Mackenzie and C. Uchida. Beverly Hills: Sage. 129–150.

Skogan, W. G., and S. M. Hartnett. 1997. *Community Policing, Chicago Style*. New York: Oxford University Press.

Smith, J. 1999. Cleaning Up Public Housing by Sweeping Out the Poor. *Habitat International* 23 (1): 49–62.

Stegman, M. A. 1992. Comment on Kathryn P. Nelson and Jill Khadduri's 'To Whom Should Limited Housing Resources be Directed?' *Housing Policy Debate* 3 (1): 57–66.

Summeries et al. v. Chicago Housing Authority (1988).

Suttles, G. 1972. *The Social Construction of Communities*. Chicago: University of Chicago Press.

Taylor, R. B. 1997. Crime and Place: What We Know, What We Can Prevent, and What Else We Need to Know. Paper presented at the National Institute of Justice Annual Research and Evaluation Conference, Washington, DC.

Taylor, R. B., and A. V. Harrell. 1996. Physical Environment and Crime. Washington, DC: National Institute of Justice.

Turner, M. A., and K. Williams. 1998. *Housing Mobility: Realizing the Promise*. Report from the Second National Conference on Assisted Housing Mobility. Washington, DC: Urban Institute Press.

Turner, M. A., and I. G. Ellen. 1998. Location, *Location, Location: How Does Neighborhood Environment Affect the Well-Being of Families and Children?* Working Paper. Washington, DC: Urban Institute.

Uchida, C. D., B. Forst, and S. O. Annan. 1992. *Modern Policing and the Control of Illegal Drugs: Testing New Strategies in Two American Cities*. Washington, DC: National Institute of Justice.

U.S. Department of Housing and Urban Development. 1996. *Expanding Housing Choices for HUD-Assisted Families: First Biennial Report to Congress*. Washington, DC: U.S. Department of Housing and Urban Development.

———. 1992. *Evaluation of Resident Management in Public Housing*. Washington, DC. U.S. Department of Housing and Urban Development.

Webster, B., and E. F. Connors. 1992. *The Police, Drugs, and Public Housing*. Washington, DC: National Institute of Justice.

Weisel, D. L. 1990. *Tackling Drug Problems in Public Housing: A Guide for Police*. Washington, DC: Police Executive Research Forum.

Wilkins, C. W. 1989. *Drugs in Housing: What Managers Can Do*. Washington, DC: U.S. Department of Housing and Urban Development.

Wilson, J. Q., and Kelling, G. L. 1982. Broken Windows. *Atlantic Monthly*, March, 29–38.

Wilson, W. J. 1987. *The Truly Disadvantaged*. Chicago: University of Chicago Press.

Index

ABLA Homes, 10, 203n29, 213n6
Ali, Muhammad, 43
American Civil Liberties Union (ACLU), and Operation Clean Sweep, 16, 18, 58, 155
Anti-Drug Abuse Act (1988), 200n15. *See also* Public Housing Drug Elimination Program (PHDEP)
Anti-Drug Initiative, 3, 17–18, 25, 36–38, 65, 203n30; costs of, 17, 20, 31–32, 65, 157, 175; in Harold Ickes Homes, 152–154, 161–167, 170–171; in Henry Horner Homes, 105–106, 124, 130–131; impact on CHA housing, 72, 80, 124, 130–131, 152–154, 161, 165–167, 175–181; and Joseph Shuldiner, 20; in Rockwell Gardens, 58, 65, 72; and Vincent Lane, 17, 31–32, 58. *See also* CADRE centers; CHA Police Department; CHA Security Force; contract security; Operation Clean Sweep; tenant patrols

Black Peace Stone Nation, *see* Gangster Stones
broken windows theory, 29
Bromley Heath, 82, 206n49. *See also* resident management
Brooke Amendments (1969, 1970), 14–15, 200n6, 207n3

Building Interdiction Team Effort (BITE) patrols, 33. *See also* CHA Police Department; Chicago Police Department; Operation Clean Sweep; swarms
Bureau of Justice Statistics, 6
Byrne, Jane, 13, 200n9

Cabrini-Green, 6, 10; resident management of, 50–51; revitalization initiatives for, 20, 82, 187, 200n16, 203n29, 213n6; tenant patrols of, 36; violent crime in, 13, 17, 76
CADRE (Combating Alcohol and Drugs through Rehabilitation and Education) centers, 36, 38; in Harold Ickes Homes, 152–154, 161–162, 171; in Henry Horner Homes, 105, 115–117, 124, 130–131; in Rockwell Gardens, 56, 58, 67–68; residents' perceptions of, 68, 116–117, 162; services provided by, 36, 67, 115–117, 161–162. *See also* Anti-Drug Initiative; drug use
CAPS (Chicago Alternative Policing Strategies), 111, 208n29. *See also* Chicago Police Department
ceiling rents, 14, 182, 200n8. *See also* Brooke Amendments; Omnibus

About the Authors

SUSAN J. POPKIN is a senior research associate in the Metropolitan Housing and Communities Policy Center of the Urban Institute. Her research focuses on a wide range of public housing issues, including crime in public housing and revitalizing distressed public housing. Currently involved in research on the impact of the transformation of public housing on residents, Dr. Popkin is a nationally recognized expert on Section 8 and mobility.

VICTORIA GWIASDA is deputy director of the Illinois Violence Prevention Authority, a state agency designed to plan, fund, evaluate, and coordinate statewide violence prevention initiatives. Ms. Gwiasda previously served as assistant director of Research Programs at the University of Illinois Survey Research Laboratory, where she coordinated several surveys focusing on neighborhood crime and interpersonal violence.

LYNN M. OLSON is codirector, Department of Research and Practice, American Academy of Pediatrics and a visiting scholar at Northwestern University's Institute for Policy Research. Dr. Olson has extensive experience studying health and social service programs in inner-city communities. Her current research covers a range of issue affecting the health and well-being of children and families.

DENNIS P. ROSENBAUM is dean of the School of Criminal Justice, University at Albany, State University of New York. His research has focused on testing models of social intervention directed at the prevention and control of crime, drug abuse, and disorder through community empowerment, community policing, school-based drug education, and the creation of communitywide partnerships.

LARRY F. BURON is a housing economist at Abt Associates. His research interests focus on housing policies and other public policies affecting the low-income population, with a special interest in mixed-income housing and income inequality.

Printed in the United States
123830LV00002BA/47/A